THE JEWISH HEROES OF CHRISTIAN HISTORY
Hebrews 11 in Literary Context

SOCIETY
OF BIBLICAL
LITERATURE

DISSERTATION SERIES

Michael V. Fox, Old Testament Editor
Pheme Perkins, New Testament Editor

Number 156

THE JEWISH HEROES OF CHRISTIAN HISTORY
Hebrews 11 in Literary Context

by
Pamela Michelle Eisenbaum

Pamela Michelle Eisenbaum

THE JEWISH HEROES OF CHRISTIAN HISTORY
Hebrews 11 in Literary Context

Scholars Press
Atlanta, Georgia

THE JEWISH HEROES OF CHRISTIAN HISTORY
Hebrews 11 in Literary Context

Pamela Michelle Eisenbaum

© 1997
The Society of Biblical Literature

Library of Congress Cataloging in Publication Data
Eisenbaum, Pamela Michelle/
   The Jewish heroes of Christian history : Hebrews 11 in literary
context / Pamela Michelle Eisenbaum.
      p.   cm. — (Dissertation series / Society of Biblical Literature ;
no. 156)
   Includes bibliographical references.
   ISBN 0-7885-0246-8 (alk. paper).
   1. Bible. N.T. Hebrews—Criticism, interpretation, etc.
I. Title. II. Series: Dissertation series (Society of Biblical
Literature ; no. 156.
BS2765.2.E57   1996
227'.8706—dc20   96-33716
                                                         CIP

Printed in the United States of America
on acid-free paper

For my loving parents
Sid and Jackie

TABLE OF CONTENTS

 దార్ ౬ద్

Figures

ACKNOWLEDGMENTS

ᥦ᥍᥌ ᥏ᥑᥒ

I am delighted to have this opportunity to thank all those who helped me complete this book. First, I gratefully acknowledge the members of my dissertation committee, Robin Scroggs, Vincent Wimbush, Celia Deutsch, Burton Vizotsky, and David Damrosch, all of whom gave the work a thorough reading and thereby made the defense one of the most satisfying experiences of my scholarly life. Professors Scroggs and Wimbush also provided important insights while the dissertation was still very much in progress. Now that I have my own students to advise, I realize how exceedingly generous they were with their time.

Many other friends and colleagues read and/or responded to parts of the work at various stages of the process and made constructive suggestions: Mary Rose D'Angelo, David Frankfurter, Deirdre Good, Amy-Jill Levine, Agneta Enermalm-Ogawa, members of the Faculty-Student Colloquium at the Columbia University Department of Religion, and my fellow graduate students in New Testament at Union Theological Seminary, especially, Cameron Afzal and Paul Germond. My colleagues at the Iliff School of Theology have become a newfound source of encouragement and support. Two deserve special mention: Dennis MacDonald, my longtime teacher, mentor, and friend, read the original draft of chapter three and helped me to solve some important problems. David Petersen was tirelessly willing to answer questions regarding editorial matters. I offer these scholars my sincere thanks.

In addition, there were others who, in one way or another, facilitated the completion of this project. Seth Kasten, the reference librarian at Union Theological Seminary's Burke Library, was always willing to help me track down elusive bibliographic references. Tom Graumen and Caroline Boss gave me much needed computer assistance on more than one occasion. My student assistant, Dale Azevedo, proofread the entire manuscript with care and enthusiasm. Sandy Smith and Susan Brayford helped me to compile the index. I would also like to thank the Mrs. Giles Whiting Foundation, whose generous support allowed for a year of full-time writing.

Finally, I wish to thank my family. My husband, Greg Horn—who has a knack for clarity of expression—cast his keen eye over many pages of this text. Most importantly, he patiently endured my obsession with this work, while always believing in me. My parents, Sid and Jackie, gave me unflagging love and support, even when they did not understand why I wanted to become a biblical scholar. To them I dedicate this book.

ABBREVIATIONS

ↄֺ Ⴙ

AB	Anchor Bible
AnBib	Analecta biblica
ANRW	*Aufstieg und Niedergang der römischen Welt*
BAGD	W. Bauer, W. F. Arndt, F. W. Gingrich, and F. W. Danker, *Greek-English Lexicon of the NT*
Bib	*Biblica*
BZ	*Biblische Zeitschrift*
CBQ	*Catholic Biblical Quarterly*
CRINT	Compendia rerum judaicarum ad novum testamentum
EvQ	*Evangelical Quarterly*
FRLANT	Forschungen zur Religion und Literatur des Alten und Neuen Testaments
HNT	Handbuch zum Neuen Testament
HTR	*Harvard Theological Review*
HUCA	*Hebrew Union College Annual*
ICC	International Critical Commentary
JBC	R. E. Brown, et al. (eds.), *The Jerome Biblical Commentary*
JBL	*Journal of Biblical Literature*
JETS	*Journal of the Evangelical Theological Society*
JQR	*Jewish Quarterly Review*
JSNTSup	Journal for the Study of the New Testament—Supplement Series
JSOTSup	Journal for the Study of the Old Testament—Supplement Series
JSPSup	Journal for the Study of the Pseudepigrapha—Supplement Series
LCL	Loeb Classical Library
LCJ	Liddell-Scott-Jones, Greek-English Lexicon
MeyerK	H. A. W. Myers, Kritischexegetischer Kommetar über das Neue Testament
Neot	*Neotestamentica*
NICNT	New International Commentary on the Old Testament
NovT	*Novum Testamentum*
NovTSup	Novum Testamentum, Supplements
NTS	*New Testament Studies*

xi

OTL	Old Testament Library
OTP	J. H. Charlesworth (ed.), *The Old Testament Pseudepigrapha*
PEQ	*Palestine Exploration Quarterly*
RB	*Revue biblique*
RevExp	*Review and Expositor*
RevQ	*Revue de Qumran*
RevScRel	*Revue des sciences religieuses*
RTP	*Revue de théologie et de philosophie*
SB	*Sources bibliques*
SBLDS	SBL Dissertation Series
SBLMS	SBL Monograph Series
SBLSCS	SBL Septuagint and Cognate Studies
SJLA	Studies in Judaism in Late Antiquity
SNTSMS	Society for New Testament Monograph Series
SPB	Studia postbiblica
StudNeot	Studia neotestamentica
TAPA	*Transactions of the American Philosophical Association*
TCGNT	B. M. Metzger, *A Textual Commentary on the Greek New Testament*
TGl	*Theologie und Glaube*
VD	*Verbum domini*
WBC	World Biblical Commentary
WUNT	Wissenschaftliche Untersuchungen zum Neuen Testament
ZNW	*Zeitschrift für die neutestamentliche Wissenschaft*

INTRODUCTION

ↀ ↀ

Significance of This Study

With the Bible of First Century Judaism as its primary source, chap. 11 of the Epistle to the Hebrews preserves a rare early Christian vision of Jewish religious history. The bulk of the text concentrates on the great heroes and moments of the Pentateuch—Noah's survival of the flood, the call of Abraham, the Israelites crossing the Red Sea, to name just a few. The historical vision of Hebrews then lists figures from Joshua, Judges, and the prophets, and ends with reference to the present community to which Hebrews is addressed. In short, Hebrews 11 constitutes a whirlwind tour of Jewish scripture or what Christians now call the Old Testament.

Still, the significance of Hebrews 11 has scarcely been noticed. Most scholars believe this chapter typifies an element of Greco-Roman rhetoric known as an 'example list.'[1] This type of list was used by ancient authors to provide numerous illustrations of a general point. Although example lists appear in all sorts of literature, they are most often found in speeches in which an orator appeals to examples of individual behavior so as to encourage such behavior in members of the audience. Because heroes exclusively populate this list, I prefer to call it a 'hero list.'

In Hebrews, the heroes listed are ostensibly examples of faith. The author initiates the hero list by defining faith and then introduces each hero with the anaphoric word *pistei*, "by faith." Thus, exegetes have concentrated solely on how chap. 11's heroes serve as illustrations of faith, rather than on the way the chapter functions as a retelling of the scriptural story.

Because scholars have seen this text as a *standard* example of a genre, and because they have judged all the heroes as *typical* Jewish heroes, they have failed to recognize the pivotal role this text plays in early Christian reinterpretation of Jewish scripture and history. Scholars have long recognized the generic similarity between the Hebrews catalog and other ancient Jewish texts,[2] but no one has undertaken a detailed analysis of the

---

[1] The most complete study of ancient example lists and their relationship to Hebrews 11 is that of Michael Cosby, *The Rhetorical Composition and Function of Hebrews 11: In Light of Example Lists in Antiquity* (Macon, GA: Mercer, 1988).

[2] The majority of commentators recognize some sort of generic relationship between Hebrews 11 and earlier texts; most recently, William L. Lane, *Hebrews 9–13* (WBC; Dallas,

1

chapter in the context of these comparable writings.[3] This study seeks to contextualize Hebrews 11 in its Greco-Jewish literary background in order to observe how its version of biblical history differs from other texts. As we will discover, when compared to cognate Jewish texts, Hebrews 11 provides a highly original reading of the heroes and history of scripture.

Although the author claims to be enumerating stellar heroes of faith, he[4] has chosen some poor examples for illustrating faithfulness, at least not the best the Bible has to offer. The list does boast well-known biblical characters, but if one compares the Hebrews 11 heroes with other Jewish catalogs, some of the choices—and some of the omissions—prove striking and atypical. Even when citing an expected hero, the author often fails to mention the deed for which the hero is best known—the sort of deed we find in comparable texts.

In addition, the concept of *pistei*, which provides the structure of Hebrews 11, can be easily explained as serving rhetorical and euphonic purposes. *Pistei* is not *necessarily* the theological or religio-historical link among all the heroes. Finally, the author, like many Jewish authors, establishes a diachronic progression which spans the religious history of Israel. The heroes of chap. 11 are not simply listed synchronically in order to illustrate the virtue of faith. Thus, when all this is taken into consideration, it becomes clear that Hebrews 11 betrays a peculiar perspective which stands apart from and extends beyond the author's stated interest in citing examples of faith.

The author of Hebrews 11, like all those who recount the past, presents history selectively. The principle of selection—that is, what criteria the writer uses to include one hero and omit another, as well as what biographical elements of a given hero are included or excluded—is the interpretive key which sets this chapter in high relief against contemporary Jewish texts. By understanding what distinguishes Hebrews' view of the religious highlights

---

TX: Word, 1991) 316–23.

[3] Cosby's study (*Rhetorical Composition*) is exclusively concerned with formal and technical aspects in his comparison of these texts; he does not pursue questions of content or ideology.

[4] Since the author of the Epistle to the Hebrews is anonymous, we cannot know for certain the gender of the author. Indeed some have suggested that Priscilla wrote Hebrews. This suggestion was first made by Adolf von Harnack (Probabilia über die Addresse und den Verfasser des Hebräerbriefes," *ZNW* 1 [1900] 16–41) and later picked up by Ruth Hoppin, *Priscilla: Author of the Epistle to the Hebrews and Other Essays* (New York: Exposition, 1969). I do not think it likely that Priscilla wrote Hebrews and will use the male pronoun when referring to the author. This is more a matter of convenience, however, than an assertion about the identity of the author.

of the past from that of other Jewish writings, one can better understand how early Christians could claim a common heritage and at the same time come to see their communities as distinct from the larger Jewish community. This connection with early Christian claims is more than just passing. The study of Hebrews 11 in its literary environs leads me to conclude that the heroes of Hebrews share in common a marginalized existence which situates them outside the national destiny of Israel. In essence, Hebrews' reading of the great heroes and events of biblical history serves both to *denationalize* Jewish scripture and to re-value the religious significance of Jewish history so that its ethnic particularity is rendered inconsequential. For the author of Hebrews, the most religiously significant deeds of the biblical heroes are not those connected with the national leadership of Israel—as they typically were on contemporary Jewish lists—but those in which the hero acts independently of the people Israel.

This reading of scripture represents one of the earliest examples of the Christian appropriation of biblical history. As we shall see, other New Testament recountings of biblical history resemble Jewish sectarian understandings far more than a distinctly Christian perspective. Furthermore, the appropriation of scripture found in Hebrews helps to explain how the 'Old Testament' became Holy Writ for Gentile Christians who lacked a connection to Israel. Once the Jewish heroes were dislodged from their nationally distinctive roles in history, Gentiles could more easily identify with them as Christian, rather than Jewish, heroes.

The Setting of Hebrews

Since chap. 11 is an integral part of Hebrews, we must briefly consider the setting of the document as a whole.[5] Unfortunately, Hebrews is a highly mysterious text with unknown origins. This fact serves to diminish the degree of certainty with which we can assert anything about its context. Nevertheless, we can argue for certain probabilities based largely on internal evidence as well as a few basic facts about the early history of the document.

First, we can be nearly certain that Paul did not write Hebrews, although all the arguments for alternative authors, such as Barnabas,[6] Apollos,[7] or

---

[5] Although several scholars have proposed or assumed that Hebrews 11 was not originally composed by the author of Hebrews, and that the hero list is derived from an independent source, I argue in chapter one that this is not a credible position.

[6] Barnabas was originally suggested by Tertullian (*De pudic.* 20). Twentieth century authors who adopted this position include Eduard Riggenbach, *Der Brief an die Hebräer* (Kommentar zum Neuen Testament 14; Leipzig: Deichert, 1922) xl-xli; and J. A. T.

Priscilla,[8] are extremely weak. As Harold Attridge observes, "The beginning of sober exegesis is a recognition of the limits of historical knowledge and those limits preclude positive identification of the author."[9] Barring the discovery of any new external evidence, the author of Hebrews will remain anonymous.

Second, although various locales have been proposed for the community of Hebrews, only three have acquired a status that transcends the idiosyncrasies of individual scholars. They are Jerusalem, Alexandria, and Rome. At one time, the first two destinations had substantial support; more recently the evidence upon which they depend has been shown to be shaky. Jerusalem emerged as a candidate[10] largely due to the title "To the Hebrews" as well as to the assumption that the recipients must have been Jewish-Christians. However, the title probably reflects ancient scribal conjecture about the addressees,[11] and the arguments for the Jewish-Christian composition of the audience are problematic.[12] Alexandria was proposed[13] on the basis of perceived connections between Philo and Hebrews.[14] Yet, in-depth comparative study of Philo and Hebrews has yielded contradictory conclusions.[15] Much of the overlap is more likely due to generic similarities in

---

Robinson, *Redating the New Testament* (Philadelphia: Westminster, 1976) 200–20.

[7] Luther first proposed Apollos as the author of Hebrews in a sermon from 1537 (see F. F. Bruce, *The Epistle to the Hebrews* [NICNT; Grand Rapids: Eerdmans, 1964] xxxix). This suggestion was picked up by several scholars, including Ceslas Spicq, "L'Epître aux Hébreux, Apollos, Jean-Baptiste, les Hellénistes et Qumrân," *RevQ* 1 (1959) 365–90; and Hugh W. Montifiore, *A Commentary on the Epistle to the Hebrews* (New York: Harper & Row, 1964) 9–11.

[8] See n. 4.

[9] Harold Attridge, *The Epistle to the Hebrews* (Hermeneia; Philadelphia: Fortress, 1989) 5.

[10] See Ceslas Spicq (*L'Epître aux Hébreux* [SB; Paris: Gabalda, 1952] 1.239 n. 1) for a complete list of modern commentators who have argued for a Jerusalem destination.

[11] See the discussions in Attridge, *Hebrews*, 12; and Paul Ellingworth, *Commentary on Hebrews* (New International Greek Testament Commentary; Grand Rapids: Eerdmans, 1993) 21–22.

[12] See my discussion of this issue on pp. 7–10.

[13] Again, see Spicq (*L'Epître*, 1.237 n. 2) for a list of those who support the Alexandrian thesis.

[14] As Ellingworth (*Hebrews*, 28) puts it, "It is difficult to distinguish between arguments for Alexandria as the place *from* which, or *to* which, Hebrews was written" (emphasis mine).

[15] Spicq has been the main advocate for an explicit connection between Philo and the author of Hebrews. (He himself, however, does not believe the destination was Alexandria, but rather Caesarea.) See Spicq, *L'Epître*, 1.39–91; and "Alexandrismes dans l'Epître aux Hébreux," *RB* 58 (1951) 481–502; and most recently, "L'Epître aux Hébreux

Hellenistic education, rhetorical training, interest in interpreting the OT, etc.[16]

Current scholarly opinion of the destination of the Letter to the Hebrews centers on Rome. The argument for a Roman address has two important pieces of evidence to support it: First, the mention of greetings of "those from Italy" at the end of the letter may indicate Italian greeters abroad who send their regards home.[17] Second, several scholars have demonstrated that *1 Clement* depends upon Hebrews[18] and thus Hebrews is first attested in Rome.

That Hebrews was not accepted in the Roman church until long after its acceptance in the Eastern church has caused some to argue against the possibility of a Roman destination.[19] This same observation, however, can be used to bolster the Roman argument further. The reason the Roman church may have been reluctant could well be due to first-hand knowledge that the document was not Pauline.[20] Conversely, Alexandrian writers were the first to ascribe authorship to Paul, although not without their own doubts.[21]

The dating of Hebrews also poses difficulties. Because *1 Clement* is dependent on Hebrews, the *terminus ad quem* must be approximately 100 CE.[22] Unfortunately, the *terminus a quo* is more difficult to fix. Most scholars

---

et Philon. Un cas d'insertion de la littérature sacrée dans la culture profane du 1er siècle (Hebr. V, 1-VI, 20 et le 'De sacrificiis Abelis et Caini'), *ANRW* 2/25.4.3602–18. In contrast, Ronald Williamson (*Philo and the Epistle to the Hebrews* [Leiden: Brill, 1970]) argues convincingly *against* a connection between Philo and Hebrews. See also the discussion by Bruce (*Epistle*, xxxiii) regarding the flaws in the Alexandrian theory.

[16] See James W. Thompson, *The Beginnings of Christian Philosophy: The Epistle to the Hebrews* (Washington D.C.: Catholic Biblical Association of America, 1982).

[17] Although, as Attridge (*Hebrews*, 10) points out, the phrase "those from Italy" (οἱ ἀπὸ τῆς Ἰταλίας) is ambiguous. It could be taken as a reference to those who are currently residing in Italy, and "greetings of those from Italy" might still mean that greetings go out to anybody in any city who knows the greeters.

[18] Donald A. Hagner, *The Use of Old and New Testaments in Clement of Rome* (NovTSup 34; Leiden: Brill, 1973) 179–95; and Paul Ellingworth, "Hebrews and 1 Clement: Literary Dependence or Common Tradition," *BZ* 23 (1979) 262–69.

[19] Spicq, *L'Epître*, 1.232–34.

[20] Attridge, *Hebrews*, 10.

[21] Both Origen and Clement attribute the document to Paul, but only indirectly, because they recognize that the style and language were not his. See Bruce, *Epistle*, xxxvi-xxxvii.

[22] The traditional dating of *1 Clement* at 96 CE has been recently questioned. J. A. T. Robinson, (*Redating the New Testament*, 327–34) argues for quite an early date of 70 CE. Attridge (*Hebrews*, 7–8) thinks the latest possible date for *1 Clement* is 120. We do not know how long Hebrews had been in circulation before *1 Clement* used it, so 100 CE can only be an approximate *terminus ad quem* for Hebrews.

think Hebrews shows too great a theological sophistication to be dated earlier than 60 CE. However, with reference to the forty year period from 60 to 100, scholars have waged a debate focused on whether Hebrews was written before or after the destruction of the temple. Those who date the document in the 60s argue that—had it already taken place—the author would have been compelled to mention the destruction in order to demonstrate the supersessionist new covenant in Christ.[23] The absence of any mention of the temple's fall points to a pre-70 date. On the other hand, those who date Hebrews after 70 assert that, of all the other writings of the NT, the document has the most affinity with Luke-Acts, placing Hebrews linguistically and spiritually in the world of post-Pauline Christianity.[24]

In this regard, it is important to realize that the author of Hebrews has no real interest in the Herodian temple. His discussions of cult focus on the tabernacle and the biblical mandate for the system of sacrifice (9–10:18). The tenor of his remarks is wholly theoretical, and his argument is based on the biblical text. Indeed, the author gives no impression of having contemporary experiential knowledge of the temple cult. He may employ the present tense, but this fact does not indicate a sacrificial cult in operation. Some post-70 Jewish authors speak in the present tense about the temple.[25] Therefore, the author's references to the sacrificial cult are virtually irrelevant for determining the date.[26]

A similar situation exists regarding the document's references to persecution. Because they are not historically specific, these references can be interpreted in various ways. While the abuse is reportedly serious—the audience has been plundered of its possessions (10:34)—they have not suffered to the point of shedding blood (12:4). For some, this is indicative of an early date (pre-64), before the Neronian persecution.[27] However, if the intended recipients of the document were in Rome's environs, they may not

---

[23] So Spicq, *L'Epître*, 1.253–65; Robinson, *Redating*, 200–20; and George Wesley Buchanan, *To The Hebrews* (AB 36; Garden City, NY: Doubleday, 1972) 261; among others. The most recent scholar to argue for this position is Barnabas Lindars, *The Theology of the Letter to the Hebrews* (Cambridge, UK-NY: Cambridge University, 1991) 19–21.

[24] For some reason, German scholars almost uniformly hold this position; see Attridge (*Hebrews*, 9) for a list.

[25] Josephus frequently uses the present tense to describe sacrifice in the *Antiquities* (e.g., *Ant.* 4.1–7 §151–87); see Attridge, *Hebrews*, 8.

[26] In addition, the author's diaspora setting may have contributed to his lack of interest in the temple. Philo, for example, has little to say about the Jerusalem temple.

[27] This is the case for William Lane, *Call to Commitment: Responding to the Message of Hebrews* (Nashville: Nelson, 1985) 22–26.

have experienced the same incendiary death suffered by the urban Christians in Rome. On the other hand, if Hebrews was written later, in 90 CE, the generation to which the author writes might not have experienced that persecution first hand. Thus, the Neronian persecution cannot function as a marker for either an early *or* a late date.

These uncertainties have led Attridge to say that a date cannot be pinned down beyond the range of 60–100 CE. While it is difficult to argue with absolute conviction, my own view is that a post-70 date is far more likely. It will become increasingly clear throughout this study that the author of Hebrews manifests a Christian identity which has utterly distinguished itself from the usual symbols that constitute Jewish identity. Such a distinction between Jewish and Christian identity betrays a context in the last quarter of the first century,[28] rather than before the destruction of the temple.

Another issue regarding the setting of Hebrews concerns the identity of the addressees. Beginning with ancient commentators, a strong scholarly tradition views the addressees as Jewish-Christians in danger of slipping into some more familiar form of Judaism.[29] A significant minority thinks the audience reflects a Gentile or mixed community who are not maintaining their initial enthusiasm and Christian commitment.[30] Again, these arguments derive only from internal evidence.

Those who argue for a Jewish-Christian community believe the author's elaborate discussion of Jewish cultic institutions and scripture imply a Jewish ethnic orientation for both author and audience. For these scholars, the fact that the writer goes into such detail about ancient Jewish institutions (including one purported mention of food regulations in 13:9) and their biblical witness indicates a Jewish-Christian community in danger of being lured back to some more conventional form of Judaism by these very institutions.

There are two flaws in this argument. First, even if it were unambiguously evident—which it is not—that a form of Judaism is the threat which Hebrews addresses, this would not necessarily mean that the people must *ipso facto* be

---

[28] See James D. G. Dunn, *The Parting of the Ways: Between Christianity and Judaism and Their Significance for the Character of Christianity* (London: SCM; Philadelphia: Trinity, 1991) 238.

[29] See Ellingworth (*Hebrews*, 22 n. 62) for a list of those who hold this position. One important recent addition to this group is Lindars (*Theology*, 4–15).

[30] Again, German scholars more often hold this position, although James Moffat (*A Critical and Exegetical Commentary on the Epistle to the Hebrews* [New York: Scribner's, 1924] xvi-xvii) positions himself in this camp; see Attridge (*Hebrews*, 11 n. 93) for a complete list. Among very recent commentators, Ellingworth may be added (*Hebrews*, 21–26).

Jewish. Gentiles attracted to Christianity might also have found something compelling about contemporary forms of Judaism. Second, there is nothing in Hebrews which states that the community actually practiced any Jewish rituals or observances. The words 'Jews' or 'Jewish' are never used,[31] and the fact that some people are said to be flagging in their attendance in the Christian assembly does not automatically indicate they were attending synagogue. In short, the author does not engage in any anti-Jewish polemics.

Recently, Barnabas Lindars has offered a thoughtfully articulated defense of the position that the readers/listeners of Hebrews were Jewish-Christians. He argues that the central theological issue for the community to which Hebrews is addressed is the problem of sin.[32] The people believe that while their sins were washed away at their baptism, they have no means of atoning for post-baptismal sins. (Initially this was not a problem, because they thought there would only be a short time between their baptism and the parousia.) As time went on, a return or partial return to Judaism became attractive because Jewish worship is predicated on a system of atonement. The author must convince the text's readers that the sacrifice of Christ is efficacious once and for all.

Although Lindars' argument accounts for the author's preoccupation with a theology of atonement, it remains far too tenuous. All the same criticisms regarding the absence in Hebrews of any mention of 'Jews' (or even 'synagogues' or specifically Jewish practices)[33] casts suspicion on the theory of a genuine threat of a reversion to Judaism. But there are also more specific objections to Lindars' proposal. Lindars argues that the audience has a heightened consciousness of sin, which the author tries to relieve by demonstrating that Christ's sacrifice is the ultimate, eternal sacrifice. The problem here is that Lindars bases his argument primarily on chap. 13, which is very pastoral and encouraging. Earlier in the text, however, the writer of Hebrews asserts that, once a Christian has sinned, there is no return:

> For it is impossible to restore again to repentance those who have once been enlightened, and tasted the heavenly gift, and have shared in the Holy Spirit, and have tasted the goodness of the word of God and the

---

[31] Ellingworth, *Hebrews*, 22.

[32] Lindars, *Theology*, 10–15.

[33] Even the food regulations mentioned in 13:9 (καλὸν γὰρ χάριτι βεβαιοῦσθαι τὴν καρδίαν, οὐ βρώμασιν ἐν οἷς ὠφελήθησαν οἱ περιπατοῦντες) give no indication of being specifically Jewish, and neither does the author accuse his readers of practicing dietary laws.

powers of the age to come, and then have fallen away, since on their own they are crucifying again the Son of God and are holding him up to contempt. (6:4–6)[34]

The severity of this attitude does not make sense if we accept Lindars' argument. This statement from chap. 6, as well as others,[35] reflect an inflexible understanding of forgiveness—one which Lindars claims the author of Hebrews tries to combat. Thus, overall, while it is impossible to rule out that the audience was made up of Jewish-Christians, nothing in Hebrews points directly to the audience's affinity with a non-Christian Jewish community.

Those who argue for a predominantly Gentile readership for Hebrews rely upon the text's references to the need for basic religious knowledge (5:11–14), as well as the fact that the author uses the expression the "living God" (10:31). While these elements are "standard fare" of preaching to Gentiles,[36] they may be due to rhetorical effect. That is, the author could be emphasizing the audience's lack of sophisticated knowledge by his use of such terms. Thus, these arguments are not conclusive either.

Far more persuasive than an argument for an exclusively Gentile congregation is the notion that the document is addressed to a mixed community. This would account for expressions oriented more toward Gentiles, like 'the living God,' as well as those oriented primarily toward Jews, "let us then go to him outside the camp" (13:13).[37] In addition, the author never polemically attacks either Jews or Gentiles, or any specific group of people within the Christian community.

Since we depend upon internal evidence for our judgment of the readership, the most productive approach is to look at the audience to which the author imagines himself speaking.[38] As one scholar has put it, what is most evident about the readership of Hebrews is that the author

---

[34] In this passage the author has in mind the sin of apostasy; even so, the author most likely has a strict definition of staying within the bounds of Christian faith. Cf. 10:26, and see the discussion by Attridge, *Hebrews*, 168–73.

[35] See 10:26–27; 12:25.

[36] Cf. 1 Thess 1:9.

[37] The use of the expression 'outside the camp' is no doubt a reference to Lev 16:28. It seems to indicate that the author presupposes Jewish categories of sacred space. As such, this verse is the strongest argument for a Jewish author. Nevertheless, as Helmut Koester, ("'Outside the Camp,' Hebrews 13.9–14," *HTR* 55 [1962] 299–315) argues, it may reflect intra-Christian debates about sacramentalism.

[38] This is commonly known as the implied reader; see Wayne Booth, *The Rhetoric of Fiction* (2nd ed.; Chicago: University of Chicago, 1983).

wrote "*to* Christians *as* Christians."[39] Beyond this, the author attempts to define what it means to have Christian faith *as distinct from* Jewish faith. A recent monograph on the new covenant in Hebrews demonstrates how this functions as a central concept in the document.[40] Because the new covenant is new, the author must describe it by distinguishing it from the old. In fact, every substantive issue discussed in Hebrews concerns the relationship between the present (post-Christ) state of affairs and the past.[41] That the past for Christians amounts to the biblical history of Israel is indicative of two things not necessarily related to the make-up of the community: the burgeoning religion's Jewish origins and the need of the first missionaries for Jewish scripture in their apologetics.

Precisely because Christians read the same scriptures as their fellow Jews, scriptures containing the same history and descriptions of laws and institutions, their identity was intertwined with that of more traditional Jews. Therefore, the author of Hebrews implicitly addresses the question of Christian identity. Throughout Hebrews, the reigning leitmotif can be summed up in the question "How are Christians rooted in Judaism and ancient Israel and yet distinct from it?" Since this issue must have been fundamental to every ancient Christian community, I strongly suspect that the author envisioned several communities benefiting from his speech.

This remark leads me to the final issue to be addressed here: genre. During the last century commentators began to view the so called Letter to the Hebrews as an exhortative speech or sermon,[42] and not as a letter at all. Today, this is without doubt the dominant position of scholars. That Hebrews bears no epistolary prescript, and that the author himself calls his text "a word of exhortation" (τοῦ λόγου τῆς παρακλήσεως) in 13:22, make the oratorical origin of Hebrews the most compelling orientation toward the text.[43] Still, occasional arguments for the epistolary character arise; again,

---

[39] Werner Georg Kümmel, *Introduction to the New Testament* (Nashville: Abingdon, 1975) 400. Emphasis mine.

[40] Susan Lehne, *The New Covenant in Hebrews* (JSNT Sup 44; Sheffield: JSOT, 1990).

[41] Perhaps the best study which demonstrates this theme is that of Graham Hughes, *Hebrews and Hermeneutics: The Epistle to the Hebrews as a New Testament Example of Biblical Interpretation* (Cambridge: Cambridge University, 1979).

[42] See Otto Michel, *Der Brief an die Hebräer* (MeyerK 13; Göttingen: Vandenhoeck & Ruprecht, 1949) 24–26; Hartwig Thyen, *Der Stil der jüdisch-hellenistischen Homilie* (FRLANT 47; Göttingen: Vandenhoeck & Ruprecht, 1955).

[43] See Koester, *Introduction to the New Testament* (Philadelphia: Fortress; Berlin and New York: Walter De Gruyter, 1982) 2.272–73; James Swetnam, "On the Literary Genre of the 'Epistle' to the Hebrews," *NovT* 11 (1969) 261–69; Lawrence Wills, "The Form of the

Lindars is a defender of this position. Lindars' argument, however, does not so much reside in demonstrating that the document has the formal characteristics of a letter, but in demonstrating that the author of Hebrews is responding to a specific, urgent situation.[44] I have two responses to Lindars' position. First, this argument, like his thesis on the situation of the addressees, depends primarily on the final paraenetic chapter, which, while an integral part of Hebrews,[45] is not representative of the thought of the whole.[46] Second, any urgency in the letter is not a sure sign that Hebrews was written for a specific occasion. Scholars of Hebrews—including those who believe the text is a speech and not a letter—traditionally assume that some situation arose which provoked the author to write.

However, while this scenario describes the circumstance associated with the writing of correspondence, it does not necessarily explain Hebrews' oratorical characteristics. Urgency and specifics can signal a specific place and time, but they can also be employed in the service of a more general rhetorical purpose. Perhaps what is necessary is the inversion of our understanding of how Hebrews came into being as a text. Writers like Isocrates, for example, often published speeches because they wanted to give lectures on some topic or other. However, the published writing was made to look as if it had been given as a speech on a certain occasion, even if it was not.[47] After all, rhetoric was such a highly developed art in Athens and later in Rome, that a writer could labor over a speech for some time—even years.[48] Yet an author would not want his text to look labored. The intended result of applying occasion-specific indicators to one's speech was to make it look fresh, spontaneous, and unstudied.

Ever since the work of Albert Vanhoye,[49] the elaborate, deliberate, highly sophisticated structure of Hebrews cannot be denied. Hebrews was not

---

Sermon in Hellenistic Judaism and Early Christianity," *HTR* 77 (1984) 277–99.

[44] Lindars, "The Rhetorical Structure of Hebrews," *NTS* 35 (1989) 382–406; and idem, *Theology*, 6–8.

[45] There have been some attempts to deny the integrity of chap. 13, like that of Buchanan (*Hebrews*, 267), but Attridge (*Hebrews*, 384–85) successfully refutes these.

[46] Although there are other paraenetic sections in Hebrews; chap. 13 has a gentler tone than the others. It functions as a rhetorical denouement.

[47] H. I. Marrou, *A History of Education in Antiquity* (Madison, WI and London: Univesity of Wisconsin, 1956) 81.

[48] Marrou, *Education in Antiquity*, 81.

[49] Primarily that of *La structure littéraire de l'Epître aux Hébreux* (Paris: Desclee de Brouwer, 1963), but see Attridge (*Hebrews*, 423) for a complete list of Vanhoye's works.

written quickly. It is a studied piece of work, having more in common with the treatises of Philo than the letters of Paul. The so-called urgent specifics, where the writer appears to address directly the needs of the community, may easily have been inserted for rhetorical effect.

In the end, Lindars' attempt to defend Hebrews as a letter is not convincing. The best analysis of Hebrews is that which construes it as an epideictic oration.[50] Epideictic oratory seeks to reaffirm a point of view currently held by the audience (but perhaps in danger of disintegrating). It often involves the praise or blame of someone or something. Since the writer of Hebrews wrote to Christians as Christians in order to praise Christ, while denouncing old forms of religiosity, the designation 'epideictic' best captures the function of the document.

I further suspect that Hebrews is a generic speech, one in which the author wanted to set forth certain ideas that he believed all Christians should hold about their faith.[51] This might explain the postscript. If Hebrews was written as a speech, but one which was circulated to other churches at remote locations, a postscript would be an appropriate way to acknowledge that the document was "sent," though it is not a letter.[52] Even if the author did have one particular community in mind, his elaborate theological and christological reflection indicates that he wanted to make a statement that could transcend any one occasion. More than this we cannot know for certain.

Method and Scope

Since Hebrews remains such a mysterious and isolated document, we possess virtually no external evidence for determining its role in early Christianity. In this examination, all research is based on the text itself, Hebrews 11, and its relation to other texts. In light of this situation, we need to marshal the best resources for making texts and relations between texts more transparent. I have, therefore, employed various critical tools at different points in the process. While I have not applied any single theoretical model to the study of Hebrews 11, those theorists who have concentrated on two particular questions have influenced me in this project.

First, studies of the dynamics of communication between a speaker or writer and an audience help to uncover the shared assumptions of a given

---

[50] Attridge, *Hebrews,* 14.

[51] Koester, *Introduction,* 273.

[52] This is essentially the position of David Aune, *The New Testament in Its Literary Environment* (Library of Early Christianity; Philadelphia: Westminster, 1987) 213.

community. This line of inquiry is commonly known as rhetorical criticism. Wilhelm Wuellner, who has written extensively on the use of this approach for biblical scholars, has the following to say about its methodological orientation:

> The rhetorical view of religious literature takes us beyond viewing language as a reflection of reality, even "ultimate reality" as understood in terms of traditional metaphysical and idealist philosophy, and takes us to "the social aspect of language which is an instrument of communication and influence on others."[53]

The word 'rhetoric'—by which I mean simply the *way* an author communicates rather than *what* s/he communicates—will appear several times throughout my discussion, but I have avoided using the term 'rhetorical criticism' because it refers to a variety of enterprises. Rhetorical criticism sometimes means nothing more than literary criticism;[54] sometimes it describes specific modes of rhetorical discourse common in antiquity;[55] it can also mean the differentiation of types of argumentation.[56]

While Hebrews is seen by scholars as possessing a high level of sophistication in its rhetorical characteristics, chap. 11 has been considered primarily a poetic interruption or appendix—present more for aesthetic effect and inspiration than as an integral part of the author's argument. But, as Wayne Booth has said, an author "cannot choose to avoid rhetoric, he can choose only the kind of rhetoric he will employ."[57] The writer of Hebrews may be recounting the heroes and history of scripture, yet he chooses precisely how to present that recounting. In chap. 11, the author's unique presentation reflects his rhetorical assumptions and interests vis-à-vis the audience, and it is these which will most interest us here.

---

[53] Wilhelm Wuellner, "Where is Rhetorical Criticism Taking Us?" *CBQ* 49 (1987) 449. The quotation he employs is taken from Ch. Perelman and L. Olbrechts-Tyteca, *The New Rhetoric: A Treatise on Argumentation* (Notre Dame: University of Notre Dame, 1969) 513.

[54] The confusion arises precisely because literary critics often use the term rhetoric as I just did—to refer to the way an author presents a story. See for example, Booth, *Rhetoric of Fiction*; and David Rhoads and Donald Michie, *Mark as Story: An Introduction to the Narrative of a Gospel* (Philadelphia: Fortress, 1982).

[55] This is the program called for by George Kennedy in *New Testament Interpretation Through Rhetorical Criticism* (Chapel Hill and London: University of North Carolina, 1984). See also Burton L. Mack, *Rhetoric and the New Testament* (Minneapolis: Fortress, 1990).

[56] As in Perelman and Olbrechts-Tyteca, *New Rhetoric*.

[57] Booth, *Rhetoric of Fiction*, 149.

The second theoretical underpinning of this work is an awareness of the role played by interpretation. Indeed, the hermeneutics of Hebrews plays an inevitable part in this study. For, not only is the author in dialogue with the biblical past itself, but surely he knows at least some of the competing interpretations of his source text(s), as well as rival understandings of the ultimate meaning of Jewish history. However, the science of hermeneutics, like that of rhetorical criticism, has a multiplicity of competing practitioners who debate both the definition of hermeneutics and what practical value it might have. Once again, I have no interest in sorting out the debate.[58] Whenever I mention the hermeneutics of Hebrews, I refer to the author's reworking of the biblical text, tradition, or history. Those scholars who have made contributions which can illumine these hermeneutical issues appear in the footnotes of this work.[59]

Furthermore, Hebrews 11 constitutes an exemplary extent case of a paradigm shift in the understanding of biblical history. If, as I assert, Hebrews 11 is one of the earliest examples of a truly Christian retelling of biblical history, then it represents the nexus between one Christian's perception of the past and his vision of the future. In that one hermeneutical moment, the author transformed the present and initiated a new future—taking one small step toward a kind of Christian identity that did not also imply Jewish identity.[60]

Although the nucleus of this study is chap. 11 of Hebrews, I have two larger aims. The first is to use my reading of chap. 11 to better situate the ever-elusive Hebrews within the early Christian literary landscape. My second aim is more grandiose: to aid in the understanding of the innovations that led to the formation of Christianity as a religion distinct from Judaism. Obviously many complex forces contributed to Christianity's evolution from a sect of Judaism into a distinct religion—more than could ever be

---

[58] The best place for biblical scholars who want to see at least an attempt at sorting it all out is in the work of Anthony C. Thiselton, *The Two Horizons: New Testament Hermeneutics and Philosophical Description* (Grand Rapids, MI: Eerdman's, 1980; and idem, *New Horizons in Hermeneutics: The Theory and Practice of Transforming Biblical Reading* (Grand Rapids, MI: Zondervan, 1992).

[59] Such as those whose work has employed the concept of intertextuality like Jonathon Culler, *The Pursuit of Signs* (Ithica: Cornell Univeristy, 1981) 100–18; and biblical scholars like Daniel Boyarin, *Intertextuality and the Reading of Midrash* and Richard Hays, *Echoes of Scripture in the Letters of Paul* (New Haven & London: Yale Univeristy, 1989).

[60] Although he does not use the language of hermeneutics, the work of Bruce Lincoln (*Discourse and the Construction of Society* [New York, Oxford: Oxford University, 1989]) contributes to the understanding of the retelling of the past and the transformation of the present. I especially make use of his ideas in chapter four.

contained in a single book. Nevertheless, Hebrews 11 captures one moment within that evolution, and I have focused my argument so as best to describe it.

The first chapter of this study will treat the Jewish and Greco-Roman literature which comprises the backdrop for understanding Hebrews 11. Jewish authors composed numerous historical summaries of the Bible, as well as a variety of hero lists. Greco-Roman writers, too, listed great individuals from the past in order to illustrate a point. The similarities and differences between these texts and Hebrews 11 serve as the foundation of this study.

While chapter one covers the broad literary horizon of various texts bearing resemblance to Hebrews 11, chapter two narrows the context to Hebrews itself. This chapter analyzes the hermeneutics of Hebrews. I identify certain principles operative in the author's treatment of the biblical text, and these aid in uncovering the agenda in chap. 11.

Chapter three is a detailed exegesis of Hebrews 11 itself. Here I demonstrate hero by hero how the figures are portrayed as marginalized individuals and how the author constructed his vision of a denationalized history of Israel.

If the first chapter looks backward toward what prefigured the composition of Hebrews 11, the fourth and final chapter looks forward to what followed the vision created by the author of Hebrews. Here I will survey the early Christian historiographic picture of Jewish scripture, beginning with NT writings roughly contemporary with Hebrews and extending to Eusebius. While direct dependence of early Christian authors on the Epistle to the Hebrews is very rare, my position is that the historiographic attitude expressed in Hebrews fostered a perception of Jewish history that became the dominant one.

Chapter One
HAGIOLOGY IN ANTIQUITY
✐ ✑

The form of Hebrews 11 bears a resemblance to texts in several other documents of the Hellenistic and Roman periods. The parallels favored by scholars are Sirach 44–50, 1 Macc 2:51–60, and Wisdom 10. Such parallels led Hans Windisch to postulate a Jewish source upon which the author of Hebrews must have depended.[1] Otto Michel elaborated upon this idea by attempting to isolate the *Vorlage*.[2] The reconstruction of the *Vorlage* encouraged Gottfried Schille to claim that the form of Hebrews 11 had its origins in a baptismal liturgy which was then redacted by the author of Hebrews into a catechetical text.[3] Although the theory that the author of Hebrews relied upon a specific source has been called into question,[4] the source theory persists.[5]

The only scholar who has actually studied Hebrews 11 comparatively with other lists is Michael Cosby, who has compared it with nearly 30 others, including Greco-Roman example lists. He concludes that there is no such formal genre, "example list of famous men," in antiquity:

> No one type of literature dominates in the use of these lists. Indeed the different styles of composition are almost as diverse as are the documents employing the lists. . . . In spite of the fact that the lists have the same rhetorical function of persuading audiences, frequently

---

[1] Hans Windisch, *Der Hebräerbrief* (HNT 14; Tubingen: Mohr [Siebeck], 1931) 98–99.

[2] Otto Michel, *Der Brief an die Hebräer* (Meyer 13; Göttingen: Vandenhoeck & Ruprecht, 1949) 422–23. The *Vorlage* allegedly includes vv. 3–12, 17–31, and 32–38.

[3] Gottfried Schille, "Katechese und Taufliturgie," *ZNW* 51 (1960) 112–31. Schille's thesis has been almost universally rejected with the exception of Robert Jewett, *Letter to Pilgrims: A Commentary on the Epistle to the Hebrews* (New York: Pilgrim, 1981) 194.

[4] Sidney Sowers (*The Hermeneutics of Philo and Hebrews* [Basel Studies of Theology 1; Zurich: EVZ, 1965] 133) has pointed out that the vocabulary and style show a natural affinity with the rest of the document. See also Paul Ellingworth, *Commentary on Hebrews* (The New International Greek Testament Commentary; Grand Rapids: Eerdmans, 1993) 558–59.

[5] The most recent commentator to accept that Hebrews 11 is an edited version of an earlier source is Harold Attridge, *The Epistle to the Hebrews* (Hermeneia; Philadelphia: Fortress, 1989) 306–7.

the only compositional similarity between them is that they give a number of examples of famous people instead of only one or two.[6]

Cosby points out that Jewish and Christian lists appeal to the authority of salvation history, but this is insufficient to constitute a definable form.[7] Since Cosby's study is concerned purely with formal characteristics of example lists, he does not pursue the question of content in Hebrews 11.

Some scholars have analyzed Hebrews 11 in terms of its resemblance to recapitulations of Jewish history which played a role in Jewish preaching. Hartwig Thyen has compared Hebrews 11 to summaries of Israelite history already found in the Bible (e.g., Ps 105; Neh 9:6–31) as well as intertestamental literature (e.g., Wis 10). He argues that in the Diaspora the focus of these summaries shifted to an emphasis on the virtues of great men,[8] in order to make such preaching more palatable in the pluralistic world of late Hellenism.[9] Lawrence Wills, in trying to pin down the type of Jewish preaching called "the word of exhortation," says that such preaching began with scriptural exempla, which were in turn followed by an exhortation to the audience; he finds repeated examples of the "word of exhortation" in Hebrews, including Heb 11:1–12:3.[10] In addition, some scholars have seen Stephen's sermon in Acts 7 as having played an influential role in the thought of Hebrews.[11] Ceslas Spicq has decided to think of Hebrews 11 as a combination of two forms: a moral exemplar list and a résumé of salvation history.[12]

Thus, the debate about whether Hebrews 11 is primarily a hagiology of virtuous exemplars or a recapitulation of biblical history has never been resolved. Some scholars, while still recognizing the influence of these kinds of texts, have avoided the problem by identifying the form of Hebrews 11 in terms of its internal formal characteristics. Harold Attridge calls Hebrews 11

---

[6] Michael Cosby, *The Rhetorical Composition and Function of Hebrews 11: In Light of Example Lists in Antiquity* (Macon: Mercer, 1988) 18.

[7] Cosby, *Rhetorical Composition*, 19.

[8] Such as Philo, *Virt.* 198–227.

[9] Hartwig Thyen, *Der Stil der Judisch-Hellenistischen Homilie* (Göttingen: Vandenhoeck & Ruprecht, 1955). Thyen, who also believes Hebrews 11 was an independent text, has been very influential upon commentators of Hebrews.

[10] Lawrence Wills, "The Form of the Sermon in Hellenistic Judaism and Early Christianity, " *HTR* 77 (1984) 277–99.

[11] William Manson, *The Epistle to the Hebrews: An Historical and Theological Reconstruction* (London: Hodder and Stoughton, 1953); and I. D. Hurst, *The Epistle to the Hebrews: Its Background of Thought* (Cambridge: Cambridge University, 1990) 89–106.

[12] Ceslas Spicq, *L'Epître aux Hébreux* (SB; Paris: Gabalda, 1952–53).

an "encomium on Faith," thus focusing on the catch-word which binds all the heroes together.[13] In addition to the fact that this designation stretches the meaning of 'encomium,'[14] the shift of focus from the heroes and their recounted deeds to faith cannot capture the substance of the text. Furthermore, an occasional feature of example lists is the catchword, because it functions to string the items on the list together. The intention is not, however, necessarily to reify the word; it is also a rhetorically effective way—and even an aesthetically pleasing way—of constructing a list.[15] One other scholar has identified Hebrews 11 as an encomium, although he understands the text to be an encomium on Jesus.[16] In this case, the biblical heroes form the genealogy of Jesus. This thesis has many flaws, the most problematic one being that the deeds (πράξεις), of the presumed subject, i.e. Jesus, are non-existent.[17]

The most compelling texts for determining the form of Hebrews 11 remain the example lists and the historical summaries. To be sure, the structure of Hebrews 11 takes on the character of a list.[18] At the same time a retelling of biblical history is contained in that structure. While Cosby's study of Hebrews 11 in terms of the example lists of antiquity is a welcome contribution, its exclusive focus on the rhetorical *techniques*[19] used by authors who compose such lists did not allow him to pursue questions about the

---

[13] Attridge, *Hebrews*, 307. This is followed by Burton Mack, *Rhetoric in the New Testament* (Minneapolis: Fortress, 1990) 75.

[14] The term 'encomium' refers to a more precise kind of oratory than many other rhetorical terms. See Theodore Burgess, "Epideictic Literature," *University of Chicago Studies in Classical Philology III* (Chicago: University of Chicago, 1902) 89–261.

[15] Although Wisdom 10 does intend the hypostatization of Sophia (the text actually repeats the pronoun αὕτη for the most part), other texts, like CD 2–3, are primarily interested in the alliterative or anaphoric effects. See discussions of the individual lists below.

[16] Merland Ray Miller, "What is the Literary Form of Hebrews 11?" *JETS* 29 (1986) 411–17.

[17] The πράξεις normally form the bulk of the encomium and are the essence of it. Thomas Lee (*Studies in the Form of Sirach 44–50* [SBLDS 75; Atlanta: Scholars, 1986] 98) and Burgess ("Epideictic Literature," 113 n. 3) quote Theon's *Progymnasmata*, which defines encomium as "a speech which elucidates the magnitude of deeds according to virtue." (ἐγκώμιόν ἐστι λόγον ἐμφανίζων μέγεθος τῶν κατ᾿ ἀρετὴν πραξέων).

[18] By a list I mean that the component parts of the text are enumerated in succession. They are usually rendered succinctly, with only brief comments following the name of the hero.

[19] Cosby's work is concerned to identify the tools of the orator's trade—especially those that facilitate oral delivery—that the author of Hebrews employs. These include, for example, anaphora, paronomasia, paromoiosis, and so on.

rhetorical *meaning* of those texts. In this inquiry we want to know what is implied by the author's particular selection of heroes or events, and what motivates him to communicate this information to the audience.

My reading of earlier recapitulations of salvation history and hero lists, especially—but not exclusively—those that may have influenced the author of Hebrews, is an attempt to reveal their complexity. More often than not, they are multi-dimensional. By 'multi-dimensional' I mean that the examples display such variety that the purpose in the author's construction of such a list cannot be merely to illustrate a single point. Conversely, a uni-dimensional list is one that displays uniformity, so that all the examples clearly illustrate one specific point, e.g., the rewards of courage, or the value of education.[20] What is needed is a comprehensive examination of the various hero lists and historical surveys in terms of their content, rhetoric, theology (in the case of Jewish texts), in addition to their function. Such an examination will comprise the bulk of this chapter. I engage these texts, for the most part, without reference to Hebrews 11. After completing the discussion of the earlier texts on their own terms, I turn to Hebrews 11 in order to demonstrate how this material helps to locate the Hebrews hero list.

Jewish Literature

Biblical Historical Summaries

While no hero lists appear in the Hebrew Bible, several recapitulations of Jewish history occur. Sometimes certain heroes are named and their particular deeds recounted, although the emphasis is still primarily on events in the historical sequence rather than the qualities of special individuals. The historical summaries pointed out by scholars usually include Pss. 78, 105, 106, 135, 136, Ezek 20:5–44, and Neh 9:6–38.[21] Most commentators on Hebrews 11 cite some or all of these biblical passages. They do not, however, explore these earlier texts in any depth, which we shall do presently. Such an endeavor should clarify in what way Hebrews 11 resembles these precursor texts.

---

[20] These are topics which appear on some of the example lists analyzed later in the chapter.

[21] There are of course summaries of biblical history outside the Hebrew canon; the best known is probably Judith 5. Since there are no radical developments in the character of these summaries, there is no reason to include them. What is significant in the literature outside the Hebrew Bible, are the hero lists, which will be addressed after the summaries.

Joshua 24

Given that at least some of the other historical summaries were probably influenced either directly or indirectly by Joshua 24, it is surprising that it is not mentioned by commentators on Hebrews 11 who have looked for biblical antecedents.[22] Joshua 24 is the premier example of covenant renewal.[23] It almost certainly contains early, pre-monarchical material, although edited by the Deuteronomist.[24]

In Joshua 24 Israel's history is not recounted as historical memory, but as the *magnalia Dei*, the mighty acts of the deity, which provide the basis upon which a vassal (Israel) can enter into a covenant with a suzerain (Yahweh).[25] The *magnalia Dei* of Joshua 24 comprise what is known as the 'antecedent history' of the covenant document.[26] The *magnalia Dei* begin with the patriarchs, noting God's guidance in leading them away from serving other gods. Then follows Egypt, the exodus, and the conquest,[27] the last of which receives relatively substantial detail. The litany of God's salvific acts is followed by Joshua's challenge to the people either to enter into the covenant with Yahweh, or, if they wish, to choose to serve other gods. The people take a formal oath to serve Yahweh, by which they entered, or re-

---

[22] I have not found a single commentator who mentions Joshua 24 as a text cognate to Hebrews 11, although in discussions of biblical historical summaries themselves, e.g. (Karlheinz Müller, "Geschichte, Heilsgeschichte und Gesetz," *Literatur und Religion des Frühjudentums* [eds. J. Maier und J. Schriener; Würzburg: Echter, 1973] 73–105) Joshua 24 is included. Other similar recitals, like Deut 26:5–9 or Exod 19:3b–6 are sometimes mentioned by scholars. I have included Joshua 24 because it is by far the most similar to the other biblical summaries in the Psalms, Ezekiel and Nehemiah, which are in turn generally seen by scholars to have a direct or indirect link to Hebrews 11.

[23] Whereas at one time many Hebrew Bible scholars presumed there was an annual ceremony of covenant renewal, its existence is now seriously doubted; see Rainer Albertz, *A History of Israelite Religion in the Old Testament* (2 vols.; OTL; Louisville: Westminster/John Knox, 1994) 230–31. Nevertheless, most scholars still believe that there were moments of covenant renewal—most likely in times of crisis—in Israelite history. Also, loyalty to covenant constituted a part of worship (Deut 26:17–19); see Dennis McCarthy, "Covenant in Narratives from Late OT Times," *The Quest for the Kingdom of God*, eds. Huffman, Spina, and Green (Winona Lake, IN: Eisenbrauns, 1983) 77–94.

[24] See the commentary in R. Boling and G. E. Wright, *Joshua: A New Translation with Introduction and Commentary* (AB 6; Garden City, NY, 1982) 543–5.

[25] F. M. Cross, *Canaanite Myth and Hebrew Epic* (Cambridge, MA: Harvard University, 1973) 84.

[26] Klaus Baltzer, *The Covenant Formulary* (Philadelphia: Fortress, 1971) 19–28.

[27] What is most important about the conquest is the 'land,' because it is evidence of God's bounty. See Baltzer, *Covenant Formulary*, 20.

entered the covenant with Yahweh. "So Joshua made a covenant with the people that day, and made statutes and ordinances for them at Shechem" (v. 25).

What is most interesting about Joshua 24 is that while the function of this text is covenant renewal, covenant does not appear in the recounting of history. Neither the covenant with Abraham nor Mt. Sinai is mentioned. The reason for the omission is precisely due to the ritual context. Because the covenant ceremony is being ritually re-enacted, there can be no reference to previous covenants, for then the recital would be a *remembrance* rather than a *re-enactment*. A re-enactment of the covenant, such as Joshua 24, relates the historical sequence as exodus-conquest-covenant. But the historical memory of Israel (at least as conveyed in the Hebrew Bible) places the event of covenant-making at Sinai in between the exodus and the conquest, which renders the scenario exodus-covenant-conquest. In covenant re-enactment rituals the conquest is a precursor to the covenant, because the covenant is predicated on the battles Yahweh has won for the people.[28] Thus, the ritualistic performance of the covenant in Joshua 24 alters the order of events in historical memory.

As we shall see, the covenant, either as an event or as a theme, plays an important role in all the later historical summaries. The inclusion of 'covenant' or individual covenants in the recitals reveals the importance of it in the historical understanding of Israel's past.

Ezekiel 20:5–44[29]

In Ezekiel 20 the elders of Israel come to the prophet to consult God. Ezekiel's prophetic tenure spans a difficult period in Israelite history; this section of Ezekiel's writings dates to 591 BCE during the period of the first exile and five years before the temple was destroyed.[30] Unfortunately for the elders, God does not want to be consulted. Instead God instructs Ezekiel to "judge" Israel, to "let them know the abominations of their ancestors." This command is fulfilled by the recitation of Israel's history[31]—God is the speaker and Ezekiel is God's mouthpiece.

---

[28] Cross, *Canaanite Myth*, 85.

[29] Sometimes Ezekiel 16 and 23 are thought of as historical summaries. But these pericopes are unlike the texts under discussion here. Ezekiel 16 and 23 are historical retellings in allegorical form, in which Yahweh tells the story of his discovery and care of a harlot, who is Israel.

[30] Ezek 20:1 introduces God's oracle with a date formula.

[31] For a discussion of the relation between Ezekiel's view of history and his historical

Like many other biblical historical résumés we will see, the bulk of Ezekiel 20 is devoted to reminding the Israelites of how badly they have behaved toward God.[32] The text begins with the statement that Yahweh chose Israel when he revealed himself in Egypt.[33] He would be their God and would lead them out of Egypt into a land flowing with milk and honey. Then God gives them a command: they must give up the idols of Egypt. The people fail to honor this first request. God becomes angry and contemplates punishing them right there in Egypt, but instead acts for the sake of his name, "that it should not be profaned in the sight of the nations." God does in fact lead them out of Egypt. This descriptive pattern of God performing a gracious salvific act, the people rebelling or acting wickedly, God contemplating punishment, but deciding to act graciously despite their bad behavior, repeats several times in Ezekiel 20.

In at least one section, however, a punishment is meted out. Although God brings them out of Egypt and into the wilderness, God swears to them that they will be scattered among the nations. This threat is of course an allusion to the situation presently faced by Israel.[34]

> I swore to them in the wilderness that I would scatter them among the nations and disperse them through the countries, because they had not executed my ordinances, but had rejected my statutes and profaned my Sabbaths, and their eyes were set on their ancestors' idols. (vv. 23–24)

The mention of idolatry and the profaning of the Sabbath occurs several times throughout the text and is consistent with Ezekiel's cultic interests.

Despite God's angry tone, the oracle ends on a note of hope. God assures Israel that she will dwell in the land, as is her rightful inheritance.[35] As we

---

situation, see Gerhard von Rad, *Old Testament Theology* (New York: Harper & Row, 1965) 2.220–30.

[32] Moshe Greenberg (*Ezekiel 1–20* [AB 22; Garden City: Doubleday, 1983] 377–78) identifies four stages of rebellion: 1) Egypt; 2) 1st Wilderness; 3) 2nd Wilderness; 4) In the Land. The fourth stage differs from the previous three in that God will direct a new exodus which will end in the realization of a true covenantal relationship between God and Israel.

[33] According to priestly tradition, Egypt (Exod 6:2–3, 28–29) is where the divine name is first revealed; see Joseph Blenkinsopp, *Ezekiel* (Louisville: John Knox, 1990).

[34] Greenberg (*Ezekiel 1–20*, 380) points out that the distinguishing feature of Ezekiel 20, when compared to historical surveys in chaps. 16 and 23, is that the present is addressed. See vv. 30–32, 39.

[35] "As a pleasing odor I will accept you, when I bring you out from the peoples, and gather you out of the countries where you have been scattered; and I will manifest my holiness among you in the sight of the nations. You shall know that I am the Lord, when I

shall see below, the theme of the reconstitution of the people in the promised land is ubiquitous in the historical résumés. The theme of the inheritance of the land, as well as the themes of profaning the Sabbath and idolatry, address the issue of Israel's identity as a nation.

Nehemiah 9:6–38

Like Ezekiel 20, Nehemiah 9 also emphasizes the people's failure to behave faithfully toward God, but the setting and mode of address are very different. Nehemiah 9 is a public prayer, a "national confession" spoken by Ezra on behalf of the people.[36] Because the form is that of a prayer, God's acts in history are recounted in the form of direct address from Ezra to God (e.g., "*you* divided the sea . . . *you* threw their pursuers into the depths"), rather than describing God's actions in the third person, or in the first person when God is the speaker, as in Ezekiel 20. Moreover, whenever the people are the active subject of a sentence they always act wickedly, as in vv. 17–19:

> *[T]hey* stiffened their necks and determined to return to their slavery in Egypt. But you are a God ready to forgive, gracious and merciful, slow to anger and abounding in steadfast love, and you did not forsake them. Even when *they* had cast an image of a calf for themselves and said, 'This is your God who brought you up out of Egypt,' and had committed great blasphemies, you in your great mercies did not forsake them in the wilderness; the pillar of cloud that led them in the way did not leave them by day, nor the pillar of fire by night that gave them light on the way by which they should go.

The scene is a powerful one: the people, having now returned from exile, are reconstituting themselves. In the previous chapter Ezra publicly read the Law of Moses. Nehemiah 9 takes place a few weeks later when the people are again assembled, but this time the mood is penitential. The narrative prelude to Ezra's prayer relates that the people of Israel were fasting and in sackcloth.

Immediately following Ezra's speech, the people renew their commitment by signing a covenant, binding them by an oath to "God's law, which

---

bring you into the land of Israel, the country that I swore to give to your ancestors" (vv. 41–42).

[36] On Nehemiah 9 as a confession, see M. Gilbert, "La place de la loi dans la prière de Néhémie 9," *De la Tôrah au Messie: Mélanges Henri Cazelles*, ed. J. Doré, P. Grelot, and M. Carrez (Paris: Desclée, 1981) 307–16; and H. G. M. Williamson, *Ezra, Nehemiah* (WBC 16; Waco, Texas: Word Books, 1985) 306–7.

was given by Moses the servant of God, and to observe and do all the commandments of the Lord our Lord and his ordinances and his statutes" (v. 29). Thus, while the form of Nehemiah 9 is a prayer, it functions as covenant renewal.[37] Because Israel is here understood to have broken the covenant in the past, the curses of the original covenant have come down on her—she has suffered. Thus, the historical review of this covenant renewal must involve repentance,[38] which is undertaken by the people's confession of sins of the past.

Beyond its form, Nehemiah 9 differs from Ezekiel 20 in two significant ways: First, it begins with a mention of creation: "You are the Lord, you alone; you have made the heaven, . . . the earth and all that is on it . . . ," whereas Ezekiel 20 began with Egypt. After creation Ezra mentions Abraham and the covenant God made with Abraham to give him the land of the Canaanites.

The second distinction from Ezekiel 20 regards the way the text ends. Nehemiah 9 closes on a pessimistic note. As harsh as Ezekiel's oracle is, it ends on a note of hope. "You shall know that I am the Lord, when I bring you into the land of Israel, the country that I swore to give to your ancestors" (Ezek 20:42). Although in the Ezekiel text the people have failed to serve God faithfully in the past, their evil ways will come to an end; they shall loathe themselves for all the evils they have committed. In contrast, Nehemiah ends with words of desperation:

> Here we are, slaves to this day—slaves in the land that you gave to our ancestors to enjoy its fruit and its good gifts. Its rich yield goes to the kings whom you have set over us because of our sins; they have power also over our bodies and over our livestock at their pleasure, and we are in great distress. (vv. 36–37)

This pessimistic outlook is surprising, given the historical context for this text of Nehemiah, especially when compared to Ezekiel 20. In Ezekiel 20 the people are in the process of going into exile; in Nehemiah the people are reassembled in the land and are in the midst of reconstituting themselves as

---

[37] Baltzer (*Covenant Formulary*) had thought Nehemiah 9–10 was an example of a covenant renewal ceremony, with chap. 9 functioning as the antecedent history. For a less dated, more nuanced view of covenant renewal in Nehemiah, see Dennis McCarthy, "Covenant and Law in Chronicles-Nehemiah," *CBQ* 44 (1984) 25–44.

[38] There seem to be examples of this kind of covenant renewal at Qumran (1QS 1.26; 5.7–9). See Baltzer, *Covenant Formulary*, 97–136; A. Jaubert, *La notion de l'alliance dans le judaisme aux abords de l'ère chrétienne* (Patristica sorbonensis 6; Paris: Seuil, 1963) 214–19; and McCarthy, "Covenant in Narratives."

the people of Yahweh, who abide by the law of Moses. Perhaps the ending was seen by its author to be in keeping with the penitential tone of the overall text.[39]

Psalm 78

Psalm 78 states its function in the introduction.

Give ear, O my people, to my teaching; incline your ears to the words of my mouth . . . I will utter dark sayings of old, things that we have heard and known, that our ancestors have told us. We will not hide them from their children; we will tell to the coming generation the glorious deeds of the Lord . . . . (vv. 1–4)

Unlike the other psalms discussed below, which begin as hymns of praise to God, the purpose of the poetic recounting of history in Psalm 78 is to be morally instructive.[40] The "dark sayings of old . . . that our ancestors told us" is similar to v. 4b of Ezekiel 20, "let them know the abominations of their ancestors . . . ." God reprimands Israel in order to correct her ways. Thus, like Nehemiah 9 and Ezekiel 20, (as well as Psalm 106 to be discussed below) the emphasis of Psalm 78 lies in the people's failure and rebellion in contrast to God's faithfulness.[41]

Like Ezekiel 20, Psalm 78 begins with the exodus from Egypt, the account of which is extraordinarily detailed, including a full account of the ten plagues. But what is most unique about the psalm is that it concludes not with entry into the land, or Israel being handed over to her enemies, but with mention of the Jerusalem temple and David. Furthermore, the psalmist explicitly demeans the tribe of Ephraim, while asserting that God has chosen the tribe of Judah to receive his inheritance. The psalm is therefore most likely dated to the fall of the Northern Kingdom.[42]

---

[39] Many scholars feel that Nehemiah 9—like much of the Ezra-Nehemiah material—does not originally belong in its present context. For this position, see Williamson, *Ezra, Nehemiah*, 375–76; and Blenkinsopp, *Ezra-Nehemiah, A Commentary* (OTL; Philadelphia: Westminster, 1988) 301–2. However, this position has been persuasively criticized by, among others, Tamara Eskenazi, *In an Age of Prose: A Literary Approach to Ezra-Nehemiah* (SBLMS 36; Atlanta: Scholars, 1988).

[40] Thus, A. A. Anderson (*The Book of Psalms* [New Century Bible; London: Oliphants, 1972] 2.561) designates it a 'didactic psalm,' as did F. Delitzsch, *Psalms* (Commentary on the Old Testament in Ten Volumes; Grand Rapids: Eerdmans, 1988) 361–62.

[41] The tone of these texts led Bent Noack (*Spätjudentum und Heilsgeschichte* [Stuttgart: W. Kohlhammer, 1971] 29) to categorize them as *Rückverweise.*

[42] See Delizsch (*Psalms*, 361–62) for a discussion of the historical situation.

Psalm 105

Psalm 105 is generally considered to be a hymn of praise.[43] It is surely a festival hymn.[44] The opening verses are a call to worship Yahweh, which will be done by rehearsing his *magnalia Dei*: "O give thanks to the Lord, call on his name, make known his deeds among the peoples. Sing praises to him; tell of all his wonderful works" (vv. 1–2). Psalm 105 is unique among the historical psalms in that it begins with the patriarchs and a retelling of the Joseph story before recounting the exodus. It ends with God giving Israel the "lands of the nations" as promised (v. 11).

Unlike the other historical résumés discussed so far, Psalm 105 has only *positive* reports of the relationship between God and Israel. The common theme of the people's violation of the covenant and their lack of faith have no role here. However, the people of Israel do not have any active role in this text. The psalm recounts only God's works in history, portraying God's devotion to Israel and commitment to the covenant, without much comment about Israel's response as a people. In this sense, Psalm 105 resembles the other summaries in its description of God, but it simply omits discussion of the people's misdeeds.

There are more individuals named in this text than the others. The purpose, however, is not to highlight any person's particular accomplishments, but rather to stress Israel's status as a chosen people and God's guiding hand in history.

[God] is mindful of his covenant forever, of the word he commanded, for a thousand generations, the covenant that he made with Abraham .... (vv.8–9)

When he summoned famine against the land, and broke every staff of bread, he had sent a man ahead of them, Joseph, who was sold as a slave .... (vv.16–17)

Psalm 105 is difficult to date. The fact that the author does not mention the people's unfaithfulness or any punishments of Israel does not necessarily

---

[43] Hermann Gunkel, *The Psalms: A Form-Critical Introduction* (Philadelphia: Fortress, 1967) 10–13.

[44] Vv. 1–15 are quoted in 1 Chr 16: 8–22, together with Psalm 96 and Ps 106:47. At one time Psalm 105, as well as all the "Heilgeschichte psalms" were believed to have been sung at covenant renewal ceremonies; see Artur Weiser (*The Psalms* [Old Testament Library; Philadelphia: Westminster, 1962] 673–74). But since the existence of such a ceremony has recently been doubted, we cannot know the specific occasion for the reciting of such psalms.

indicate a pre-exilic date. The psalm shows dependence on the final form of the Pentateuch and probably dates to the post-exilic period.

Psalm 106

Psalm 106 has been associated with Ezekiel 20, Nehemiah 9, and Psalm 78, because like those texts it highlights the people's misdeeds in contrast to God's salvific acts.[45] The psalm reminds the reader particularly of Nehemiah 9 because of its confessional tone.

> Remember me, O Lord, when you show favor to your people; help me when you deliver them; that I may see the prosperity of your chosen ones, . . . that I may glory in your heritage. (vv. 4–5)

> Both we and our ancestors have sinned; we have committed iniquity, have done wickedly. (v. 6)

Despite this tone, the psalm, like Psalm 105, begins and ends like a hymn of praise.[46]

The author begins the historical résumé with the people's rebelliousness during the exodus and ends with Israel's subjection to her enemies. However, it ends, not on a note of hopelessness, but with a positive attitude in the midst of this subjection.

> Nevertheless [God] regarded their distress when he heard their cry. For their sake he remembered his covenant, and showed compassion according to the abundance of his steadfast love. He caused them to be pitied by all who held them captive. (vv. 44–46)

Given this attitude, as well as its dependence on the Pentateuch, the psalm can be placed in the post-exilic period.

What is most noteworthy about Psalm 106 is that it distinguishes certain individuals who set themselves apart from the people by their noble actions. Moreover, these figures act as intercessors between God and the people.

> They were jealous of Moses in the camp, and of Aaron, the holy one of the Lord. (v. 16)

> They forgot God, their Savior, who had done great things in Egypt, wondrous works in the land of Ham, and awesome deeds by the Red

---

[45] Lee, *Form of Sirach 44–50*, 26–27.

[46] Psalm 106 is not classified as a hymn of praise because of the recounting of the people's misdeeds. Scholars who possess the category of 'historical psalms' put it in this category, although this is a category based on content, not form. See John Kselman and Michael Barré, "Psalms," *JBC*, 526.

Sea. Therefore he said he would destroy them—had not Moses, his chosen one, stood in the breach before him, to turn away his wrath from destroying them. (vv. 21–23)

[T]hey provoked the Lord to anger with their deeds, and a plague broke out among them. Then Phinehas stood up and interceded, and the plague was stopped. (v. 30)

Although notable individuals from Israelite history are sometimes named in other summaries, they always act as agents of God; they are never credited with independent action or virtuous qualities. Chronologically, Psalm 106 is the first text which ascribes to a few individuals self-motivated actions.[47] Furthermore, it is important to recognize that the will of these individuals, e.g., Moses and Phinehas, is *not* in harmony with the will of the people. This development is significant, because later sectarian texts that summarize biblical history believe the genealogy of the remnant of Israel is preserved only through certain individuals, and not the whole of Israel.

Psalms 135 and 136

Both of these psalms are considered hymns of praise, and can therefore be categorized with Psalm 105. The people are only the recipients of God's mighty acts; they are never active agents. Both psalms begin with creation, to which several lines are devoted, then they move on to the exodus and conclude with the settlement of the land, as is typical. Both mention the defeat of Kings Sihon and Og. Psalm 136 is much longer than Psalm 135, because it includes more details about the exodus story, and because it includes a refrain following every act of God recited:

who spread out the earth on the waters, for his steadfast love endures forever; . . . who made the great lights, for his steadfast love endures forever; . . . . (vv. 6–7)

who struck Egypt through their first born, for his steadfast love endures forever; . . . and brought Israel out from them, for his steadfast love endures forever; . . . . (vv. 10–11)

---

[47] Those scholars who see a great chasm between the biblical historical summaries and the Hellenistic hero lists, such as Lee (*Form of Sirach 44–50*), Müller ("Geschichte"), and Noack (*Spätjudentum*), do not seem to have noticed the significance of Psalm 106, which may stand as a critical developmental stage between the collective history of the summaries and the emphasis on individuals in the Hellenistic lists.

Common Themes and Development Among the Summaries

While each of these texts has idiosyncrasies that are connected with their historical contexts, several important themes occur repeatedly in all or most of them.

1) Covenant: First, Joshua 24 is an important text, not only because it is one of the earliest thorough recitals of Israel's history up to that point, but because its function—that of covenant renewal—is also a likely function for many of the later texts. This function is most obvious in Nehemiah 9.[48] Because the Nehemiah recital is followed by a scene where at least certain individuals sign the covenant and bind themselves to the law of Yahweh, the contextual similarity between Joshua 24 and Nehemiah 9 is clear.

Covenant renewal is not, however, just one potential function of the reciting of these summaries; 'covenant' is more importantly a theme within the recital. The word 'covenant' (ברית) occurs in all the summaries mentioned, with the exception of Psalms 135 and 136. Sometimes it serves as part of a thematic introduction or conclusion:

> The Ephraimites, armed with the bow, turned back on the day of battle. They did not keep God's *covenant,* but refused to walk according to his law [torah]. (Ps 78:9–10)

> Many times he delivered them, but they were rebellious in their purposes, and were brought low through their iniquity. Nevertheless, he regarded their distress when he heard their cry. For their sake he remembered his *covenant,* . . . . (Ps 106:43–45)

At other times the text names a specific covenant.

> You are the Lord, the God who chose Abram and brought him out of Ur of the Chaldeans and gave him the name Abraham; and you found his heart faithful before you, and made with him a *covenant* to give to his descendants the land of the Canaanite, the Hittite, the Amorite, the Perizzite, and the Girgashite; and you have fulfilled your promise, for you are righteous. (Neh 9:7–8)

> He is mindful of his *covenant* forever, of the word that he commanded, for a thousand generations, the *covenant* that he made with Abraham, his sworn promise to Isaac, which he confirmed to Jacob as a statute, to Israel as an everlasting covenant, saying, "To you I will give the land of Canaan as your portion for an inheritance." (Ps 105:8–11)

---

[48] See McCarthy ("Covenant and Law," 34–36) who identifies the constituent parts of covenant renewal in Nehemiah 8–10.

While the earliest résumé we looked at, Joshua 24, does not list the making of any of the covenants in the summary of events, the later texts include God's covenant with Israel as part of history retold. Joshua can skip over the Sinai experience in his listing of great historical moments, because the covenant is not contained in history; it is literally re-enacted at the moment Joshua speaks. In this case the covenant is not part of the past but the present. However, for all the texts after Joshua 24, the covenant becomes an element *within* history to be remembered.[49]

2) *The Land:* Closely tied to the theme of covenant—and even more prominent—stands the theme of the inheritance of the land. In the quotations cited earlier from Neh 9:7–8 and Ps 105:8–11, we can see the explicit connection between the Abrahamic covenant and the promise of the land. Since most of our texts date to exilic or post-exilic times, the importance of the land is not surprising. In the case of Nehemiah 9, the mention of the land not only comes at the beginning and at the end, but reference to the promise about the land occurs twice during the historical sequence (vv. 15, 22–25; the latter being a very detailed account of entry into the land). Similarly, Ezekiel 20 mentions the land at the beginning and the end and several times in between.

While the theme of possessing the land occurs most frequently in Nehemiah and Ezekiel, it also appears in the other texts. Indeed, nearly all of the texts begin and end with a reference to the possession of the land as part of Israel's promised inheritance. The following is a list of these references from the ends of the texts.

Here we are, slaves to this day—slaves in the *land* that you gave to our ancestors to enjoy its fruit and its good gifts. (Neh 9:36)

You shall know that I am the Lord, when I bring you into the *land of Israel,* the country that I swore to give to your ancestors. (Ezek 20:42)

He drove out nations before them; he apportioned them for a *possession* and settled the tribes of Israel. (Ps 78:55)

For he remembered his holy promise, and Abraham his servant. So he brought his people out with joy, his chosen ones with singing. He gave

---

[49] Perhaps significantly, none of the résumés use the word בְּרִית to describe the Sinai event in particular. It is beyond the scope of this paper, however, to address the debate among Hebrew Bible scholars regarding conflicting covenant traditions (e.g., whether or not the Davidic covenant superceded the Mosaic). See Jon D. Levenson, "The Davidic Covenant and Its Modern Interpreters," *CBQ* 41 (1979) 205–19.

them the *lands* of the nations, and they took possession of the wealth of the peoples . . . . (Ps 105:42–44)

He struck down many nations and killed many kings—Sihon, king of the Amorites, and Og, king of Bashan, and all the kingdoms of Canaan—and gave their *land as a heritage*, a heritage to his people Israel. (Ps 135:10–12)

and killed famous kings . . . Sihon, king of the Amorites . . . and Og, king of Bashan . . . and gave their *land as a heritage* . . . a heritage to his servant Israel. (Ps 136:18–22)

From this list of quotations we can see that the entry into the land plays a significant role in both kinds of summaries, those that highlight the bad behavior of the Israelites and those that do not. In the first kind of text there is often anxiety expressed about the status of this promised inheritance (as is the case with Neh 9:36), or the ultimate possession of the land is pushed forward into eschatological time (Ezek 20:42[50]). Nevertheless, the fact that reference to the inheritance of the land is made usually at the beginning and at the end of these texts indicates that land possession serves a teleological function in the retelling of history. In other words, the inheritance of the land is the goal toward which Israelite history is directed.

3) Corporate Identity: In Joshua 24, the identity of the people presently addressed in the recital and the "ancestors" are conflated. While Joshua recounts past events, and therefore knows that there is a temporal distinction between the time of Abraham and the present people whom he now addresses, he nevertheless uses the pronouns 'you' (i.e., the people who are the audience) and 'they' (i.e., the people's ancestors) almost interchangeably, as in vv. 6–7.[51]

When I brought *your ancestors* out of Egypt, *you* came to the sea; and the Egyptians pursued *your ancestors* with chariots and horsemen to the

---

[50] From Ezek 20:33ff., God speaks in the future tense, reflecting a utopian time when Israel will dwell in the land while keeping God's commandments. The implication of Ezekiel's oracle is that the exodus/conquest scenario has not been properly completed up to that point. The 'conquest' has been delayed. Ezekiel most likely envisions the return to the land after being exiled as the opportunity for the ultimate and rightful settling of the land. On the eschatology of Ezekiel, see Paul D. Hanson, *The Dawn of Apocalyptic: The Historical and Sociological Roots of Jewish Apocalyptic Eschatology* (Philadelphia: Fortress, 1979) 228–40.

[51] Boling and Wright (*Joshua*, 534) point out that the term 'ancestors' forms an "envelope construction," where the term occurs six times in vv. 2–6 and three times in vv. 14–17; while the intervening passages use the pronoun 'you.'

Red Sea. When *they* cried out to the Lord, he put darkness between *you* and the Egyptians, and made the sea come upon them and cover them; and *your eyes* saw what I did to Egypt. Afterwards *you* lived in the wilderness a long time.

Historical time is collapsed in the service of generational solidarity. The interchangeable use of the third person 'ancestors' and the second person 'you' indicate that there is no significant sense of historical distance between generations in Joshua's recitation of God's acts in history.

This historical telescoping is partially in evidence in Ezekiel 20 and Nehemiah 9 as well. In both texts the speakers use the third person (e.g., 'Israel' or 'ancestors') consistently to recount the deeds of the past, but they easily make the transition to the second person at certain points.[52] The switch of pronouns implicitly equates Israel's past sins (committed by the ancestors) with the audience's. For the bulk of the recital, Nehemiah 9 recounts the sins of the ancestors as the ancestors' own doing: "our ancestors acted presumptuously and stiffened their necks and did not obey your commandments" (v.16); and "they were disobedient and rebelled against you and cast your law behind their backs and killed your prophets . . . . Therefore, you gave them into the hands of their enemies, who made them suffer" (vv. 26–27). At the end, however, we find the present people identifying the ancestors' sins as their own: "Here we are, slaves to this day— slaves in the land that you gave to our ancestors to enjoy its fruit and its good gifts. Its rich yield goes to the kings whom you have set over us because of *our* sins . . ." (vv. 36–37). Thus, while the ancestors' sins are treated as the people's sins at the end, the speaker does not create the same kind of conflation throughout the recital of history that occurs in Joshua 24.[53] The speaker, Ezra, allows for more historical distance between the people and the ancestors.

4) Historical Distancing and the Coverage of Events: The later texts in general seem more aware of the temporal distance between them and the history they recount. The best example of this historical distancing is the prelude in Psalm 78:

---

[52] In Ezekiel 20 this transition happens in vv. 30–35; 37–40; 41–44. In Nehemiah 9 it only happens at the end, from v. 32ff.

[53] Cf. Ps 106:6, which explicitly identifies the sins of former generations with the current generation, "Both we and our ancestors have sinned . . ." Nevertheless, the historical recital itself speaks of the ancestors in the third person.

I will utter dark sayings from of old, things that we have heard and
known, that our ancestors have told us. (vv. 2–3)

He established a decree in Jacob, and appointed a law in Israel, which
he commanded our ancestors to teach to their children; that the next
generation might know them and the children yet unborn. (vv. 5–6)

In this instance the progression of time itself is understood as the reason for
recounting this historical memory. Indeed, the psalmist here recounts a
memory. History itself is memorialized in such psalmic résumés. This
memorializing of history represents a significant development from the
ritualized re-enactment of history in Joshua 24. Furthermore, history is not
kept up to date, i.e., almost all the summaries that are exilic or post-exilic
end with the conquest of the land, or, in the résumés where Israel acts
unfaithfully, with Israel falling victim to her enemies. Recent history is
largely ignored.

The overwhelming bulk of every summary focuses on the exodus story,
which is usually followed by the possession of the land, as stated above.
While the degree of detail varies from very detailed (Psalm 78) to very brief
(Psalm 135), the proportionate majority of a given summary is consumed by
the exodus narrative. Interestingly, it is the earliest text, Joshua 24, that has
the most evenly distributed coverage of events, including mention of several
post-exodus details. This helps bring the sequence of events up to the
moment when the historical summary is recited. After all, the text of Joshua
24 is spoken in pre-monarchical times; there was not yet much to tell beyond
the conquest of the land.

Later texts usually end their historical summary earlier than Joshua 24,
even though, ironically, there is more history to tell. Of all the biblical
summaries, only Psalm 78 makes any mention of a monarch, viz., David in v.
70. And none of the events that lead up to the time of David are
enumerated. For the most part, the summaries begin history with the exodus
after a prelude, although Nehemiah 9 and Psalms 135 and 136 begin with
creation, while Psalm 105 initiates the historical sequence with Abraham and
the patriarchs. The historical summaries reflect their historical context not
by bringing history up to date, but by their perspective on early Israelite
history or by grafting the current situation onto the historical retelling.
When writers do make reference to their current situation, history retold
does not build up to the present, but is appended on to the exodus-conquest
scenario. In other words, the authors who write in the exilic period or later
do not cover the historical events leading up to their own time (like the

period of the judges, or the rise and fall of the monarchy). Nehemiah 9, for example, takes us through the period of the conquest and into some vague time when Israel began to be the victim of her enemies, which turns out to be the current post-exilic situation. No events between the conquest and the exile are described.

Most of the Hellenistic hero lists, which we will review in a moment, move beyond the exodus story to include judges and monarchs and prophets. The main list in Hebrews 11, however, does not make it past Rahab, who follows Moses and the Israelites. Thus, like the biblical summaries, the historic climax of Hebrews 11 is the period of the exodus/conquest. Nevertheless, the two most important themes that traditionally accompany the recounting of this momentous period of Israelite history are missing in Hebrews 11: the covenant at Sinai and the taking of the land. The fact that the author covers the same span of history as the biblical summaries, and yet omits the two most significant moments within that history is one key to understanding Hebrews 11.

Hellenistic Hero Lists

Sirach 44–50

If there is one text scholars are reminded of when they study Hebrews 11, it is Sirach 44–50, "The Hymn in Honor of Our Ancestors."[54] Dated ca. 180 BCE, it stands as the earliest example of a Jewish Hellenistic hero list. As such it represents a departure from the historical summaries of the Hebrew canon. While the summaries recounted historical events as the *magnalia Dei,* the hero lists enumerate the accomplishments of individuals. Because Sirach 44–50 and the other texts considered in this section are structured as lists, rather than as narrative[55] retellings of historical events, they are sometimes referred to as *Beispielreihen,* or 'example lists.' Scholars who use this term wish to emphasize the dissimilarity between the hero lists of the Hellenistic period and the biblical summaries.[56] Although most scholars recognize a

---

54 The title πατέρων ὑμνος is found in the Greek text.

55 I do not use the word 'narrative' here in the sense of prose (as opposed to poetry). To be sure, many of the summaries are poetic. Rather, I mean that the résumés in the Hebrew Bible tell a story; they have a beginning, a middle, and an end.

56 Lee (*Form of Sirach 44–50*) following Thyen (*Homilie,* 112), believes the *Beispielreihen* are related to the παραδείγματα of Greek rhetoric—which explains why only Hellenistic texts use this form. Lee (32–41) believes that biblical historical summaries should not be considered cognate antecedents to Sirach 44–50, as are *Beilspielreihen* such as 1 Macc 2:51–60 and Wisdom 10. (Since Lee classifes Hebrews 11 as a *Beispielreihe* [32], he would probably come to the same conclusions about Hebrews 11's relationship to the biblical

literary relationship between the summaries and the hero lists,[57] those who designate the Hellenistic texts 'Beispielreihen' believe that the function of these lists is to assemble examples to illustrate a general point.[58] From this point of view the hero lists possess a synchronic structure, while the summaries are diachronic. In other words, the summaries tell a story, and the hero lists do not. In the analysis that follows, I wish to demonstrate that some of the Hellenistic hero lists are more similar to the summaries than has been traditionally thought. In these lists, the author is not just synchronically listing heroes, but telling the story of Israelite history. Perhaps nowhere else is this more obvious than in Sirach 44–50.

The hymn is the longest and most complete text[59] we will consider. After a lengthy proem (44:1–15), the list of individuals praised in the hymn begins with Noah,[60] and ends with the praising of Simon II. Many scholars previously considered the praising of Simon an appendix, because he could not be considered one of the 'ancestors.'[61] However, a trend toward seeing the section on Simon as part of the original hymn has developed.[62] There

---

summaries.)

[57] In spite of the fact that they stress the dissimilarity between the biblical summaries and the Hellenistic hero lists, Thyen (Homilie) and Lee (Form of Sirach 44–50) assume that the Beispielreihe is an evolution from the historical summary. This assessment, therefore, puts the historical summaries on the same literary trajectory as the example lists.

[58] Interestingly, Cosby (Rhetorical Composition, 14) whose study of example lists is quite comprehensive, and who calls Hebrews 11 an 'example list,' omits Sirach 44–50 on the grounds that as an encomium-type list, it is not truly an example list.

[59] That is, it has the most extensive coverage of Israelite history.

[60] In the Greek, Enoch precedes Noah, and thus Enoch heads the list. However, our earliest Hebrew texts of Sirach do not include this initial mention of Enoch. Therefore, most scholars assume he was not part of the original composition. The same is true of 49:14–16, wherein Enoch is mentioned again along with Joseph, Shem, Seth, and Enosh. See P. Skehan and A. Di Lella (The Wisdom of Ben Sira [AB; New York: Doubleday, 1987] 499) who point out that these additions form an interesting inclusio.

[61] See G. H. Box and W. O. E. Oesterley, "The Book of Sirach" in The Apocrypha and Pseudepigrapha of the Old Testament in English, ed. R. H. Charles (London: Oxford University, 1971) 1.279; Thierry Maertens, L'Eloge des pères (Ecclèsiastique XLIV-L) (Bruges: Editions de L'Abbaye de Saint-André, 1956) 195–96; Helmut Lamparter, Die Apokryphen I: Das Buch Jesus Sirach (Die Botschaft des Alten Testament 25.1; Stuttgart: Calwer, 1972) 211; and Skehan and Di Lella, Ben Sira, 499.

[62] See Robert T. Siebeneck, "May Their Bones Return to Life!—Sirach's Praise of the Fathers, " CBQ 21 (1959) 415; Noack, Spätjudentum, 42–3; Enno Janssen, Das Gottesvolk und seine Geschichte: Geschichtsbild und Selbstverstandnis im palästinensischen Schrittum von Jesus Sirach bis Jehuda ha-Nasi (Neukirchen-Vluyn: Neukirchener, 1971) 16–33; Lee, Form of Sirach 44–50, 10–12; Burton Mack, Wisdom and the Hebrew Epic: Ben Sira's Hymn in Praise of the Fathers (Chicago and London: University of Chicago, 1985) 195–8.

has also been some discussion about the relationship of the preceding hymn praising God's creation (Sir 42:15–43:35) to Sirach 40–55. Burton Mack believes that the hymn of creation and the hymn in praise of the ancestors are discrete textual units, but that they are intentionally juxtaposed and work to complement each other.[63]

I find Mack's study on Sirach 44–50 to be the most exegetically sensitive reading of the text. He has concluded that although many descriptions of the heroes are detailed and can be read as miniature eulogized biographies,[64] an overall pattern of characterization nevertheless exists.

> Ben Sira worked with types of heroes or functions of heroes in history and used the devices of type recurrence, success and failure of type functions, juxtapositions, comparisons, escalations, and so forth, in order to delineate the course of "the heroic" from beginning to end in a systematic way.[65]

Mack designates seven components that make up the pattern of characterization: 1) designation of office; 2) mention of divine approbation or election; 3) a reference to covenant; 4) mention of the person's character or piety, 5) an account of the deeds; 6) reference to the historical situation; and 7) mention of rewards.[66]

Of these seven, he finds that the concept of office plays the most dominant role in the text.[67] "The assignment of a figure to an office is so consistently emphasized that one must ask whether it is not the office that makes the man for Ben Sira."[68] In some cases—specifically the offices of priest, king, and Moses[69]—the office is directly tied to the covenant. So, for example, Ben Sira says of Aaron, "He made an everlasting covenant with him, and gave him the priesthood of the people" (45:7). And of Phinehas he says, "therefore a covenant of friendship was established with him, that he should be leader of the sanctuary and of his people, that he and his descendants should have the dignity of the priesthood forever" (45:24). In chap. 50 Simon performs the same functions in the office of priest as Aaron

---

[63] Mack, *Wisdom and Hebrew Epic,* 189–93.

[64] Lee (*Form of Sirach 44–50,* 54–79) has dealt most comprehensively with the influence of biography on Sirach 44–50.

[65] Mack, *Wisdom and Hebrew Epic,* 17.

[66] Mack, *Wisdom and Hebrew Epic,* 18–26, 205–14.

[67] Mack, *Wisdom and Hebrew Epic,* 18.

[68] Mack, *Wisdom and Hebrew Epic,* 19.

[69] Mack (*Wisdom and Hebrew Epic,* 30–32) believes Moses is a unique figure on the list, and he therefore has a *sui generis* office.

does. Thus, the heroes are heroic because they participate in an authoritative office or covenant. This association between hero and office implicitly—or explicitly as in the example of an inherited office above—creates genealogies, sequencing, and lines of succession among the heroes.[70]

More than continuity, this emphasis on offices helps to create historical development and teleology. In other words, Sirach 44–50 possesses diachronic movement which guides the reader through Israelite history. Such movement is not due solely to the fact that the heroes of Sirach 44–50 are listed in chronological order; to be sure, Jewish hero lists are almost always in chronological order.[71] Rather, the author achieves historical continuity and development by making the heroes part of one coherent and evolving story, even as he relates their individual biographies. The listing by Ben Sira of great individuals with their respective accomplishments is not simply a list, but a historical composition possessing movement and drama.

Historical coherence and evolution in Sirach 44–50 is conveyed by several different means. First, the text breaks down into five broad periods of history according to Mack: 1) the establishment of the covenants; 2) the conquest of the land; 3) the history of kings and prophets; 4) the restoration; and 5) the climax, which refers to the rule of Simon.[72] The first period, for example, includes Noah, Abraham, Isaac, Jacob, Moses, Aaron, and Phinehas. Each of these men is said to have been given a covenant.[73]

Mack also identifies something he calls "serialization," by which he means nothing more than the connecting of figures by means of a theme.[74] For example, he points out that the sub-series which runs from Abraham to Isaac is held together by the promise of blessing. Of Abraham Ben Sira says "that the nations would be blessed through his offspring" (44:21). He concludes the series by saying

---

[70] Cf. Lee (*Form of Sirach 44–50*, 79) who ardently downplays the importance of succession in Sirach.

[71] The only exception is 4 Macc 18:11–19.

[72] Mack, *Wisdom and Hebrew Epic*, 37–41. Cf. Maertens (*L'Eloge des pères*) who identifies three periods. Other commentators are strikingly disinterested in assessing the compositional flow of the hymn. Since Lee (*Form of Sirach 44–50*) sees the text as an encomium praising Simon, he sees 44:15–49:16 as one unit.

[73] In fact, Ben Sira breaks the chronological sequence after Phinehas in order to mention the covenant with David before moving onto Joshua (45:25). This break is a major clue that this first section should be thought of as a unit, encompassing the establishment of covenants.

[74] Mack, *Wisdom and Hebrew Epic*, 42.

To Isaac also he gave the same assurance for the sake of his father
Abraham. The blessing of all people and the covenant he made to rest
on the head of Jacob; he acknowledged him with his blessings, and
gave him his inheritance; he divided his portions, and distributed
them among twelve tribes. (44:22–23)

Here explicit successive connection occurs between figures as well as
historical development—the text describes how the promise to Abraham
concerning possession of the land was realized at a later point.

It is not clear whether Mack intended for serialization to cross historical
periods (or whether doing so would undermine his five-part historical
breakdown), but the theme of inheritance certainly connects figures across
periods. By inheritance I refer to the tangible part of the promise made to
Abraham: the land and the constitution of nationhood that accompanies
it.[75] The theme turns up in the verses extending from Abraham to Caleb—
the latter naturally comes after Phinehas and Joshua, which in turn falls in
the period of the conquest of the land (period 2 in Mack's scheme), while
Abraham falls in the period of covenants (period 1). Caleb is said to have led
"the people into their inheritance, the land flowing with milk and honey"
(46:8). Furthermore, "The Lord gave Caleb strength, which remained with
him in his old age, so he went up to the hill country, and his children
obtained it for an inheritance, . . ." (46:9). Thus, what God first promises to
Abraham becomes a reality in Caleb's time. The fact that the theme of
inheritance plays no significant role after this section indicates that with
Caleb and the conquest of the land the matter of inheritance is brought to a
close.

We can further demonstrate the role of biblical history in Ben Sira's
hymn to the ancestors by pointing out that he includes mention of undesir-
able figures in his hero list in order to fill out the historical sequence. These
undesirables occur in the section covering kings and prophets:

Solomon rested with his ancestors, and left behind one of his sons,
broad in folly and lacking in sense, Rehoboam, whose policy drove the
people to revolt. Then Jeroboam son of Nebat led Israel into sin and
started Ephraim on its sinful ways. Their sins increased more and
more, until they were exiled from their land. (47:23–24)

Neither are the kings of Judah exempt from this criticism:

---

[75] In other words, the same important concept of inheritance as we saw in the
historical summaries.

Except for David and Hezekiah and Josiah, all of them were great sinners, for they abandoned the law of the Most High; the kings of Judah came to an end. They gave their power to others, and their glory to a foreign nation, who set fire to the chosen city of the sanctuary, and made its streets desolate, as Jeremiah had foretold. (49:4–6)

The inclusion of anti-heroes indicates a motivation beyond the praising of Israel's greatest heroes. Although these anti-heroes may partly function as contrasting models, Ben Sira's inclusion of such information also allows him to be historically comprehensive. That is, he does not want to leave out certain historical events, even if they are not an integral part of any of the heroes' biographies. He includes events (such as the destruction of the temple) which he connects to various individuals (such as the bad kings of Judah and Jeremiah) but which are ultimately important *as events* in the collective history of the nation. Indeed, because the heroes are leaders (hence the importance of offices) throughout the history of Israel, their deeds and honors are often coextensive or at least bound up with great events in Israel's history.

One final comment about Ben Sira's understanding of history in this text is in order. When we discussed the historical summaries above, we noted that the earliest ones were highly ritualistic, and therefore historical time was collapsed in them. The *magnalia Dei* of the covenant renewal ceremony were recited not as a memorial, but as a living myth. However, in some later historical résumés a sense of historical distance was detected. The proem of Sirach 44–50 makes it very clear that the hymn is a memorial to heroes and history past.[76] This does not mean that there are not important continuities between Ben Sira's time and the past. After all, the hymn does conclude by eulogizing Simon in such a way that he is portrayed as a new Aaron.[77] Nevertheless, the very notion of succession and historical development in the text points to the author's awareness of the progression of historical time. Much has changed since the time of Noah and the Patriarchs; a nation was established and a temple was built. Ben Sira's hero list thus tells the story of the birth of a nation and its greatest institution, the temple.

---

[76] Note that Ben Sira regards the heroes as great in their own time as well as in historical memory. "[All these men] were honored in their generations, and were the pride of their times. Some of them have left behind a name so that others declare their praise" (44:7–8). As we shall see, the author of Hebrews praises his heroes as if they were previously unsung .

[77] See Lee, *Form of Sirach 44–50*, 10–18.

Although Sirach 44–50 is structured as a list of Israel's heroes, it shares with the biblical summaries an interest in telling Israel's story. The fact that Ben Sira includes sinful kings and the destruction they visited upon the people shows the influence of the summaries that include the failures and sins of the people. If Ben Sira was only interested in the virtues of Israel's rulers, then he would have chosen only virtuous figures for his list. Furthermore, at least two themes that were prominent in the summaries are prominent in Sirach: covenant and inheritance of the land.

1 Maccabees 2:51–60

As he lay dying, Mattathias, patriarch of the Maccabees and a military hero himself, gives a farewell speech which includes a list of Jewish heroes, beginning with Abraham and ending with Daniel.

The opening line "remember the deeds of your ancestors, which they did in their generations . . ." is reminiscent of the introduction to Sirach 44–50. However, both the literary and historical setting of this text differ from Sirach. While Sirach 44–50 reflects a scholastic and liturgical setting written for the glorification of Israel, 1 Macc 2:51–60 stands in the context of military and political interest. The list also has a far more consistent and less complex pattern than the list in Sirach. Every hero on the list is remembered for an act of bravery for which he is rewarded. (See figure 1.) Although the text is laconic about some of the accomplishments of the heroes, particular incidents are most likely being remembered. For example, Joseph is said to have "kept the commandment," therefore he becomes lord of Egypt. This "commandment" refers to the incident in Potiphar's house in which Joseph resists the wiles of Mrs. Potiphar.[78] The heroes of 1 Macc 2:51–60 follow Torah, or some aspect thereof, very strictly in the face of adversity. As a result God rewards the hero in a concrete and public way, so that he can be recognized for the hero he is. Phinehas zealously routs out sin; his reward is therefore the covenant of the priesthood. Elijah never stops defying the sinful king, so he is taken up to heaven. In about half the cases, the reward is a position of leadership ordained by God.

---

[78] Cf. 4 Macc 2:1–4 and see James Kugel, *In Potiphar's House* (San Francisco: Harper San Francisco, 1990) 21.

Figure 1. Heroes of 1 Macc 2:51-60 w/Deeds and Rewards

Hero	Deed	Reward
Abraham	tested	righteousness
Joseph	kept commandment	lord of Egypt
Phinehas	zealous	covenant of priesthood
Joshua	fulfilled commandment	became judge
Caleb	testified	inheritance of land
David	merciful	throne
Elijah	zeal for law	taken up to heaven
Hannaniah, Azariah, & Mishael	believed	saved from flame
Daniel	innocent	delivered from lion

The opening line of 1 Macc 2:51-60 quoted above is followed by the statement, "and you will receive great honor and an everlasting name." Thus, the rewards mentioned for each hero are there to inspire the listener that uncompromising fidelity to the covenant will be rewarded.[79] Indeed some of the figures mentioned on the hero list have undergone trials noticeably similar to events in the life of Mattathias.[80] The lives of the heroes are therefore primarily remembered for their military and political conquests.

1 Macc 2:51-60 is not the multi-dimensional text of Sirach 44-50.[81] Nevertheless, important historical themes we saw in Sirach 44-50 and in the summaries—like covenant and inheritance of the land—appear here. Although the heroes appear in chronological order, there is no historical

---

[79] Verse 50 of this same chapter says, "Now my children, show zeal for the law, and give your lives for the covenant of our ancestors."

[80] For example, J. A. Goldstein (*1 Maccabees* [AB 41; Garden City, NY: Doubleday, 1976] 7, 230-31) points out that the description of Mattathias fleeing to the hills (2:28) or leading a band of fugitive outlaws (2:44) intentionally resonates with stories in the military life of David (see 1 Sam 22:1-2; 23:1-5; 25:14-16). Also 2:19-22, which describes Mattathias determination to remain loyal to God and covenant, even if everyone else does otherwise, parallels the story of Joshua and Caleb in Numbers 13-14. The reader should note that Joshua and Caleb were also mentioned in Sirach for their loyalty, despite the crowd's tendency to go the other way. Furthermore, Mattathias is explicitly compared to Phinehas in 2:26.

[81] It is not, however, as simple a list as we will see among Greco-Roman writers. The author of this list has included a variety of characters who do *different* sorts of deeds and receive *different* rewards. The variety may just be rhetorical, or it may indicate the author's striving for a broad coverage of biblical history.

progression or genealogical succession from Abraham to Daniel.[82] In this sense, 1 Macc 2:51–60 can be substantially differentiated from the summaries of the Hebrew canon. The designation of *Beispielreihe* can be unambiguously applied here.

Wisdom 10

Wisdom 10 possesses two stylistic features that have not appeared thus far. First, the heroes are not identified by name, but the descriptions given of each figure are not enigmatic—they clearly point to one particular biblical figure in each case.[83] For example vv. 13–14 relate some of the biographical details from the life of Joseph:

> When a righteous man was sold, wisdom did not desert him, but delivered him from sin. She descended with him into the dungeon, and when he was in prison she did not leave him, until she brought him the scepter of a kingdom and authority over his masters. Those who accused him she showed to be false, and she gave him everlasting honor.

This device occurs elsewhere in the book of Wisdom. Its intended effect is probably poetic or aesthetic.[84]

A second notable stylistic feature is the anaphoric use of the pronoun αὕτη to introduce each character. αὕτη refers to the figure of Sophia who guides and protects the heroes. This anaphora is notable because it plays the same stylistic role that πίστει plays in Hebrews 11,[85] although πίστις is not a personified agent.

The intent of Wisdom 10 is not simply to describe Sophia, but rather to highlight those special individuals who have been blessed by her presence

---

[82] However Phinehas is called "our ancestor," meaning that since Mattathias is a priest he is descended from him.

[83] The assertion by J. M. Reese (*Hellenistic Influence on the Book of Wisdom and Its Consequences* [AnBib 41; Rome: Pontifical Biblical Institute, 1970] 119) that the author avoids naming the heroes because he is interested in types rather than the particular individuals fails to take account of the historical specifics surrounding the discussion of each hero. Also, cf. 1 Macc 2:51–60 where the deeds of the heroes are not specifically identified but nevertheless specific incidents are being referred to.

[84] See David Winston, *The Wisdom of Solomon* (AB; Garden City, NY: Doubleday, 1979) 139 n. 10.

[85] Lee (*Form of Sirach 44–50*, 48) believes that Hebrews 11, Wisdom 10, and CD 2:17–3:12 are a particular kind of *Beispielreihe*, which is structured around the repeated use of a catchword. Although I would not call these texts merely *Beispielreihen*, the catch-word as a stylistic feature is unmistakable.

and to show how she has steered their course through history.[86] At the same time, Wisdom 10 is not *merely* a *Beispielreihe*, but, like Sirach 44–50, shows marked similarities with the historical summaries, and is, therefore, a historical reading as well. In this case, historical continuity and development is clear because Sophia is a historical agent who links all the heroes together into one narrative.

Since Sophia herself is ultimately responsible for the course of events, Wisdom 10 parallels the summaries which recount the *magnalia Dei*. Comparisons like the following abound:

> Then [Yahweh] brought Israel out with silver and gold, and there was no one among their tribes who stumbled. Egypt was glad when they departed, for dread of them had fallen upon it. He spread a cloud for a covering, and fire to give light by night. (Ps 105:37–39)

> [Wisdom] gave to holy people the reward of their labors; she guided them along a marvelous way, and became a shelter to them by day, and a starry flame through the night. (Wis 10:17)

Wisdom is now credited for acts that were previously stated as the work of Yahweh.[87] Individual heroes are singled out, but a single principle provides continuity, both thematic and historical.

Furthermore, covenantal theology, which played a significant role in the summaries, provides both a synchronic and diachronic structure to the text. First, a synchronic pattern emerges which pairs each righteous hero with an opposing wicked individual or group.[88]

Adam	Cain
Noah	Generation of the Flood
Abraham	Nations in confusion (Babel)
Lot	People of Sodom

---

[86] Francois Bovon ("Le Christ, la foi et la sagasse dans L'Epître aux Hébreux" *RThPh* 18 (1968) 135–36) believes the sapiential context of Wisdom 10, as well as Sirach 44–50 and 4 Macc 16–18, is essential for understanding the texts. He thinks it is the sapiential background which has influenced Hebrews 11 as well. While a sapiential context or influence is entirely possible for Hebrews 11, some of Bovon's criteria are too general to be applied only to sapiential texts.

[87] As M. J. Suggs (*Wisdom, Christology, and Law in Mathew's Gospel* [Cambridge: 1970] 21) says (also quoted by Winston [*Wisdom*, 211]) "The idea of Wisdom's repeated efforts among men through her envoys is elaborated in Wis 10–11 into a new interpretation of *Heilsgeschichte*, in which Israel's history is seen as determined by Sophia's providential guidance of the people through chosen vessels in each generation."

[88] Winston, *Wisdom*, 211.

Jacob	Esau
Joseph	His brothers and other enemies
Moses/Israel	Egypt = the nation of oppressors

Thus, each of the heroes is under the special protection of Sophia against some evil or chaotic part of the world.[89]

Second, the text possesses diachronic movement, that is, historical development. Wisdom 10:1 opens with Adam, who is described as "the first-fashioned father of the world, created alone."[90] The emphasis on the aloneness of Adam allows for the gradual expansion of the world and a progression toward ethnic particularity as the author proceeds with the description of each figure. Adam is alone, but Abraham lives among other (generic) nations. Joseph lives among the nation of oppressors. Then Israel, a holy people and a blameless race (10:15), arises from within the "nation of oppressors." Thus, through Sophia's guidance, God's holy people is established from the father of the world; a specific trajectory is isolated within world history.[91] Therefore, Wisdom 10 is not only a list of biblical examples, but a historical review which seeks to explain the genesis of the people Israel.[92]

4 Maccabees 16:16–23; 18:11–19

The two hero lists in 4 Maccabees are frequently cited as parallels to Hebrews 11. Attridge has pointed out that the first one, in chap. 16, resembles Hebrews 11 because it has a similar paraenetic interest:[93] "you ought to endure any suffering for the sake of God . . ." (v. 19); "you too must have the same faith in God and not be grieved" (v. 22). The theme of

---

[89] Thyen (*Homilie*, 114–15), who identified what he believed were two kinds of *Beispielreihen*, type 'a' which is composed of standard positive examples and type 'b', which is the "Historische Exempla für die Bestrafung von Frevlern." He believes Wisdom 10 is a combination of the two types. See also the discussion in Lee, *Form of Sirach 44–50*, 42.

[90] Translation from Winston (*Wisdom*, 210).

[91] Interestingly, each section of Wisdom 10 becomes progressively longer with each successive hero. The mention of each hero is gradually accompanied by more and more detail about events contemporary with the hero's life. In vv. 15–21 only one line is actually devoted to Moses (v. 16); the remainder of the verses concern the exodus events and the people of Israel.

[92] Chapter 11 of Wisdom continues the deuteronomic historical sequence with more detailed descriptions of the exodus, the wilderness, and the conquest. It would be tempting to see it all as one section but for the fact that the anaphora is discontinued. Cf. R. T. Siebeneck, "The Midrash of Wisdom 10–19" *CBQ* 22 (1969) 176–82.

[93] Attridge, *Hebrews*, 306.

suffering clearly ties all the figures listed together.[94] The list includes Abraham, who was asked to sacrifice his son Isaac, who is also named for his bravery when he realized his father was about to take his life; Daniel and the well-known threesome, Hananiah, Azariah, and Mishael are the others who appear here—they are mentioned for the same sufferings named on the list in 1 Maccabees.

4 Macc 16:16–23 most resembles 1 Macc 2:51–60 of the texts we have studied so far. 4 Macc 16:16–23 has no interest in salvation history; it is simply a uni-dimensional list of well-known individuals who have suffered on account of their religion. Its only *raison d'être* is as exempla for the point being made, and therefore it is properly labeled a *Beispielreihe*.

More so than 1 Macc 2:51–60 the list here is very short and makes no attempt to be historically comprehensive. Because there is no variety in the kinds of people listed, i.e., because everyone appears here for exactly the same reason (suffering which they nobly endured), the writer of 4 Maccabees is not interested in the historical circumstances of any one figure or even in their individuality. They are merely types.

The list in 4 Macc 18:11–19 is longer and more varied. The mother of the seven martyred children relates how her husband, Eleazar, used to teach her children "the Law and the Prophets." What follows is a listing of examples which presumably represent a sampling of what he taught. It begins, "He read to you of Abel, slain by Cain, of Isaac, offered as a burnt offering, and of Joseph, in prison" (v. 11). Phinehas and Hananiah, Azariah, Mishael, and Daniel follow. After Daniel several other figures are named, although not as biblical characters, but as *authors* of memorable verses of scripture,[95] with the quoted verses included, e.g.,

> He reminded you of the scripture of Isaiah which says, "Even though you walk through the fire, the flame shall not burn you." He sang to you of the psalm of David which says, "Many are the afflictions of the righteous." (vv. 14–15)

That the figures named are the authors of scripture and not objects of it in the second half of the list make it unique. However, it fits in with the opening line about teaching the Law and the Prophets. Still, it is unusual that the author does not follow chronological order in the second half of the

---

[94] The primary theme of 4 Maccabees is the triumph of reason over the passions, and it is in this context that the martyrdoms of the heroes must be understood.

[95] A few commentators, such as Attridge (*Hebrews*, 306) do not regard vv. 14–19 as part of the same unit as vv. 9–13.

list. The disregard for chronology probably indicates the author's disinterest once again in salvation history. Yet, while I would not say that the author desires to be comprehensive, he does strive for variety—the goal appears to be to construct a representative sample of biblical characters.[96]

The Covenant of Damascus 2–3

This section of the Covenant of Damascus stands out along with Sirach 44–50 and Wisdom 10, as being both a listing of examples and a diachronic reading of biblical history. At first glance it looks similar to the biblical historical summaries which highlight the failure of the people, but like Wisdom 10, certain individuals stand apart as having resisted the evil that otherwise possessed all the people.

Lee has shown that this text is a list constructed in a catch-word format much like Wisdom 10. The author introduces this section of the text with an exhortative plea for the listener to know what it is God rejects and what God favors. The examples follow—there are those who followed thoughts triggered by the eyes of lust and those who did not. The catch-word is first the preposition-plus-pronoun בם "in them," which refers to the "eyes of lust" (עיני זנות); then it switches to בה "in it," which refers to the "stubbornness of their hearts" (שרירות לבם). The following is an abbreviated outline of the examples:[97]

A. Pre-patriarchal period
   1. General
      a. Many went astray through them
      b. Mighty heroes stumbled in them
   2. Specific examples of stubbornness of heart
      a. Heavenly watchers caught in it
      b. Sons of Noah went astray through it
      c. Their families were cut off through it
B. Patriarchs
   Abraham did not walk in it
   Isaac
   Jacob

---

[96] This list seems to be particularly influenced by who is included on other lists, particularly the one in 1 Macc. While the majority of figures in the first half of the list are suffering figures, the inclusion of Phinehas stands apart; he is not known for suffering, but for zealousness. The reader should also note that Hananiah, Azariah, Mishael, and Daniel appear on all three Maccabees lists.

[97] This outline is a modified version of Lee's (*Form of Sirach 44–50*, 45–47).

C. Israel
  1. General
      Sons of Jacob went astray through them
  2. Specific examples of stubbornness of heart
      a. Their sons perished through it[98]
      b. Their kings were cut off in it
      c. Their mighty men perished through it
      d. Their land was ravaged through it
D. Summary
  Through it the first members of the covenant sinned.

Lee's perceptive analysis of this text allows him to categorize it along with Wisdom 10 and Hebrews 11 as a subset of the *Beispielreihen*—that subset being those example lists strung together by a catch-word. Such an analysis is useful for our purposes because it points to the formal motivation an author may have had in choosing such a catch-word, rather than, or in addition to, a theological motive. In other words, while Wisdom 10 has at times been viewed as an aretology on Sophia,[99] and Hebrews 11 been seen as an encomium on faith, the primary function of the recurring word may be primarily aesthetic.

Because Lee does not read this text as a historical retelling, his only explanation for the appearance of positive and negative examples is an appeal to Thyen's mixed *Beispielreihen*, in which heroes and wrongdoers are sometimes listed together.[100] But the author of the Covenant of Damascus is also formulating a historical genealogy to explain the origin and development of both the corrupt faction of Israel and the remnant, with which the sect identifies itself.

For the author of the Covenant of Damascus, the story of Israelite history goes like this: In the primeval period, nearly everyone fell short of God's expectations. Then, for the sake of the patriarchs, God made a covenant with Israel (presumably Sinai). Israel sins anyway after this, but God forgives them and builds them a temple. The "stubbornness of their hearts," however, resumes among the people. After this, those who are "members of the covenant forever"—the patriarchs and those who follow in their

---

[98] Although the referent appears to be the same, the gender of the Hebrew pronoun switches here.

[99] See Winston, *Wisdom,* 211–13.

[100] See n. 89.

footsteps—become a distinct group *apart from* the children of Israel.[101] For this author then, two separate trajectories exist within the history of Israel. Given that the text ends by identifying the elect as the Qumran community,[102] I think it likely that the example series was intended as an etiological history of the sect. The reason for positive and negative examples is not simply the construction of illustrations, by similarity and contrast, for moral behavior. The author clearly displays a historiographical interest. That is, he wishes to retell the biblical story in such a way so as to explain the contemporary fractious environment of Judaism in the last two centuries BCE.

4 Ezra 7:105–111

4 Ezra contains the following example list:

"[S]o no one shall ever pray for another on that day, neither shall anyone lay a burden on another; for then everyone shall bear his own righteousness or unrighteousness." I answered and said, "How then do we find that first Abraham prayed for the people of Sodom, and Moses for our fathers who sinned in the desert, and Joshua after him for Israel in the days of Achan, and Samuel in the days of Saul, and David for the plague, and Solomon for those in the sanctuary, and Elijah for those who received the rain, and for the one who was dead, that he might live, and Hezekiah for the people in the days of Sennacherib, and many others prayed for many? If therefore the righteous have prayed for the ungodly now, when corruption has increased and unrighteousness has multiplied, why will it not be so then as well?"[103]

The angel then responds to Ezra's question by telling him that in the "immortal age to come" there can be no corruption of any kind. Therefore, unrighteous individuals cannot exist.

This text is no doubt a *Beispielreihe*. That is, all the examples synchronically illustrate one type of action—prayer—with no significant diachronic movement, or narrative. In this sense, 4 Ezra 105–111 is similar to the list of martyrs in 4 Maccabees, although the descriptions of each hero are not as consistent. One would expect that all the prayers would be prayers for the

---

[101] At the end of the passage the author quotes from Ezek 44:15: "The Priests, the Levites, and the sons of Zadok who kept the charge of my sanctuary when the children of Israel strayed from me, they shall offer me fat and blood." After the quotation the writer tells us that the priests are the "converts of Israel who departed from the land of Judah." The Levites joined them, and the sons of Zadok are the elect of Israel "who shall stand at the end of days."

[102] See the last line of note above.

[103] Translation from Bruce Metzger, "The Fourth Book of Ezra," *OTP*, 1.540–41.

benefit of others; most are, but some are not.[104] Furthermore, most of his examples refer to situations where there was a contest or conflict of some kind between the hero, along with his allies, and the opposing group who was defying God.[105] The figure of Ezra himself is implicitly part of the historical lineage of the righteous because he, too, is portrayed as someone exceptionally merciful throughout 4 Ezra.[106] The fourth book of Ezra is fundamentally concerned with the fate of the unrighteous, and, as we see in the hero list, with defining the relationship between the righteous and the unrighteous.[107]

Philo

Two texts from the works of Philo, *De Praemiis et Poenis* 11–51 and *De Virtutibus* 198–227, are often listed by commentators as example lists which bear a resemblance to Hebrews 11.[108] These texts from Philo represent a shift from the previous texts. It is my contention that texts from Philo are mentioned too glibly in discussions of *Beispielreihen*[109] and in relation to Hebrews 11.[110] We shall look briefly at Philo's lists in order to clarify what the similarities and differences are.

---

[104] Joshua inquires why he has lost in battle (Josh 7:6–9); David repents of his own sin (2 Sam 24:17); and Hezekiah prays for victory (2 Kings 19:15–19).

[105] Abraham and his kinsman Lot vs. Sodom (Gen 18–19, prayer 18:23); Moses vs. the wilderness generation (Exod 32, prayer 32:11); Joshua vs. Achan who kept some of the devoted things and thereby caused destruction for the Israelites in the battle immediately following at Ai (Joshua 7, prayer 7:6–9); Samuel is not in harmony with the people who want a king, even though he complies and comes into conflict with Saul (1 Sam 7, prayer 7:9; see also 1 Sam 15); Elijah vs. the prophets of Baal (1 Kings 18, prayer 18:36–39); and Hezekiah vs. Sennacherib the King of Assyria (2 Kings 19, prayer 19:15–19). With David and Solomon there does not appear to be specific opposition, although Solomon's prayer at the time of the dedication of the temple devotes substantial verbage to the potential reconciliation that can come following sin because of the presence of a temple. David's prayer constitutes repentence for his own sin.

[106] See especially chap. 8.

[107] Since 4 Ezra is dated ca. 100 CE (see Metzger, "Fourth Ezra," 520), the interest in defining the relationship between the righteous and unrighteous probably reflects the domestic dissension between different Jewish groups, as well as complex relations with other ethnic groups. See also M. E. Stone, "Introduction," *Jewish Writings of the Second Temple Period*, 24–31.

[108] Lee (*Form of Sirach 44–50*, 32) also cites *Quod Omn. Prob.* 62–130, but see my comment in n. 116.

[109] E.g. Lee, *Form of Sirach 44–50*, 37–42; Windisch, *Hebräerbrief*, 98–99.

[110] Attridge, *Hebrews*, 306.

First, *De Praemiis et Poenis* 11 is sometimes cited by itself as a parallel, because here Philo lists a series of examples all introduced by the word "hope," ἐλπίς. After telling his reader that the Creator God has first sown the seed of hope in the human rational soul, Philo starts naming examples.

In hope of gain the tradesman arms himself for the manifold forms of money getting. In hope of a successful voyage the skipper crosses the wide open seas. In hope of glory the ambitious man chooses political life and the charge of public affairs. The hope of prizes and crowns moves the training athlete to endure the contests of the arena. The hope of happiness incites also the devotees of virtue to study wisdom, believing that thus they will be able to discern the nature of all that exists and to act in accordance with nature . . . .

Philo goes on to say that "he alone is worthy of approval who sets his hope on God . . . ." Although Philo does use anaphora here, which is similar to Hebrews 11,[111] the kind of example used by Philo does not parallel the examples used in Hebrews or in any of the texts seen so far. These examples are of a general type, in this case, professions, which do not resemble the *specific* persons drawn from history in the other texts. Besides the repeated theme of 'hope,' the only parallel between this particular text and the others is that examples are cited.

Later in the same treatise, however, Philo does name specific biblical characters who illustrate abstract qualities,[112] but these involve such extended narration, commentary, and argumentation that a reader would hardly recognize that s/he is in the midst of a list. One list, which only includes Abraham, Isaac, and Jacob, covers nine pages of text in the Loeb edition, thus placing the Philo 'example lists' in a class by themselves. A similar situation exists in *De Virtutibus*.[113]

What makes the lists from Philo different from the other Jewish Hellenistic hero lists is their form in relation to the literary context. Both *De Virtutibus* and *De Praemiis et Poenis* are lengthy treatises, on topics covered by their respective titles. Especially in *De Praemiis et Poenis*, the figures discussed are not historical examples of an abstract subject but are the subjects

---

[111] Philo, however, is not as consistent as the author of Hebrews. The first three examples begin with ἐλπίδι, then Philo uses δι᾽ ἐλπίδα, and finally ἐλπίς.

[112] In *Praem.* 13–51 Philo discusses two groups of three examples The first includes Enosh, Enoch, and Noah; the second includes Abraham, Isaac, and Jacob.

[113] In order to prove that virtue is not an inherited trait, Philo lists examples first of individuals who were born of noble parents but led ignoble lives (199–210), and second, figures who had humble beginnings but led virtuous lives (211–227). These two lists together also comprise more than nine pages of text in the Loeb edition.

themselves. For Philo, history is the story of reward and punishment.[114] Almost every character is discussed at length and in substantial detail, and often because they illustrate a point peculiar to themselves, and not simply a general point. Enosh, Enoch, and Noah are unique examples of particular traits (hope, repentance and justice) as much as they are examples of the fact that they are rewarded.

Although it may be difficult to make brevity a hard and fast criterion for judging a 'list,' if the figures are not listed in a consistent and predictable succession, the reader or listener will not perceive that s/he has encountered a list of examples illustrating a common point. If too much detail is provided by the author, the focus will be on the particulars of a given case rather than on the general point being illustrated. Indeed, as Cosby has shown, it is the rapid fire listing of multiple examples that gives an example list its rhetorical power.[115] The list creates the impression that the author has innumerable examples that could prove the point at his/her disposal but s/he does not have enough time or space to list them all. In contrast, Philo frequently pauses to bask in the special qualities of certain Jewish heroes.

We must keep in mind that the use of multiple examples or heroes in a text is not sufficient to make it an 'example list' or a 'hero list.' With the exception of the psalms, which are individual compositions, all the lists we have studied so far are an integral part of larger texts, even though they can be identified as sub-units having distinctive rhetorical techniques.[116] Aside from the use of more than one figure in a row, the texts from Philo bear little resemblance to the other Jewish Hellenistic hero lists. Not surprisingly, Philo's 'lists' bear the most resemblance to Greco-Roman lists.

Comparison and Contrast of Jewish Hero Catalogs

Perhaps what is most noteworthy about all these lists is that they always reflect the interests of the author and thereby display an ideology consistent with their literary context. Since these catalogs are intended to gather

---

[114] As Philo himself says regarding the historical part of the Bible, "The historical part is a record of good and bad lives and of the sentences passed in each generation on both, rewards in one case, punishments in the other" (*Praem.*, 2).

[115] Cosby, *Rhetorical Composition,* 19.

[116] Interestingly, Cosby (*Rhetorical Composition,* 12–14) includes the texts from *De Virtutibus* in his study but comments that *De Praemiis et Poenis* as well as *Quod Omnis Probus Liber sit,* which is listed by Lee (*Form of Sirach 44–50,* 32), do not stand out enough from their contexts to warrant consideration as a distinct unit.

together certain heroes to illustrate a certain point(s), we should not be surprised at their variety.[117] By looking at their similarities and differences, we can expose their common function(s) as well as important deviations.

1) Characters: The two most common characters that appear are Abraham and Joseph. That an audience always expected the mention of Abraham is evident from his ubiquitous presence on these lists; he must be considered the hero *par excellence.* I have collected each text's mention of Abraham in figure 2, enumerating the events from his life that appear in each list. (I have included Abrahamic events from the biblical summaries as well as Acts 7 and Hebrews 11 for comparison.) In this way it is easy to identify the most popular events, as well as idiosyncratic entries.

Figure 2. Descriptions of Abraham on Hero Lists

Neh 9	Psalm 105	Sir 44–50	1 Macc 2	Wis 10
Choosing/ Naming		Father of Nations		Presence at Babel
		kept law		
covenant	covenant	covenant		
land	land/inheritance	offering of Isaac	offering of Isaac	offering of Isaac
promise		promise		
		nations blessed		
		numerous descendants	reckoned as righteous	
		inheritance		

4 Macc 16	CD 2–3	4 Ezra 7	Acts 7	Heb 11
father	friend of God	prayed for Sodom	Migration	Migration
			inheritance	inheritance/ land
	kept law		promise	promise
			Foretelling of Egypt and exodus	foreigner
	covenant		covenant	
			bore & circumcised Isaac	conception of Isaac
				Numerous descendants
offering of Isaac				offering of Isaac

---

117 In Appendix B I have listed the heroes from each list in parallel columns.

We note, for example that the covenant and the offering of Isaac are the most popular incidents recorded from Abraham's life on these lists. While the offering of Isaac was not mentioned in the biblical summaries, it occurs on every list from the Hellenistic period, with the exception of 4 Ezra and the Covenant of Damascus.

We must note that of all the lists, Hebrews 11 has most in common with Sirach 44–50 regarding Abraham (as is true of Joseph). They share the following biographic elements: The offering of Isaac, God's promise or oath to Abraham, and two of the contents of that promise—topographic inheritance[118] and numerous descendants.[119] Hebrews additionally includes the migration (which Acts 7 also has) and the conception of Isaac, which is unique to Hebrews.

The character of Joseph is also praised effusively on the hero lists. In Wisdom 10 Sophia "brought him the scepter of a kingdom and authority over his masters." In 1 Macc 2:53 he is called 'Lord of Egypt.' This title and the authority that comes with it function as Joseph's honor or reward. Figure 3 is a comparative rendering of the events in Joseph's life on those hero lists where he appears. We must note that Joseph does not appear on those texts that have sectarian orientation, namely the Covenant of Damascus and 4 Ezra. From figure 3 we can not only see the honors typically bestowed upon Joseph, but also the idiosyncrasies of the authors. For example, I suspect that the same thoughts that kept Joseph off the sectarian lists have affected the presentation of Joseph on other lists. Wisdom 10 mentions that Joseph received the scepter of a kingdom, but the kingdom goes unnamed. If we consider the interests and provenance of the Wisdom of Solomon as a whole, this comes as no surprise. The likely tension between Jews and Gentiles in Alexandria at the time[120] and the author's theological interest in portraying a chasm between Jews and "pagans," would make Joseph's intimate connection with the Egyptian kingdom disturbing.

---

[118] Although the word ἐπαγγελία, because of its different connotations in the LXX, does not appear in Genesis 15 to refer to God's oath, and does not appear in the historical summaries, in NT times it was commonly used to refer to God's promise to Abraham about the land. Cf. Rom 4:13–17 and Gal 3:18. Several references in Hebrews itself make clear the connection between ἐπαγγελία and the specific oath to Abraham regarding the inheritance of the land: 6:13, 7:6, 11:9, 17. See BAGD 280–81.

[119] Wisdom 10 and the Covenant of Damacus do not make use of the promises to Abraham.

[120] Winston, *Wisdom*, 21–25.

Figure 3. Descriptions of Joseph on Hero Lists

Psalm 105	Sir 44–50	1 Macc 2	Wis 10
sold			sold
		Mrs. Potiphar incident	Mrs. Potiphar incident
prison			prison
prophesied			
Lord of Egypt	bones cared for	Lord of Egypt	Lord

4 Macc 18	Acts 7	Heb 11
prison	sold	
	wisdom before Pharaoh	
	Lord of Egypt	mention of exodus
	Reunited w/brothers	
	bodies returned to Shechem	instructions about his bones

Joseph is absent from the original text of Sirach. Perhaps this should not surprise us either, since national offices are so important to the author of Sirach, and the one office Joseph held was in another nation, i.e., Egypt. However, mention of him was added near the end of the text (49:15); it reads: "Nor was anyone ever born like Joseph; even his bones were cared for." Reference to his bones occurs in Hebrews 11 as well. When we consider all the biographical facts to choose from in the biblical Joseph story, mention of his bones is puzzling. Joseph's virtue or heroism would be better illustrated by his resistance to Mrs. Potiphar (1 Macc 2; Wis 10) or his endurance and eventual release from prison (Ps 105; Wis 10). There may well be some cross-influence among these lists which caused authors to include certain biographic elements about a hero.[121]

2) Rewards: In spite of the many idiosyncrasies of each list, at least one theme is consistent: The heroes are usually said to have been honored or rewarded in some way.[122] In the list from 1 Macc 2:51–60, the rewards actually structured the text, but we can find mention of rewards or honors in almost every catalog. That rewards play such a consistent role points to the fact that lists like this are displays of national pride.[123] That the heroes are a source of national pride is true even for those few lists that do not explicitly

---

[121] Kugel (*Potiphar's House*, 28–29) points out that because Jospeh's bones are mentioned in Gen 50:24–26, and then in Exod 13:19 when Moses brings them out of Egypt, and then in Josh 24:32 when they are taken to Shechem, exegetes frequently focused on the theme of Joseph's remains.

[122] The only exceptions to this are the lists in 4 Macc and 4 Ezra, but even in these cases rewards are implicit.

[123] Siebeneck, "May Their Bones Return to Life," 414.

mention the honors these men received in their own lifetime, such as 4 Macc 16:18–23. Just before the mother of the seven commences her list of biblical martyrs in order to encourage her sons, she says, "My sons, noble is the contest to which you are called to bear witness for the *nation*. Fight zealously for our ancestral law" (4 Macc 16:16).

3) Interest in Retelling the Story of Israelite History: As will become increasingly clear, Sirach 44–50, Wisdom 10, and the Covenant of Damascus are the most closely related antecedents to Hebrews 11. They are longer, more complex lists that display an overt interest in retelling the history of Israel. In fact, the two most important themes in the biblical résumés, the covenant and the land, play a major role on the longer lists.[124] The shorter lists function only as example-series which illustrate one precise concept. In other words, those lists are uni-dimensional, while Hebrews, Sirach, Wisdom, and the Covenant of Damascus are multi-dimensional. Most importantly, the heroes on these multi-dimensional lists form historical genealogies for the community being addressed by the hero catalog. Communities find legitimation and even etiological explanations of their origins in these texts. In our discussion of Sirach we saw how the heroes were the originators of national offices, institutions, and covenants. Most significant for the author is the institution of the priesthood. In order to eulogize Simon II with maximum effect, he must show that Simon is the true heir to Aaron and Phinehas. It is not just that Simon, Aaron, and Phinehas are exemplary priests; a genealogy is being drawn. As such, it is the story of an ecclesiastical dynasty and the institution it upholds. We saw also how Wisdom 10 is an account of the evolution of the people Israel into a distinct, chosen nation. Sophia functions as a structural link which not only allows for the praise of heroes, but describes them as playing a part in the birth of the nation. In this sense, a genealogy is established here, too.

The Covenant of Damascus is also a text that explains the origins and development of a community, but it represents a new stage in perceptions of the past and the role of the heroes. The advent of Jewish sectarianism led to the radical reinterpretation of Israelite history. Sirach 44–50 and Wisdom 10 give no indications of sectarian interests. Ben Sira may have a priestly bias, and Wisdom a sapiential one, but they still think of Israel as a nation, as a whole. For the author of the Covenant of Damascus, the nation is now

---

[124] The land does not play a role in the Covenant of Damascus, because of that text's sectarian orientation (see below). These themes can turn up on shorter lists, too, as they do on the list in 1 Maccabees 2.

divided between disobedient Israel and the remnant or the elect who have not strayed from the covenant. What is important to recognize here is that the heroes must now be shown to be separate from greater, sinning Israel. The sect legitimates itself by reinterpreting the past. The heroes can no longer be seen as representative of the offices and institutions of Israel, as they are in Sirach, but as *separate* from the sinning community. Notice that the author of Covenant of Damascus does not mention the promises to Abraham or their contents, i.e., the numerous descendants and the inheritance of the land. Neither of these elements would fit with an ideology of separatism, because the 'multiple descendants' is associated with the nations of the world and the 'inheritance of the land' with collective Israel as a complete nation.

Excursus on Genealogical Function

Although Jewish hero lists and Hebrews 11 are themselves not genealogies,[125] hero lists sometimes share an important function with genealogies. The main purpose of a genealogy is to express "the descent of a person or group of persons from an ancestor or ancestors,"[126] while the main purpose of a hero list is to enumerate and proclaim the great deeds of the individuals listed. But genealogies and hero lists also serve social and political ends. In the case of genealogies, these range from the legitimation of power and status through pedigree to fixing kinship rights and privileges. The genealogies of the Hebrew Bible also serve a number of specific purposes. Robert Wilson has made the point that "for the Yahwist, genealogies not only introduce and relate some of the people mentioned in his later narratives but also make the eponymous ancestors of the tribes the inheritors of the promise given to Abraham, Isaac and Jacob."[127] Marshall Johnson has pointed out that biblical genealogies often have a historiographical purpose. That is, they help construct an orderly understanding of biblical history. As Johnson says of the genealogies in the P source:

> [T]he special concern to reveal the continuity of the cultus through the period of disruption is in harmony with the desire of the priestly narrative of the Pentateuch to trace the origins of the sacerdotal cultus

---

[125] Although if Lee (*Form of Sirach 44–50*) is correct in seeing Sirach 44–50 as an encomium on Simon II, then the heroes there indeed form a genealogy.

[126] Robert R. Wilson, *Genealogy and History in the Biblical World* (New Haven and London: Yale, 1977) 9.

[127] Wilson, *Genealogy and History*, 193.

to Aaron and, in turn, to reveal Aaron as the culmination of a long genealogical process. Thus the genealogical form was well adapted to express the priestly concern for order and arrangement; for a genealogy is, by its very nature, entwined in history and the order of history. Beyond this, however, the priestly genealogies revel the conviction that the course of history is governed and ordered according to a pre-arranged plan. The generations come and pass; epochs begin and end. But the worship of God through the cultus ordained by him in previous epochs continues.[128]

Indeed, genealogies help create continuity when there is anxiety about radical change, as was the case during and after the exile.[129]

Related to the interest in creating historical continuity is the phenomenon of telescoping. Telescoping constitutes the omission of middle generations, in order to incorporate new people into the genealogy, while still maintaining a constant length.[130] The founding ancestors usually comprise the most important figures for establishing status, and recent ancestors cannot be omitted either because they are still living or, having died only recently, are alive in the memories of those using the genealogy. Thus, the middle generations fall out. Telescoping can help explain why the biblical summaries and many of the hero lists stress the early history of Israel and then append recent or current events/people to it, while at the same time neglecting the monarchy or the exilic period.[131] Those "middle periods" have lost their relevance in constructing the ancestry. We must keep in mind that those who construct genealogies or hero lists are always fundamentally concerned with their own identity in relation to those who came before them.[132]

Since we have already demonstrated that a number of hero lists display a historiographical interest, the functional connection between hero lists and genealogies can now be made explicit. The lists in Sirach, Wisdom, and the

---

[128] Marshall Johnson, *The Purpose of Biblical Genealogies, with Special Reference to the Genealogies of Jesus* (SNTSMS; Cambridge: Cambridge University, 1988) 81.

[129] For Ezra-Nehemiah, the genealogies serve to establish that individuals are genuinely Israelites, untainted by the peoples of the land. Indeed, Johnson believes that the issue of ethnic purity becomes the primary purpose of genealogies in later biblical and post-biblical material. See Johnson, *Purpose of Biblical Genealogies*, 85–99.

[130] Wilson, *Genealogy and History*, 33–36. Cross-cultural data indicate that the standard maximal depth of lineage genealogies is 10–14 generations, the average being twelve. Interestingly, the main list in Hebrews 11 is twelve generations long.

[131] The most glaring case of this is probably 4 Macc 16:19–22, which jumps from Abraham and Isaac to Daniel.

[132] Walter Ong, *Orality and Literacy* (New York and London: Methuen, 1982) 48–49.

Covenant of Damascus, like the summaries of biblical history before them, all display an interest in the inheritance of the divine promise or blessing. While Ben Sira concerns himself with the election and blessings of Israel's elites and Wisdom 10 focuses on the emergence of the people Israel as God's elect, the Covenant of Damascus tells the story of the divine favor and eventual salvation of the remnant of Israel (as well as the condemnation of the rest of Israel). In each case, the community addressed by these texts legitimates itself by portraying the heroes as the ancestors of the community. In sectarian literature, the issue of rightful heirs becomes polemical. So, for example, the Covenant of Damascus list creates a lineage between the patriarchs and the remnant and implies that the patriarchs are no longer the true ancestors of all Israel, but only of the elect.[133] Most importantly, the listing of the heroes legitimates the self-understanding of the Qumran community as the elect.[134]

A similar kind of genealogical legitimation is present in Hebrews 11. In the beginning of the Hebrews list (11:2), the heroes are introduced as "our ancestors." At the end of the text, the heroes stand implicitly as ancient members of the community of Hebrews, when the author says, "apart from us, they would not be made perfect." Although it is implicit, it is hardly subtle; the author of Hebrews, like the author of the Covenant of Damascus, constructs a lineage for his community. In the case of a hero list, the concern is not for a literal, biological lineage, but for a spiritual one. Thus, while we would not want to confuse hero lists with genealogies, the hero lists sometimes possess this important genealogical function.

Greco-Roman Literature

Theoretical Discussion of Examples

The use of examples to illustrate a point is hardly unique. Indeed the use of examples or *paradeigmata* was given rhetorical analysis by ancient orators and philosophers. Since we have available to us theoretical discussions concerning the use of examples by Greco-Roman authors (and we lack such

---

[133] Cf. the argument of Paul in Romans 9.

[134] This kind of legitmation is analogous to the rabbinic list in *m. Abot* 1–2. The rabbis, of course, do not think of themselves as the elect the way that Qumranites do, but they believe they are the rightful keepers (i.e., interpreters) of Torah. They legitimate this self-perception by the *Abot* chain of individuals, who are said to have passed down the Torah from one to another. In its present mishnaic form, the list extends thirteen generations from Moses to Johanan b. Zakkai. See Johnson, *Purpose of Biblical Genealogies,* 202–4.

information from Jewish writers) it will be useful to look at some pertinent literature before viewing the example lists.

Aristotle, commenting on what he calls the two kinds of proofs, enthymemes and examples, has this to say:

> If we can argue by Enthymeme, we should use our Examples as subsequent supplementary evidence. They should not precede the Enthymemes: that will give the argument an inductive air, which only rarely suits the conditions of speech-making. If they follow the Enthymemes, they have the effect of witnesses giving evidence, and this always tells. For the same reason, if you put your examples first *you must give a large number of them*; if you put them last, a single one is sufficient; even a single witness will serve if he is a good one. (*Rhet.* 2.20/1394a; emphasis added)

This quotation is significant not only because it discusses the logical place of examples, but also because it is one of the few times a writer mentions the use of multiple examples.

Although not everyone followed Aristotle's advice in practice, most subsequent scholars of rhetoric were theoretically influenced by his discussion.[135] Rhetorical critics of the Hellenistic and Roman periods focused less and less on the logical and philosophical implications of examples and more on their pure rhetorical value.[136] Discussions of rhetoric in general and examples in particular became progressively more complicated,[137] so that even the notion of what counted as an example could vary. The *Rhetorica ad Alexandrum*, which considers *paradeigmata* a subspecies of inventive proof, has the following definition: "Examples are actions that have occurred previously and are similar to, or the opposite of, those which we are now discussing."[138] While we commonly assume that examples are similar to the situation or the issue under discussion, this definition rightly recognizes that examples can be used to illustrate the opposite. For instance, if we are trying to argue for the virtue of courage, we need not only use examples illustrating courage, but might well use some

---

[135] B. Brice, "Paradeigma and Exemplum in Ancient Rhetorical Theory," Ph.D. Diss., University of California, Berkeley, 1975, 14.

[136] Kennedy, *The Art of Persuasion in Greece* (Princeton: Princeton University, 1963) 267.

[137] Plato and Aristotle engaged the topic of rhetoric more theoretically and generally; the systemization of rhetoric occurs with the Hellenistic and Roman handbooks. See D. L. Clark, *Rhetoric in Greco-Roman Education* (Westport, CT: Greenwood, 1957) 67–143.

[138] παραδείγματα δ' ἐστι πράξεις ὁμοίαι γεγενήμεναι καὶ ἐναντίαι ταῖς νῦν ὑφ' ἡμῶν λεγόμεναις (cf. 34.1–2, also quoted in Brice, "Paradeigma," 15).

examples of cowardice, which would shame the audience into avoiding such behavior.

Quintilian developed the most sophisticated classification of exempla. He identifies five types of example: the similar, dissimilar, contrary, from the greater to the lesser, and from the lesser to the greater.[139] By making this classification, Quintilian recognizes that an example can sometimes have more argumentative power if there is not a point-for-point correspondence between the example (*illustrans*) and what it is that is being illustrated (*illustrandum*).[140] While it is obvious what a similar or contrary example would be, the nature of a dissimilar example is more elusive.[141] Quintilian simply says that unlikes may differ regarding kind, manner, time, place, etc.[142] To illustrate how an example would work as an argument from the greater to the lesser, Quintilian says the following:

> Courage is more remarkable in a woman than in a man. Therefore, if we wish to kindle someone's ambition to the performance of heroic deeds, we shall find that parallels drawn from the cases of Horatius and Torquatus will carry less weight than that of the woman by whose hand Pyrrhus was slain, and if we wish to urge a man to meet death, the cases of Cato and Scipio will carry less weight than that of Lucretia. (*Inst. Ort.* 5.11.10)

A woman's display of courage is a greater example of courage, because it is contrary to expectation.[143] Implicit in this argument is that women are inferior. If a woman can be courageous, how much easier it is for a man! The lesser to the greater would of course follow the same logic only in reverse. For example, if ill fate has befallen a city due to a trivial immorality, imagine how great a tragedy could result from adultery.

---

139 *Inst. Ort.* 5.11.6–7.

140 Brice uses these terms throughout his study.

141 Brice ("Paradeigma,"158–63) points out that Quintilian never adequately explains what he means by a dissimilar example. While he gives both short and long examples for the other types, he gives only one short one for the dissimilar type: "Brutus killed his sons for plotting against the state, while Manlius condemned his son to death for his valor" (5.11.7). As Brice says, from this mysterious illustration, we cannot even tell the *illustrans* from the *illustrandum*.

142 *Dissimile plures causas habet, fit enim genere, modo, tempore, loco, ceteris . . .* (5.11.13).

143 The *Rhetorica ad Alexandrum* (8.34.7–11) discusses similar situations, but casts the discussion in terms of examples which confirm expectations, thus making probabilities credible, and those which discedit probabilities, causing the audience to doubt their expectations. See also Brice, 17.

The *Rhetorica ad Herennium* moves completely away from example as a kind of proof and considers it instead a stylistic embellishment.[144] For this author, a proof should be provided following a proposition; following the proof, the speaker should use "comparisons, examples, amplifications, previous judgments, and other means which serve to expand and enrich the argument."[145] I suspect that the anonymous author of the *Rhetorica ad Herennium* can make this claim because traditional commentary on *paradeigmata* and *exemplum* had consistently determined one important facet of example: examples were never confused with 'evidence' or non-artificial proofs like witnesses or documents, etc. Examples were thereby always considered artificial proof.[146] While the use of examples, both theoretically and practically speaking, can apply to judicial as well as to deliberative and exhortative speeches, their function lies in their power to affect one's thinking about a current situation. Accurately recounting historical events is not the function of using examples. Their ultimate purpose lies in moving the audience toward some sort of action or belief in the present. Thus, the description of an example from the past will always be colored by an interest in the present.[147]

Ancient commentators were aware of the propagandistic potential of historical examples. Quintilian warned that the orator should be selective not only about choosing an example but about what to include within the example.[148] Quintilian knew that different kinds of examples are appropriate for different kinds of speeches. For example, 'similar' examples should be used in deliberative oratory,[149] while "arguments from unlikes are most useful in exhortation."[150] He was also aware that different kinds of examples were suited to different kinds of audiences. The historical example was for the serious minded, while the fable was for the uneducated.[151]

---

[144] Brice, "Paradeigma," 88.

[145] *Rher. Her.* 2.29.46, quoted in Brice, "Paradeigma," 88.

[146] This categorization is found in almost all the rhetorical theoreticians, see Brice, "Paradeigma," 52.

[147] See the influential article by S. Perlman, "The Historical Example, Its Use and Importance as Political Propaganda in the Attic Orators," *Scripta Hierosolymitana* VII, ed. A. Fuks and I. Halpern (Jerusalem: Magnes, 1961) 150–66.

[148] *Inst. Ort.* 5.11.16.

[149] *Inst. Ort.* 3.8.66.

[150] *Inst. Ort.* 5.11.10.

[151] "[F]ables are specially attractive to rude and uneducated minds, which are less suspicious than others in their reception of fictions, and, when pleased, readily agree with arguments from which their pleasure is derived" (5.11.19). Similarly, Aristotle, when

Because they are a type of artificial proof, discussions of examples are often tied up with fables, analogies, similes, and comparisons. Nevertheless, an example usually means a real, specific historical event.[152] While Quintilian allows for the use of mythological or quasi-historical examples, they have a lower status than historical examples.[153] If possible, the event should be from the recent past; the assumption is that a more recent example is a more convincing one.[154] It is not uncommon, as we shall see below, for example lists to conclude with a contemporary example.

While actual instances of authors using multiple examples to prove a point abound in antiquity, there is no substantive discussion (beyond the comments quoted earlier from Aristotle) about the significance of using multiple examples to prove the same point. We may assume that much of what is said about examples in general apply to example lists, but the best way to grasp the particular nature of the lists in Greco-Roman literature, is to analyze at least some of them, just as we did the Jewish lists. Of course, we are interested not merely in example lists in general, but in lists of exemplary figures.

Lists of Exemplary Figures

Unlike the lists from Jewish literature, which themselves were quite varied, the example lists from Greco-Roman literature do not share a single body of literature from which they draw examples. Michael Cosby has done the most extensive study of example lists from antiquity and, recognizing their immeasurable diversity, analyzes them with his eye turned toward

considering examples to be used in deliberative speeches thinks only of historical examples (*Rhet.* 1.9/68a; 3.17/18a).

[152] Aristotle (*Rhet.* 2.20/93a) included fables, λόγοι, and fictions, παραβολαί, (illustrations made up by the speaker) as one kind of example (the historical parallel was the other). Quintilian's very definition of historical example may include fictions (*Inst. Ort.* 5.11.6). However, both the *Rhetorica ad Alexandrum* and the *Rhetorical ad Herennium* allow for only historical examples, while Cicero considered *ficta exempla* a type of *similitudo*; see Brice ("Paradeigma," 149–50). Furthermore in *Rhet, Her.* 4.49.62, the author states that an example should always be specific and not generic (i.e., "there once was a man who"). What is most telling is that in actual speeches, fables and fictions are rare, see Brice, "Paradeigma," 45.

[153] *Inst. Ort.* 5.11.17, discussed by Brice ("Paradeigma," 190–92). Quintilian is in fact the only one who acknowledges material from the poets as being valid for use in examples. Aristotle, while acknowledging fables or fictions, never discusses using material from the poets, e.g., Homer, as examples.

[154] Quintilian (*Inst. Ort.* 5.13.24), in explaining how to refute examples, says "Examples drawn from facts, if damaging to our case, must be treated in various ways; if they are ancient history, we may call them legendary."

specific rhetorical techniques.[155] I am heavily dependent upon Cosby's work here,[156] but I am interested in different questions. Although Greco-Roman texts which make use of examples can not be compared very often with one another in terms of content, as we have done with Jewish texts, there is more of interest in these lists than just their technical-rhetorical qualities. Since our ultimate concern here is the form and rhetoric—that is, rhetoric in terms of communication—of Hebrews 11, we will discuss a sampling of lists which can help us focus on two questions: 1) whether the form of Hebrews 11 is related to, and most influenced by, Greco-Roman oratory (as opposed to the Jewish literary context), and 2) whether the rhetorical aims of such texts can illumine our understanding of Hebrews 11. The most important aspect of the second question regards the treatment of the figures in relation to what it is that the author is illustrating. As we shall see, that which was consciously stated by the theoreticians can help us illumine the subtle rhetorical finesse with which orators handle examples.

Aristotle, *Rhetoric* 2.23.11

The following excerpt is from a section of the *Rhetoric* where Aristotle discusses types of induction, and since *paradeigmata* are a form of induction, Aristotle is essentially citing examples of the use of examples:

> [I]n order to prove that men of talent are everywhere honored, Alcidamas said, "The Parians honoured Archilochus, in spite of his evil-speaking; the Chians Homer, although he had rendered no public services; the Mytilenaeans Sappho, although she was a woman; the Lacedaemonians, by no means a people fond of learning, elected Chilon one of their senators; the Italiotes honoured Pythagoras, and the Lampsacenes buried Anaxagoras, although he was a foreigner, and still hold him in honour."

With the exception of the first example, each honoree is introduced by καί and stands immediately adjacent to the community who honored him or her.[157] As Cosby repeatedly points out, a stylistic device like this helps to make this piece of text into a list-like unit.

---

[155] Such as anaphora, asyndeton, paronomasia, and more. Cosby (*Rhetorical Composition,* 4–7) is particularly interested in those techniques that make the greatest impact on a listening audience.

[156] I have selected the lists for my analysis from Cosby's book. Cosby (*Rhetorical Composition*), Lee (*Form of Sirach 44–50*), and Von Armin Schmitt (Struktur, Herkunft und Bedeutung der Beispielreihe in Weish 10," *BZ* 21 [1977] 1–22) are the primary scholars to have dealt with Greco-Roman example lists.

[157] This is not evident from the English translation, but can be seen plainly in the

Although some of these figures became the stuff of legend, they are all human figures from verifiable history. The first three are poets, while the final three are philosophers.[158] They all lived sometime during the eighth to the fifth centuries BCE and appear here, for the most part, in chronological order.[159] What is striking is that the virtue of the individual does not appear to be significant. That is, Alcidamas—the original speaker of this quotation—is not concerned to show that the heroes named *deserve* honor, only that that *were* honored. Although Aristotle uses this citation in order to show how examples function as inductive proofs, he is not clear about what it is exactly that is proved by these examples. Aristotle introduces this quotation with "So as to show that all people honor the wise, Alcidamas says . . . ." It would seem that the examples are designed to prove that "all people honor the wise." Yet, the very first person named to illustrate this point is Archilochus, who is called a βλάσφημον—hardly the description of a wise man deserving of honor. In fact, the first three examples, the poets, appear to be named as examples precisely because they were *not* deserving of honor—at least in the traditional sense—and yet received it anyway.[160] Indeed, by highlighting weaknesses in some of the heroes, while not mentioning what any of them were respected for, the author stresses the tendency of peoples (who are perhaps unwitting) to bestow honors, but he neglects to prove by example that the recipients of those honors were indeed wise.

Isocrates, *Archidamas* 40–48

The masterful orator Isocrates also used example lists as inductive proofs of persuasion. In this speech written on behalf of Archidamas and directed to the people of Sparta, Isocrates tries to persuade the audience that the invasion of Thebes can be overcome.[161] Although the passage is too long to

---

Greek.

[158] Chilon was also an ephor of Sparta.

[159] Although the date of Archilochus is uncertain, Homer may well pre-date him. See Anthony J. Podlecki, *The Early Greek Poets and Their Times* (Vancouver: University of British Columbia, 1984) 29–32.

[160] Archilochus was famous for his biting sarcasm and invective. Horace said of him, "Fury armed Archilochus with her own satiric iambic," quoted by Podlecki, *Early Greek Poets*, 50. Sappho, while uniformly praised for the beauty of her poetry was sometimes derided over issues concerning her sexuality and morality. See Jeffery Duban, *Ancient and Modern Images of Sappho* (Lanham, MD: University Presses of America, 1983) 28–36.

[161] Early in the second quarter of the fourth century, Thebes was the pre-eminent power in Greece, and had taken territory from the Spartans. Sparta and Athens allied to

quote here in entirety, Isocrates uses a series of examples which are intended to demonstrate that other nations, when threatened by a stronger power, succeeded in fending them off. In some cases he simply speaks of the people as a whole, as in the case of the "Athenians,"[162] while at other times he focuses on the actions of the king.

He introduces his list to his audience by stressing that the lessons of history are instructive regarding the situation in which Sparta now finds itself.

If no people, after meeting with misfortune, ever recovered themselves or mastered their enemies, then we cannot reasonably hope to win victory in battle; but if on many occasions it has happened that the stronger power has been vanquished by the weaker, and that the besiegers have been destroyed by those confined within the walls, what wonder if our own circumstances likewise should undergo a change?

He then cleverly adds that he can offer no examples from Sparta's own history, because in the past she was always the strongest nation, so he must turn to others, first of which is Athens.

Isocrates spends most of his time on the example of Athens. In that discussion he comments about the inadequacy of examples far back in antiquity:

Now if I were to recount the wars of old which they fought against the Amazons or the Thracians or the Peloponnesians who under the leadership of Eurystheus invaded Attica, no doubt I should be thought to speak on matters ancient and remote from the present situation; but in their war against the Persians, who does not know from what hardships they arose to great good-fortune?

Isocrates' attitude is by no means unique; he spells out the bias orators have against using ancient examples, which we saw in the theoretical material. A recent example is more persuasive.

After the example of Athens, Isocrates has two others, but they are individual leaders, rather than nations. He first mentions Dionysius, tyrant of Syracuse, who eventually managed to take the upper hand against the Carthaginians. His final example is Amyntas, king of Macedonia 393–370 BCE.[163] and father of Philip II, who saved his country from invading

---

invade Thebes in 362 BCE.

[162] This would be analogous to mention of the people Israel collectively, which sometimes occurs on hero lists, as is the case with Heb 11:29.

[163] Note how recent this example is; it is practically contemporary with Isocrates' speech.

"barbarians." Isocrates tells us that both these men were initially tempted to flee for their lives when the country was threatened, but by staying and defending their people, they acquired greater power and respect than they had before.

These last two examples are about half the length of the discussion of Athens. However, in all cases there is more rhetorical flourish and narrative in excess of what is needed to make the point. Isocrates does not quite reach the point of turning an example into a digression as Philo was wont to do, but his list of examples here does not display the consistent succession found in Aristotle above and in most of the Jewish-Hellenistic lists.[164] Nevertheless, this series of examples is held firmly together by the *sameness of the narrative elements* that make up each example. Each figure/nation is confronted with a seriously threatening situation; they contemplate making a difficult choice— in two cases this choice explicitly entails a move to fight rather than flee— they make the decision to confront the aggressor, and, as a result, their situation ends up more favorable than when the incident began. There is only variety in the names and places; the story is the same in each case. Not surprisingly, that story matches the situation Sparta faces.[165]

Isocrates ends his list with the well-known rhetorical tactic of implying that he could think of countless more examples, but listing them would only cause fatigue.[166]

Isocrates, *Antidosis* 230–36

The *Antidosis*[167] contains a series of examples, which are listed in more consistent succession than those found in the previous list. In this text

---

[164] Cosby (*Rhetorical Composition*, 20) points out that Greco-Roman lists vary in their length of example much more than Jewish ones.

[165] Early in his *Rhetoric*, (1.2/1357b), Aristotle defines an argument by example as one of "part to part or like to like." In other words, such an argument "moves from particular to particular." Although Aristotle considers the use of examples a form of induction, the principle or universal to which the example may aspire does not necessarily factor into the argument. The rhetorical prinicple at work in this series of examples from Isocrates is exactly what Aristotle described: the identification of the current situation with examples from the past. As Perlman ("Historical Example," 152) says, "the historical example is chiefly a means of explanation of the contemporary politics and a method of political propaganda."

[166] This tactic turns up in Heb 11:32, where our author asks "And what more shall I say?" which he follows with a rapid fire succession of names. The goal is to give the impression that there are countless examples the author could draw upon.

[167] The *Antidosis* is an apologia Isocrates wrote for himself under pressure from his rivals. Written late in life, it is Isocrates' primary work which bears witness to his system of

Isocrates wishes to demonstrate that those who are versed in the "cleverness of speech" are not necessarily evil manipulators. On the contrary, Isocrates claims, "it was the greatest and most illustrious orators who brought to the city most of her blessings."

He names four individuals in chronological order and in explicit succession, Solon, Cleisthenes, Themistocles and Pericles.[168] All of them are Athenian statesmen who were for the most part highly respected. Three of them were military men (all but Solon) who endeavored into serious foreign intrigue or diplomacy (depending upon how you look at it).

Isocrates defends himself and his profession; " . . . it was the greatest and the most illustrious orators (ῥήτορας) who brought to the city most of her blessings." His examples, however, are not orators, but statesmen. Isocrates himself was never a statesmen and apparently did not speak in public for lack of presence.[169] Thus, while the individuals chosen by Isocrates do not exactly parallel himself, he obviously chose them because he believed he would achieve the greatest possible rhetorical effect. By using statesmen rather than great orators and educators—of which there was no shortage to be found—Isocrates focuses on the gains to society to be had from oratory, and ignores the issue of whether those who possess oratorical skill are really virtuous.

Cicero, *De Oratore* 3.32–34

In this text there are actually four successive lists of exemplary figures, all of which are offered as proofs on variously related issues concerning liberal education and the place of oratory in it. The lists are related, but not repetitious; each list has its own particular theme or moral which holds the figures in that particular grouping together.

In the first list, the characters are very similar to one another, they are all sophists of the same early period. Cicero (through the voice of Catulus) introduces the series with the following remark:

---

paideia. See Werner Jaeger, *Paideia: The Ideals of Greek Culture* (3 vols.; New York: Oxford, 1981) 3.132–55.

[168] Isocrates uses expressions like μετὰ ταῦτα when moving from one example to another, and Pericles is introduced with the phrase to δε τελευταῖον.

[169] Jaeger (*Paideia*, 2.127; 3.52, 82–105) compares Isocrates with Socrates because both felt there was something fundamental in their character that kept them out of politics. However, to be fair to Isocrates, there was also an Athenian tradition, which began with Gorgias but which was a recurring issue in the fourth century, that an educator was a a kind of statesman, because he trained future politicians.

For in the good old days, as we are told, the professors and masters of rhetoric considered no kind of discourse to lie outside their province, and continually occupied themselves with every system of oratory.

The section of *De Oratore* in which this series of lists falls is concerned to point out that specialization or too narrow a field of vision makes for a weak education.[170] The sophists are viewed as the ancestral orators, the forefathers of the discipline, so it is natural that Cicero should begin with them. Cicero spends most of his time on his first and last example. Of his first character, Hippias, Cicero says

> . . . Hippias of Elis, visiting Olympia on the occasion of the quadrennial celebration of the famous games, boasted before an audience containing virtually the whole of Greece that there was not a single fact included in any system of encyclopaedic knowledge with which he was not acquainted; and that he had not only acquired the accomplishments that form the basis of the liberal education of a gentleman, mathematics, music, knowledge of literature and poetry, and the doctrines of natural science, ethics and political science, but had made with his own hand the ring he had on, the cloak he was dressed in and the boots he was wearing. No doubt Hippias went too far, but the story of itself makes it easy for us to guess how keen an appetite the orators of old had for the most distinguished accomplishments, if they did not spurn even the meaner ones.

This passage is worthy of our consideration because while Hippias is the first example of an orator with breadth, he is also a caricature of such an orator. Indeed, Cicero is obviously aware of the absurdity of Hippias's claims, when Cicero says "No doubt Hippias went too far . . . ." Furthermore, Cicero did not have to include all the detail which creates the caricature; we must remember that every author chooses what s/he wishes to include regarding his/her example. Why then does he include what he does? I suspect that Cicero provides his readers with more information about the liberal education he espouses within the example. In other words, the details he provides about Hippias are not important as aspects of Hippias, but as aspects of Cicero's system of education.[171] For instance, the naming of the various disciplines of liberal education—math, literature, natural science,

---

[170] This is the main theme of Book 1 of *De Oratore*.

[171] Cicero's vision of education is broad and inclusivist, tending toward the encyclopaedic (with rhetoric at the top, so that one could employ the acquired information in the affairs of the state). See Renato Barilli, *Rhetoric* (Theory and History of Literature 63; Minneapolis: University of Minnesota, 1989) 26–27.

etc.—remind the reader of Cicero's interest in breadth. The fact that Hippias was also an alleged artisan demonstrates that such skills should not be devalued by the orator. In addition, examples that are extreme or exaggerated are more entertaining and thereby more memorable. Cicero does not realistically expect his readers to imitate Hippias, for the example of Hippias is over-the-top. He sees in Hippias's desire to possess all knowledge, however, a source of inspiration.

The final and most important reason why Cicero practically caricatures the sophists becomes clear at the conclusion of the pericope. After Cicero finishes his examples in this group, he acknowledges that while he has produced several examples, they were all ancient Greek orators. Therefore, the list constitutes a narrow body of evidence which stands far removed from the current Roman world. He reflects on this situation:

> [The sophists] are evidence that what you say, Crassus, is the case—a larger or perhaps more famous list adorned the name of 'orator' in Greece in the old days. This indeed makes me the more doubtful whether to decide that more praise is to be assigned to you or more blame to the Greeks; inasmuch as you who have another native language and were born under a different form of society, in spite of your dwelling in an extremely busy community and being engrossed in almost every sort of private business or else government of the entire world and administration of a vast empire, have succeeded in acquiring and grasping so vast a range of facts, and have coupled with all this the knowledge and the practical activity of one whose wisdom and oratory give him influence in the state; whereas the Greeks, though born in a world of literature and enthusiasts for these studies, are yet demoralized by sloth and have not only made no further acquisitions but have not even preserved their own heritage that came down to them.

It is quite clear that while the Greek sophists function in one sense as models of the kind of educated orator Cicero would like to promote, they also function as a contrasting model. They were old-world Greeks who for all their bragging were wholly impractical and did not build on their advancements. However, as a present day Roman orator, Crassus may be a rarer breed in his society, but he is superior to the ancient Greeks because of his worldliness. In other words, the Roman orators combine a high level of education with "practical activity" in the affairs of the state. Not surprisingly, while the Romans looked to the Greeks as models, they still saw themselves as superior.[172] But such an attitude was not unique to the Romans. The ambivalence toward examples from the past, even if its one's own past, is common—for the present often stands as the most privileged historical position.

Further evidence of this mixed attitude toward examples from the past can be seen in the second list. The second and third lists of heroes stand almost back to back and are closely related. The second is comprised again of all Greeks, however, they are not from the same period nor of the same vocation. The third list includes only Romans, all of whom are politicians/orators.[173]

In the second list of great Greeks, Crassus (who is now speaking in reply to Catulus) names highly revered professionals other than orators, in order to show that even if one has expertise in a given area, a general embrace of knowledge is still worthwhile. He chooses to name Hippocrates, the physician, Euclid and Archimedes as mathematicians, Damon and Aristoxenus as musicians, and Aristophanes and Callimachus as literary scholars. Cicero does not provide information about any of them, as he did in the first list, but simply names them and expects that the reader will recognize them as famous experts in their respective fields. He does not claim that men such as Hippocrates are themselves examples of broad learning. Rather, his point is that even when such individuals develop advanced learning in a particular field, there is still a place for some individuals to "embrace all subjects." A society that produces such specialists should not preclude the existence of generalists.

It is, of course, the orators (and philosophers) who are capable of such embrace. Thus, the third list is comprised of Roman (not Greek) heroes possessed of substantial oratorical powers. The combination of the first three lists has the effect of subtly devaluing Greek scholars in comparison with

---

[172] Debates over Atticism in literary style are indicative of Roman pride vis-à-vis the Greeks. Cicero himself was a Latin purist who avoided Atticisms. See Giam Biagro Conte, *Latin Literature: A History* (Baltimore and London: Johns Hopkins University, 1994) 199; and Barilli, *Rhetoric*, 29. See also Conte's discussion (*Latin Literature*, 89–90) of Cato and Roman national anti-Greek bias.

[173] Cicero does not put these two lists in chronological order. On the second list, for example, Hippocrates, the first one named, is a contemporary of Socrates, while Callimachus dates are 305–240 BCE and he is listed last, but in between are Archimedes, whose dates are 287–212 BCE, and Damon who is also a contemporary of Socrates. On his third list, Cicero begins with Sextus Aelius and Manius Manilius who were active ca. 200 and 150 BCE, respectively, while his last two names are Scipio (236–184 BCE) and Cato (234–149 BCE).

Roman ones. Keep in mind that in the first list the sophists were men of great breadth of education but had no inclination to put that knowledge to public use. The second series was comprised of Greeks very much involved in the practical side of knowledge—physicians, musicians, mathematicians, but who were specialists, not scholars of breadth. Finally, when we come to the Roman heroes in the third list, we see figures who are public leaders with the practical power to influence events and who are generalists in their educational background. Thus, it is the Romans who effectively combine practical worldliness *and* a breadth of knowledge. Of the Roman jurist, Manius Manilius, Cicero says

> [W]hile we have actually seen Manius Manilius walking across the forum, and the remarkable thing was that in doing this he was putting his wisdom at the service of all his fellow-citizens; and in old days persons resorted to these men both when they were going a walk as described and when seated in their chairs of state at home, not only to consult them on points of law but also about marrying off a daughter, buying a farm, tilling their estates, and in short every sort of liability or business.

Most striking is Cicero's use of Marcus Cato as the final example. On the one hand, Cato's example best illustrates the relationship between general, abstract knowledge and its useful application:

> Did his study of law cause him to refrain from appearing in court? Did his ability as a pleader make him neglect the science of jurisprudence? No, he was an ardent worker in both fields, and won distinction in both. Did the influence thus acquired from doing the business of private clients make him backward in taking part in public life?

On the other hand, Cato was a notorious anti-Hellenist. He was a conservative who tried to rid the Romans of all things Greek.[174] Cicero may even be alluding to this fact when he says of Cato "For what did Marcus Cato lack except our present day super-refinement of culture which we have imported from overseas." That Cicero should conclude this example list with Cato is once again a subtle devaluation of the Greek examples. At the very least, he is trying to distance the Roman examples from the Greek ones, thereby distinguishing the Romans from the Greeks.[175] Perhaps that is why

---

[174] See Conte, *Latin Literature*, 89–90.

[175] It is worth noting that the second series of Greek examples (the professionals) serves as a buffer between the list of Greek orators and the list of Roman orators. The fame of the Greek orators was legendary, while the Romans did not quite have that status. By placing the list of Greek professionals in between, the reader is less likely to make too

Cicero speaks only of sophists in the first list and does not include any orators who were involved in public life, such as Isocrates, who would have been a more appropriate parallel to the Roman orators on the third list. Thus, the Greeks who make no use of their knowledge for the public good stand in unclouded contrast to the Romans who do.

Cicero does cite examples of Greek statesman in the fourth list. However, he does not introduce them as statesmen, but as examples of learning who have been trained by the best educators; "For just as we have to go to our fellow countrymen for examples of virtue so we have to turn to the Greeks for models of learning . . . ." This allows him to discuss figures such as Plato and Isocrates and their role in training politicians in the course of his discussion of examples. He also includes great figures such as Pisistratus and Pericles. Cicero mentions that Pisistratus arranged the previously disordered books of Homer, but otherwise "did no service to his fellow-citizens." Pericles stands as a more straightforward example; Cicero acknowledges his political finesse, while stressing his oratorical powers and the fact that Anaxagoras was his teacher.

One can not help wondering why, if Cicero wanted to list examples of Greek learning, he did not just list men like Plato, Aristotle, and Isocrates in the first place. It could be argued that the other examples he lists after Pisistratus and Pericles, such as Critias and Alcibiades, are not even good examples of statecraft. Perhaps, once again, Cicero wishes Roman politicians to have exclusive claim to high-level political skill, even as he is forced to recognize the superiority of the Greeks in the advancement of knowledge.

In general, it is important to recognize that what an author says is the general rule which is illustrated or proved by the examples does not necessarily correspond directly with the examples themselves. Cicero is among the most self-conscious of orators; it is not an accident that his examples do not function as simple illustrations of the explicitly stated rule. Rhetorical communication operates at many levels; what is unsaid may be as important as what is said, what is implied may mean more than what is stated explicitly.

Greco-Roman and Jewish Texts Compared

While hero lists in Greco-Roman literature vary more than those in Jewish literature, we can observe some rhetorical patterns which define these lists as distinct from Jewish ones.

---

direct a comparison; rather the comparison is guided by Cicero's subtle rhetorical skill.

1) Ancient versus Recent Examples: The majority of exemplary figures on Greco-Roman lists are from verifiable, secular, and often recent history. Because the Greeks and the Romans conceived a broad categorical distinction between history and mythology, and mythology was seen as philosophically (and eventually historically) unreliable,[176] it is no surprise that this bias comes out in hero lists, too. In contrast, ancient Jewish cultural elites did not differentiate between history and mythology.[177] The Bible was a reliable, historical source; at the same time it was a divine document which contained information about the acts of God. No Jew in antiquity ever thought to condemn the Bible as a resource because it contained ancient material. Thus, the heroes on the Jewish lists were almost exclusively from biblical literature. Hardly any exilic or post-exilic figures turn up as illustrations on these lists,[178] even though most of the lists are from the post-exilic period. Lists from the orators, on the other hand, usually end with very recent and sometimes contemporary examples.[179]

2) Length and Structure: While the listing of exemplary figures in general calls for a similar structure,[180] the Greco-Roman example lists differ in length, on the average, from the Jewish texts of the Hellenistic period. For example, the average number of examples on the Greco-Roman lists is only about four to six heroes. While the lists from the Maccabean literature are fairly succinct, Wisdom 10, Sirach 44–50, Covenant of Damascus 2–3, and Hebrews 11, list a large number of figures. Furthermore, some Greco-

---

[176] The relationship between, on the one hand, Greek epic poetry, e.g., in the form of Homer and mythology, e.g., in the form of Hesiod and, on the other hand, the burgeoning field of historiography in the sixth century BCE Greece, e.g. in the form of Herodotus, is complicated, and I do not mean to oversimplify it. Nevertheless, Herodotus displays a critical spirit about "what actually happened" which is not present in myth or epic. See John Van Seters, *In Search of History: Historiography in the Ancient World and the Origins of Biblical History* (New Haven: Yale University, 1983) 8–31.

[177] The typical understanding, as expressed by Cross in *Canaanite Myth and Hebrew Epic*, of the sources that constitute the Pentateuch is that they are historicized prose versions of earlier, poetic myth and/or epic. (Cf. the critque of Van Seters, *In Search of History*, 18–22.) See also the discussion by David Damrosch, *The Narrative Covenant: Transformations of Genre in the Growth of Biblical Literature* (San Francisco: Harper & Row, 1987) 51–87.

[178] The one major exception is Daniel and his three friends who consistently appear on the Maccabean lists.

[179] Dionysius, who is listed by Isocrates, is essentially his contemporary. Dionysius died in 367 BCE and Isocrates's dates are 436–338 BCE. Cicero, who uses Cato as an example, knew his great grandson, see Michael Grant, *History of Rome* (New York: Charles Scribner's Sons, 1978) 201.

[180] See n. 18.

Roman authors can become very detailed in their discussion of one individual, while only perhaps referring to two or three others. At times, an author can become so involved in recounting the details regarding a certain figure,[181] that one loses the sense that the text is a list at all—as I suggested was the case with Philo. This tendency of Greco-Roman authors means that often their lists form a longer text with fewer examples, while the Jewish lists have more examples in less space. With the exception of Philo, most Jewish authors, however, maintain a consistent rhythm in enumerating examples. If the length of the descriptions of the examples varies, it does so in a predictable way and forms a literary pattern. So, Ben Sira, for example, spends more verbiage on Aaron because Simon, with whom the list culminates, most resembles Aaron. The two heroes of Aaron and Simon then form a parallel. Similarly, Abraham and Moses receive more lines than the other examples on the Hebrews list. They, too, form a poetic parallel. In any case, a predictable rhythm is maintained.

   3) Historiographic Interest: There is a significant distinction between Greco-Roman and Jewish authors regarding the importance of history in these lists. I said earlier that it was important for Greco-Roman authors that the exemplary heroes be from recent, secular history, rather than from ancient mythological sources. However, the significance of using such historical figures is that they are assumed to be more reliable for proving the point. Hellenistic and Roman authors describe one or two individual incidents related to the hero, which are historical in that they happened in the past, but there is no historiographic narrative encompassing all the heroes on the list. In other words, there is no diachronic movement from the first example to the last, no *single historia* which encapsulates all the examples.

   By contrast, there was such diachronic interest among some of the Jewish authors. While the Jewish heroes model certain behaviors or represent certain virtues, professions, or noble upbringings, there is also a story which unfolds, beginning with the first example and ending with the last. Furthermore, those Jewish authors who display this diachronic interest use their lists to legitimate the author's own community. But even in those uni-dimensional lists that did not have an interest in retelling the biblical story, the assumption is that they are all part of one *historia,* because all the heroes

---

[181] Perhaps it is significant that Quintilian could at times confuse *exemplum* and *narratio,* and thus he sometimes conflates historical examples with *historia.* See Brice, "Paradeigma,"151, 192. It seems that those giving the speeches sometimes confused them as well.

come from the Bible. For Greco-Roman authors, each exemplary figure has its own mini-*historia*, a discrete narrative unit. There is no single narrative that can encompass Chilon and Sappho or Euclid and Aristophanes. Although many of the Greco-Roman lists also enumerate the examples in chronological order, starting with the oldest and moving toward the most recent, this seems to be nothing more than a convenience; the lists might just as well be in alphabetical order. Chronology in Jewish lists is not just convenient; it offers an implicit narrative structure, because all the characters are part of one story.

4) Types of Modeling: With the possible exception of Isocrates' list of war heroes, the heroes of Greco-Roman hero lists are *not* virtuous exemplars or models of *ideal* behavior which the author would like to instill in his audience. In the list discussed from Aristotle, Aristotle is not at all concerned to show that the figures on his list possess the virtue of wisdom. Although he attempts to demonstrate that societies always honor the wise, the burden of proof for Aristotle lies not on the quality of the individual, but resides in the fact that citizens honor people who (they think) are wise.

I do not mean to say that the context is not exhortative in Greco-Roman texts. Indeed, the function of examples is to move people to action or create a perception or belief regarding an issue in the present. In other words, the heroes serve as examples because they prove some point of fact or because some circumstances surrounding the life of the hero match (either by similarity or contrast) the circumstances of the present. But the heroes are not ideal models which a general audience is encouraged to emulate. The heroes in Aristotle's list do not inspire others to seek out wisdom. However, they might inspire communities not to neglect their responsibility to honor men of learning. Thus, the audience identifies with the *communities* who honored the wise, not with the wise hero himself. When Isocrates in the *Antidosis* lists individuals of oratorical skill, it is not to encourage more people to become orators. Rather it is to demonstrate that orators are not political subversives but actually contribute to the benefits of a city. By arguing this way, Isocrates exhorts the audience not to chastise him or other orators because of their rhetorical powers.

While not all the lists from Jewish authors exhort the audience to emulate a particular virtue or type of behavior, the majority of them do.[182] The lists

---

[182] The one major exception, i.e., the case of a Jewish list not functioing to persuade the audience to imitate the behavior of the heroes, is Sirach 44–50. To praise the memory of the heroes seems to be the ultimate purpose of the text. However, one must also bear

in the Maccabean literature, for example, exhort the listeners to piety and endurance of adverse circumstances. They are models of behavior. In the case of 1 Macc 2:51–60, where the rewards the heroes received are listed in addition to their admirable actions, the audience knows that the same rewards can be theirs if they imitate the qualities and behaviors of the heroes. This kind of modeling can even be claimed for the biblical historical summaries. The audience identifies with their ancestors as fellow members of the covenant. When Israel—past or present—is faithful, those faithful deeds lead to reward; when Israel sins, she is punished. Thus, the recounting of history points the audience in the right direction. Israel must emulate the faithful and reject the unfaithful.[183]

Moreover, the historical figures employed as examples by Greek and Roman writers are quite human, while the biblical figures are always examples of perfection or, in the case of negative examples, evil. They are always either paradigmatic types or anti-types; there are no in-betweens. This is not at all the case with the Greco-Roman lists. As we have already noted, the *ultimate* virtue of a particular hero on a Greco-Roman list is of no consequence. A hero on those lists is used for one particular aspect of his/her person, or because a circumstance involving the individual is relative to the current situation. The over-all quality of the individual is irrelevant. So, for example, Cicero can praise the tyrant Pisistratus for his eloquence, even if as Cicero tells us "he did no service to his fellow citizens." Many of the figures that occur on Greco-Roman lists have checkered histories and mixed reputations. This may be partly due to the fact that we are dealing with secular history which is often preserved from multiple points of view,[184]

---

in mind that the overall context of Sirach is an exhortative one—one within which the author pedagogically encourages prudent and faithful living. Furthermore, for Ben Sira, each hero is an idealized super-human figure, a paradigmatic representation of an office or covenant.

[183] Müller ("Geschichte," 74), who in his discussion sees all the summaries (both those that focus only on the *magnalia Dei* and those that emphasize the unfaithfulness of Israel) as having one important common goal:

In mehr oder minder abgewandelter (vgl. Jos 24,2b–13; I Sam 12,8) und auch erweiterer Form (vgl. Ex 15,4–16; Ps 78; 105f; 135; 136,1–26) ist für alle Geschichtssummarien des hebräischen Kanons bis hin zum Bußgebet des Nehemia (Neh 9,5–37) derselbe Grundansatz charakteristisch: Indem die göttlichen Geschichtstaten in ihrer Einmaligkeit und Kontingenz bekannt werden, bereut Israel seinen Ungehorsam in der Gegenwart oder sucht in den vergangenen Eingriffen Gottes den Beweggrund für erneute göttliche Heilssetzungen in der Zukunft.

[184] Among the Greeks, for example, there were always rivaling intellectual movements,

while this is not the case with Israelite history. In any case, they are not idealized in general, but praised for certain particular qualities.

Another way to describe the fallibility of the Greco-Roman heroes is to say that, from the author's point of view, their alleged exemplary qualities have been relativized. We noted that in the theoretical discussions, particularly that of Quintilian, there were a variety of different ways in which an example could relate to a principle, or a quality, or a situation, which was being illumined by the example. Examples could sometimes implicitly contain the lesser-to-greater or greater-to-lesser argument. So, for instance, when Cicero uses his list of ancient Greek sophists to demonstrate that orators should have a breadth of learning, he also subtly distinguishes them from what he ultimately wants to illustrate—breadth of learning combined with public service—and thereby detracts from any temptation a reader might have to seeing these figures as role models. Thus, the sophists are exemplary for their own time, but relative to Cicero's time, i.e., to the kinds of orators the Romans have produced, they are imperfect as models. This subtle use of exemplary figures may be at least partly due to a desire to distinguish and elevate the present from the past—a desire that most likely arises from a confused identity in the present, as the Romans sometimes had vis-à-vis the Greeks.

By contrast, Jewish authors are unequivocal in their praise of biblical heroes. Even though the Bible itself possesses stories which demonstrate the human failings of virtually all its characters, biblical figures do not appear on hero lists as mere mortals. Even on uni-dimensional lists, in which merely one trait or patterned course of action is all that counts, an author never mentions anything about the character that is not flattering. One never finds, for example, that although David was an adulterer, he was a great king.[185] The heroes as they appear on the lists are the objects of unrestrained praise (or scorn, in the case of negative examples).

---

like that between orators and philosophers. Among Romans there were conflicting political parties, like that between Scipio and Cato. Thus, disparate writings are preserved which sometimes provide widely divergent images of famous figures.

[185] The only exception I can find among any of the lists is in Ben Sira's recounting of Solomon's reign. Ben Sira praises Solomon for reigning in peace, building the temple, and being wise, but then he changes his tone: he admonishes the king for his sexual license, which led to the defilement of the family line. Nevertheless, because of his promise to David, Yahweh did not destroy the royal line. This is the only case where a hero on a Jewish list possesses a complex moral character, virtuous in some matters and villlainous in others.

Hebrews 11 in Literary Context

It is my contention that Hebrews 11 shares far more characteristics with Jewish lists than with Greco-Roman lists. Nevertheless, the Hebrews hero list possesses a rhetorical sophistication that allows for a more complex portrayal of the biblical heroes than had heretofore been seen in Jewish lists of exemplary heroes. In other words, Hebrews 11 is most influenced by the Jewish material in its form and content, but we must add to this evidence of influence from Greco-Roman methods of rhetorical communication. We shall again take up the qualities that allowed us to compare and contrast the Greco-Roman and Jewish lists, in order to assess their relevance for Hebrews 11.

1) Ancient versus Recent Examples: Like most of the Jewish texts, the heroes in Hebrews 11 are from ancient Israelite history. There is no compunction on the part of any Jewish author or the author of Hebrews to acquire recent examples as somehow being more effective in proving the point. Significantly, the author of Hebrews concludes his list early in Israelite history—earlier than almost all the Jewish hero lists—with the peculiar figure of Rahab. Although David is mentioned in a mini-list appended onto the main list, his name—nothing is said about him—appears more as an after thought than as an integral part of the hero list. Most Jewish lists of the magnitude of Hebrews extend beyond the exodus/conquest. The fact that Hebrews 11 ends where it does may partly indicate that Hebrews 11 was more influenced by the biblical summaries, in which the climax of history is always the exodus/conquest. It may also be the result of telescoping, which, as we shall see later, is due to the author's conscious exclusion of figures who are no longer relevant for the author's Christian vision of Jewish history.

2) Length and Structure: Like the Jewish lists, Hebrews is lengthy but highly rhythmic and even poetic. Besides the use of the anaphoric πίστει, which structures the whole text and allows the reader to recognize the start of each new example, there is a beautiful balance and symmetry to the list.[186] Abel, Enoch, and Noah comprise the first grouping of three. After them comes Abraham, who is given far more attention—about equal to Abel, Enoch and Noah combined. Following Abraham, there is another minor grouping of three, Isaac, Jacob, and Joseph. Then follows Moses, who receives about the same amount of attention as Abraham. The recounting of both Abraham and Moses is punctuated by the author's commentary which breaks up their

---

[186] See my outline of Hebrews 11 in Appendix A.

respective miniature biographies into two parts. Another grouping of three comes after Moses, the people who crossed the Red Sea, the walls of Jericho, and Rahab. Thus, the over-all pattern is 3–1–3–1–3.

3) Historiographic Interest: The most important resemblance that I wish to argue for between the Hebrews list and Jewish lists is the presentation of a diachronic history that encompasses all the heroes on the list, so that they are part of one story or historical sequence. The importance of history in Hebrews 11 has traditionally been either taken for granted or ignored. The scholars who take it for granted see Hebrews 11 as typically Jewish, similar to all the Jewish precursor texts in one way or another.[187] Many of these assume that Hebrews 11 relied upon a Jewish source. Since the document of Hebrews in general is seen to be christologically absorbed, as well as anti-Judaic (because of its supersessionist theology), and since Hebrews 11 ostensibly does not betray that perspective, the assumption is that Hebrews 11 must have some other derivation apart from the author. Scholars who do not perceive a historiographic interest in the list see it as simply a catalog of examples of faith, similar to any of the Greco-Roman lists and some of the Jewish lists.[188]

That Hebrews 11 is a retelling of biblical history can be demonstrated from the following evidence: First, that the author includes a variety of 'faithful acts,' and that this variety allows him to include well-known highlights from biblical history, points to his historiographic interest. One of the differences we noted between Jewish and Greco-Roman lists was that Jewish lists offered a variety of types of person, as well as variety in describing what makes the heroes exemplary. We designated these kinds of lists 'multi-dimensional.' Greco-Roman lists, by contrast, followed a particular type of example more closely—orators who are knowledgeable, statesmen who saved their countries, etc. One well-defined trait was usually at stake, and this kind of list we labeled 'uni-dimensional.'

Although the heroes of Hebrews are people who have somehow acted in faith, the author includes several *different* sorts of characters from Israelite history who are listed for a *variety* of behaviors. In this way, Hebrews 11 is a multi-dimensional list. The list includes staple characters like Abraham and Moses, but also included are more rare figures like Abel and Enoch, not to

---

187 E.g., Windisch, *Hebräerbrief*.

188 So Cosby (*Rhetorical Composition*) for example, like Lee (*Form of Sirach 44–50*) in his study of Sirach 44–50, omits all the texts that are primarily historical summaries.

mention the highly unusual inclusion of women[189] Furthermore, no two characters perform the same deed, and the deeds they do perform are often momentous events in historical memory: Noah's building the ark, the offering of Isaac, the crossing of the Red Sea, to name a few. Thus, the variety in presentation, along with the attempt to cover significant events, point to the author's interest in retelling the story of Israel's history.

Second, most of the heroes' faith involves some ability to perceive the future, and this ability often forms a historical link between one character and the next. Noah, for example, heeds God's warning regarding events unseen and as a result becomes an 'heir.' Abraham and Sarah are promised descendants numerous as the sea, and they believe. Isaac and Jacob invoke special blessings on their sons at the time of their death, and Joseph is even said to make "mention of the exodus" at the time of his death. In this way earlier heroes are made an explicit part of the same narrative world as later heroes. The biographic descriptions of each hero are not independent *historia*, as they are on the Greco-Roman lists, but part of one comprehensive *historia*.

Indeed, the notion of promise and inheritance or reward, which was such an important theme in the biblical summaries and turns up on many of the post-biblical hero lists, is a major theme in Hebrews 11 and the third and most important reason why history plays a key role in the Hebrews hero list. The promises made to Abraham function as prophecies regarding the future course of history. Hebrews, however, has a unique view of the role of God's promise, which appears in vv. 13 and 39, the latter of which reads "Yet all these [heroes] though they were commended for their faith, did not receive what was promised." Just how significant these words are will be taken up in detail later. What is important to note here is that with these words the author lets us know that the heroes on the list also have a *collective* historical trajectory (even if it is left unfulfilled).

4) Types of Modeling: The final relationship between the Hebrews list and the other lists from antiquity I wish to discuss involves the issue of whether or not the heroes are models for behavior, as they typically are on Jewish lists, or whether they are illustrations about a conceptual point, as is more typical on the Greco-Roman lists. As I said earlier, Jewish heroes are not just models to be imitated, they are paragons of perfection. The humanity of biblical characters so evident in the biblical stories is not to be found on the lists of exemplary figures. Greco-Roman lists, on the other hand, do not recoil from

---

[189] See Appendix B for a comparison of the occurrences of these characters.

mentioning the short-comings of a hero, even as they stress a particular positive quality. Indeed, the Greco-Roman texts allow for more human, complex characterizations of the heroes. The author of Hebrews 11, I believe, has blended these two tendencies together, allowing for a subtle departure from the standard presentation of heroes as usually cataloged by Jewish authors.

On the one hand, the author of Hebrews has chosen these particular figures because they are the heroes of biblical tradition. Many of the heroes, like Noah, Abraham, and Moses are natural choices; they are the pride of the tradition. On the other hand, some of the author's selections are surprising, most notably Rahab. Furthermore, as some scholars have realized, the author frequently has not necessarily made the most appropriate choices for illustrating faith.[190] Why should David be merely an afterthought? He was the composer of the psalms and reckoned as one of God's intimates. Why should Rahab appear as the figure from the period of the Judges, while Joshua and Caleb are left off the list? On that part of the list where Moses and the Israelites are covered, where are Aaron and Phinehas? Even more striking than these omissions is that the author does not exploit the full potential of many of the examples he does use. Abraham, for instance, seems like a good choice for illustrating faith, but when the author of Hebrews recounts how Abraham was promised descendants as numerous as the sea (11:11–12), he neglects to mention the now famous quotation, that "Abraham *believed* God and it was reckoned to him as righteousness" (Gen 15:6). Although the author of Hebrews may not have wanted to use a quotation here,[191] it is puzzling that he would not take full advantage of the expression, since it is one of the few times the biblical text *literally* expresses the faith of a character.

As if these enigmas of the text were not enough, the author of Hebrews makes one particular statement, already referred to, which is so out of the ordinary that it is impossible to imagine that it could have been said by a Jew: "Yet, all these, though they were commended for their faith, *did not receive what was promised,*" at which point the author says "since God provided something better so that they would not, apart from us, be made perfect"

---

190 Spicq's remark is typical of those that occasionally turn up in commentaries: "Dans le détail, on ne distingue pas toujous très bien d'alleurs par quoi se manifeste spécialement la foi des personnages mis en cause . . ." (*L'Epître*, 2.335).

191 In the following chapter I discuss the author's bifurcated use of quotations and retellings. When the author discusses biblical narrative, he often avoids the use of quotations.

(11:39–40). This remark has profound implications for understanding Hebrews 11. By saying that the heroes did not receive what was promised them, the author implies that the heroes, relative to his perspective, were somehow disadvantaged. They were not honored and rewarded in their own lifetime. The lack of honor accorded the heroes of Hebrews diverges substantially from the consistent interest of Jewish texts in naming the honors and rewards which the heroes received.[192] The author believes that he speaks from a privileged position. The heroes, therefore, can only be models in a limited way. Similar to at least some of the Greco-Roman texts, the heroes are localized, historicized, and ultimately relativized.[193] The heroes are indeed models of faith, and the author of Hebrews presumably wants his audience to emulate their faith. To be sure, the audience is directed to identify with the heroes themselves, and not with the 'people,' since the people of Israel are not depicted as honoring the heroes. However, since that faith is described with such variety and thereby in such generality, an imitation of the heroes' behavior can not be what the author strives for, except in the most general, vague way. Rather, like Quintilian in theory and Cicero in practice, the author of Hebrews conveys some sort of *dissimilarity* between the examples he uses and the ultimate form of faith which he is trying to illustrate. When Cicero employed the early Greek sophists as examples of orators with a great breadth of knowledge, he was also quick to point out their deficiencies (that they made no practical use of their education) relative to the Roman ideal he wanted to promote. Cicero also implied that this was an inherent problem of the Greeks. In other words, these sophists, however exemplary, were products of a time and place regarded by Cicero as obsolete and inferior.

I find the same phenomenon, *mutatis mutandis*, in Hebrews 11. The heroes of Hebrews live in a time prior to the advent of Christ. Their world is an inferior one from the point of view of the Christian author of Hebrews. What they can accomplish is limited by their place in divine history. The divine and human honors bestowed upon the heroes, which played such an important role in the Jewish lists, is gravely diminished in Hebrews.

However, even this sort of modeling, in which the examples are less than perfect, possesses the power to persuade a listener toward imitative action.

---

[192] Cf. Sirach 44:7–8, where the heroes are explicitly said to have been honored in their own time.

[193] Bovon's remark ("Le Christ, la foi, et la sagasse," 136) about sapiential hero lists that "le fait même que l'on reprenne des example du passé comme norm de la foi et de la vie pour aujourd'hui," does not apply to Hebrews 11 the way it does to other lists.

We could dub the use of examples in Hebrews 11 a case of 'the lesser to the greater:' if even these men and women, who live prior to the time of Christ, can live a life of faith, how much more feasible it is for individuals who live in the time of Christ to be faithful!

Thus, Hebrews 11 resembles Jewish hero lists in the following ways: 1) the author is primarily interested in ancient, rather than recent examples; 2) the structure is poetic, rhythmic, and includes a large number of examples, but is multi-dimensional in its use of a variety of figures and actions; 3) a diachronic-historiographic interest is evident. However, Hebrews 11 is more like the Greco-Roman texts in its more complex characterization of the heroes and in the relationship of the heroes to the ideal principle of faith. In other words, the heroes of Hebrews are not the ideal models of earlier Jewish lists; from the author's point of view, their esteem is mitigated by their historically inferior position. This deviation from Jewish lists is highly significant, because it contributes to the new Christian vision of Jewish heroes and history that I contend Hebrews 11 represents.

The Form and Function of Hebrews 11

Having completed our survey of hero lists in antiquity, we can address the genre of Hebrews 11. The first issue, which I think can be permanently resolved on the basis of this study, is whether or not Hebrews 11 constitutes an edited version of an earlier source. The evidence from all the lists we have examined points toward the authors' producing their own examples. The fingerprints of each author occur on every list. Given the purpose of using examples, which is to be relevant to the issue at hand, it seems quite natural that the author of a given work is in the best position of selecting his/her own examples. Since an earlier source cannot possibly match the current conditions of a given speaker or writer, there is no advantage in using one. To be sure, the fact that the author chooses the exemplary figures for him/her/self does not mean that there are not stock examples or stock heroes, which are popular and therefore used again and again. But even commonly used examples are tailored to a particular situation, to the precise needs of the author for making the point.[194]

There is no reason to believe that Hebrews is any different in this regard. The various internal reasons that have been amassed to argue for a source, such as that Jesus is mentioned only once in the course of 40 verses, or the

---

[194] Thus, a figure like Abraham is so commonly appealed to that we could think of him as a stock example. However, we saw from figure 2 that different elements of his life were employed for different purposes.

so-called contradiction between the statement in vv. 13 and 39 that the heroes did not receive the promises and the remark in v. 33 that they did,[195] are extremely weak. The author of Hebrews neglects to make mention of Jesus in other sections of his text, primarily when he is engaged in interpreting a text from Jewish scripture (e.g., 3:7–4:13 has only one reference to Jesus, in 3:14). As for the problem of reconciling vv. 13 and 39 with 33, this can be accounted for by the specific contexts of each case. Each verse, for example, has a different verb for "receiving" the promises, and occurs in a very different place on the list. As I will argue in the following chapter, the author probably refers to the act of promising in v. 33, while meaning the fulfillment of those promises in vv. 13 and 39.[196]

The argument that the heroes are poor examples of faith and therefore the author grafted the anaphoric structure of faith onto an existing catalog, does not have much potency either. As we saw in the Greco-Roman texts, there can be varying degrees of similarity between the *illustrans* and the *illustrandum*. A perfect parallel between the example and the principle may not be the most advantageous relation, especially if the author has some rhetorical sophistication. Furthermore, the author of Hebrews probably has more than one agenda in the composition of his list. A historiographic interest would cause him to include or exclude on the basis of the historiographic picture he wanted to convey.[197] The historiographic agenda would then affect the selection of heroes.

Since we conclude that the author composed the list himself, we must see Hebrews 11 first and foremost as part of Hebrews. That is, the catalog of heroes in Hebrews—however prominently it stands out as a distinct unit—cannot possess its own *independent* genre. It is a rhetorical form that an author employs in order to build up his overall argument(s). In the texts we have seen, hagiologies, or lists of exemplary figures in general, do not circulate by themselves;[198] they are always found embedded in some larger work. A hero list is not a kind of literature in antiquity.

---

[195] These were two of the arguments put forth by Michel (*Der Brief*, 244) in his construction of the source hypothesis. For a complete rebuttal of all the arguments for Hebrews' dependence on an earlier source, see Ellingworth, *Hebrews*, 558–59.

[196] This is essentially the position of F. F. Bruce, *The Epistle to the Hebrews* (Grand Rapids: Eerdmans, 1964) 343.

[197] A better way to assess whether the examples are consistent with the author's agenda would be to see if they dovetail with the thought of Hebrews as a whole—which is largely the goal of chapter two of this study—and not simply the faith principle.

[198] Other kinds of lists do circulate as independent pieces of ancient literature: There are lists of citizens, see William Harris, *Ancient Literacy* (Cambridge: Harvard, 1989) 27,

Furthermore, as is evident from the Greco-Roman material, examples are part of the stock-in-trade of rhetoricians. A trained rhetorician exercised great care in the employment of examples. Such a carefully constructed series of exemplary figures as Hebrews 11 was not a spontaneous jotting. Most scholars believe that the author of the document now known as the Epistle to the Hebrews had formal rhetorical training, and Hebrews 11 confirms this assessment. Since we assume that Hebrews as a whole is an epideictic oration, and since examples are fairly common in such speeches,[199] the text of Hebrews 11 would seem to be consistent with its present context.

Many scholars refer to Hebrews 11 as an example list, but often they want to identify it as something more.[200] This tendency does not come as a surprise, since Hebrews 11 is a complex, multi-dimensional collection of examples with a diachronic as well as a synchronic angle. Unfortunately, the encomiums[201] or baptismal liturgies[202] that have been proposed do not capture the historical element. Thyen's notion that Hebrews 11 was an independent sermon did take into account the influence of *Heilsgeschichte*,[203] but his thesis about the form of Hebrews 11 also fails. Not only is he wrong to assume that Hebrews 11 could have had an independent existence—for we now see that there is neither evidence that Hebrews 11 came from a source nor that hero lists circulated as documents by themselves—but he fallaciously assumed that Greek ideas about human virtue were what transformed the *Heilgeschichte* into a hero list. My reading of Greco-Roman hero lists indicates that they are never about ultimate virtues. In fact, most of the lists display an indifference to virtue. Greco-Roman authors are only interested in the qualities of individuals that lead to success in the public arena. Success in the public arena is not something for which *any* of

---

209; lists of magical spells, see H. D. Betz (ed.), *Greek Magical Papyri* (Chicago: University of Chicago, 1986); and lists of miracles in early Christian circles, see David Frankfurter, "The Origin of the Miracle List Tradition and Its Medium of Circulation," *SBL Seminar Papers* (1990) 344–71.

199 *Synkrisis*, the comparison of the subject to something else is common in epideictic rhetoric, and examples often count as comparisons; see George Kennedy, *New Testament Interpretation Through Rhetorical Criticism* (Chapel Hill and London: University of North Carolina, 1984) 24. Texts such as Plutarch's *On the Bravery of Women* and Dio Chrysostom's *Encomium on Hair,* are good illustrations of this use of example series.

200 E.g., Attridge (*Hebrews*, 306).

201 The designation used by Attridge (*Hebrews*, 306–307) and Mack (*Rhetoric*, 75).

202 As used by Schille, "Katechese und Taufliturgie."

203 See n. 57.

Hebrews' heroes are listed. Indeed, what the author of Hebrews does seem to have inherited from the Greco-Roman tradition was the ability to see the biblical figures in a more human, less heroic light, and the rhetorical sophistication to express this while still maintaining the figures as models of behavior.

Spicq was perhaps most accurate in his simple assertion that Hebrews 11 is a combination of the moral exemplar list and a retelling of salvation history.[204] At the very least, we can say that Hebrews was inspired by more than one of these earlier forms.[205] Formally speaking, Hebrews 11 is no doubt a list, and I will continue to refer to it as such. But we must bear in mind that the text also possesses a narrative quality, which allows for the retelling of biblical history, as was fairly typical of those Jewish lists we defined as multi-dimensional. I prefer 'hero list' to 'example list' because the emphasis then lies on the characters themselves,[206] rather than on some vague principle of which the heroes are mere illustrations. The author of Hebrews himself never says he is citing *paradeigmata*; rather, he says "by faith the ancestors (πρεσβύτεροι) were attested to" (11:2). 'Hero list' also captures the genealogical function implicit in the text; the heroes are the community's πρεσβύτεροι.

To be sure, that the heroes are examples of an abstract principle, such as faith, is one function of a hero list. In my assessment, however, the primary function of a multi-dimensional hero list is *to explain and legitimate the existence of the community which is being addressed, by grounding the members of that community in a significant genealogical history.*

---

[204] See n. 12.

[205] As Attridge himself admits (*Hebrews*, 306). See also the discussion by William Lane, *Hebrews 9–13* (WBC; Dallas, TX: Word, 1991) 316–23.

[206] The label applies even if the heroes of Hebrews are somewhat less "heroic" than their counterparts on Jewish lists. As will become clear in the following chapter, the author's effort to alter the status of the biblical figures also functions to redefine the portrait of the Jewish hero.

Chapter Two
HEBREWS AND HERMENEUTICS
෴ ๑๒

In the previous chapter we evaluated the broad literary context of which Hebrews 11 is a part. In this chapter we will study a context more immediate: Hebrews itself. Having determined that our hero catalog bears greatest resemblance to those Jewish Hellenistic lists which also function as retellings of biblical history, such as Sirach 44–50, Wisdom 10, and Covenant of Damascus 2–3, we must now study the hermeneutical relationship between our author and his source, i.e., Jewish scripture. The construction of the hero list in chap. 11 is just one of many instances in Hebrews where the author engages the biblical text. Numerous 'retellings' of biblical episodes appear throughout the pages of Hebrews. Thus, an investigation into the hermeneutics of Hebrews in general can only deepen our understanding of chap. 11 in particular.[1]

Hebrews is indeed a document characterized by the interpretation of scripture. Yet, surprisingly few complete studies of Hebrews' use of the biblical text are available. Most previous analyses of scripture in Hebrews focus on the document's biblical citations.[2] The problem with these studies

---

[1] A discussion of where chap. 11 fits in the argument of Hebrews will appear at the start of the following chapter.

[2] See P. Padva, *Les citations de l'Ancien Testament dans l'Epître aux Hébreux* (Paris: N.L. Danzig, 1904). L. Vernard, "L'utilisation des Psaumes dans l'Epître aux Hébreux," in *Mélanges E. Podechard* (Lyon: Facultés Catholiques, 1945) 253–64; J. van der Ploeg, "L'Exégès de l'Ancien Testament dans l'Epître aux Hébreux," *RB* 54 (1947) 187–228; Robert Rendall, "The Method of the Writer to the Hebrews in Using Old Testament Quotations," *EvQ* 27 (1955) 214–220; K. J. Thomas, "The Old Testament Citations in Hebrews," *NTS* 11 (1964–65) 303–25; Simon J. Kistemaker, *The Psalm Citations in the Epistle to the Hebrews* (Amsterdam: Soest, 1961); G. Caird, "The Exegetical Method of the Epistle to the Hebrews," *CJT* 5 (1959) 44–51; P. Katz, "The Quotations from Deuteronomy in Hebrews," *ZNW* 49 (1958) 213–23; and H. J. Combrink, "Some Thoughts on the OT Citations in the Epistle to the Hebrews," *Neot* 5 (1971) 22–36. There are two significant exceptions, i.e., studies which are more comprehensive in their assessment of the OT in Hebrews: Friedrich Schröger, *Der Verfasser des Hebräerbriefes als Schriftausleger* (BU 4; Regensburg: Pustet, 1968) and "Das hermeneutische Instrumentarium des Hebräerbriefverfassers," *ThGl* 60 (1970) 344–59; and George W. Buchanan, *To the Hebrews: Translation, Comment and Conclusions* (AB 36; Garden City, NY: Doubleday, 1972). Unfortunately, both of these scholars suffer from tendentious attempts to demonstrate parallels with Jewish technique: Schröger is overly concerned with the pesharim, and Buchanan believes the entire text of Hebrews is a midrash on

is that they are not at all comprehensive, since Hebrews also contains significant discussion of scriptural themes and stories almost completely devoid of quotations. Indeed, Hebrews 11 is an example of such discussion.[3] In these texts, rather than resort to direct quotations, the author retells biblical episodes in his own words. Because the author so faithfully renders scripture when he does choose to quote, the absence of quotations in such paraphrases is conspicuous. What follows then is a comprehensive analysis of the pattern of quotation and retelling in Hebrews.

Quotations and Retellings

While the interpretive strategy in Hebrews may not be consistent, it is not arbitrary. Significantly, the author's treatment of scripture does not vary according to a text's category. For example, he does not treat a text from the Pentateuch differently from a psalm, simply because it is part of the Pentateuch (as we find in Philo, who tends to quote exclusively from the Pentateuch[4]). Rather, the hermeneutical distinction that motivates our author to quote directly in one place and to retell in another depends upon *whether or not he wants to render the biblical text as speech or as narrative.* Thus, the first section of this chapter will map out the author's two contrasting methods of approaching the biblical text. The following section will then explore the rhetorical function of biblical interpretation in Hebrews.

Quotations as Divine Speech

My criteria for recognizing explicit citations in Hebrews are strict,[5] so as to clearly distinguish between a citation and a paraphrase. The first and

---

Psalm 110. Other exceptions include M. Barth, ("The Old Testament in Hebrews: An Essay in Biblical Hermeneutics" in W. Klassen and G. F. Snyder, eds., *Current Issues in New Testament Interpretation* [New York: Harper, 1962] 53–78) and F.C. Synge (*Hebrews and the Scriptures* [London: SPCK, 1959]) but their readings are superficial and apologetic.

[3] Because scholars have focused their attention on the document's citations, Hebrews 11—which has only two explicit citations—has not enjoyed much attention as a work of interpretation. In other words, the hermeneutical presuppositions, attitudes, and interests of the author regarding the biblical text have not been explored, with the possible exception of Barth, "Old Testament in Hebrews."

[4] See Yehoshua Amir, "Authority and Interpretation of Scripture in the Writings of Philo," in *Mikra: Text Translation, Reading and Interpretation of the Hebrew Bible in Ancient Judaism and Chrisitianity*, M. J. Mulder, ed. (CRINT 2.1; Minneapolis: Fortress, 1990) 422–3.

[5] Not surprisingly, different commentators on Hebrews tally the total number of citations differently. See Kistemaker (*Psalm Citations*, 16) for a brief overview of who counts what and how.

simplest is that a citation must be formally introduced; this usually occurs
with a verb of saying, like λέγω or λαλέω, as we shall see below.[6] The second
is that the integrity of the text must be largely intact. That is, the majority of
the words must be the same in the quoted text and in the source text, and
they must generally follow the order of the LXX. Subtle alterations, like the
changed tense of a verb which can be easily explained by the author's
theological or cosmetic interest, do not disqualify the text from counting as
a citation.[7]

The second criterion confirms the validity of the first. In other words,
those texts which are imprecise in following the source text—thus they do
not meet the second criterion—do not formally introduce the biblical text—
and so do not meet the first criterion either. If a completely different word
order is used from the LXX, with significant omissions or additions, it is
better counted as a paraphrase. For example, the most significant
disagreement I have with Simon Kistemaker concerns Heb 7:1–2, which he
considers a direct citation of Gen 14:17–20.[8] I have labeled it a paraphrase.[9]
It is not formally introduced and there are significant omissions—the author
of Hebrews has obviously compressed the story. Second, he is not faithful to
the word order for more than two or three words in a row, and often these
are titles or phrases that naturally go together, e.g., "Melchizedek, King of
Salem," or "God of the Most High." If the author of Hebrews is such a
reliable quoter of texts at the times he chooses to be, then his free form

---

[6] Some have argued that Heb 10:36 is not a formal introduction to the citation of
Isaiah and Habakkuk in 10:37–38. 10:36 reads: "For you need endurance, so that when
you have done the will of God, you may receive what was promised." The quotation that
follows is "what was promised." To be sure, this is not an introduction like the others in
Hebrews. However, it is not exactly an exception either. The verb "to promise" is a verb of
speaking, which elswhere is used to introduce a citation directly (12:26). Since the author
ended his sentence with the word "promised," he probably did not want to be redundant
by then using a formal introduction. Thus, 10:37–38 counts as a formal citation.

[7] See e.g., K. H. Jobes, "Rhetorical Achievement in the Hebrews 10 'Misquote' of
Psalm 40," *Bib* 72 (1991) 387–96. I am also indebted to a conversation with Agneta
Enermalm-Ogawa, who pointed out that several alterations, such as the word ἀνομιῶν
added in 10:17, derive from liturgical style, in which poetic embellishment is desirable.
Attempts to explain discrepencies by crediting the MT, such as is found in George
Howard ("Hebrews and the Old Testament Quotations," *NovT* 10 [1968] 208–16); and
Buchanan, (*Hebrews*, xxvii-xxviii) are improbable, see Harold Attridge (*The Epistle to the
Hebrews* [Hermeneia; Philadelphia: Fortress, 1989] 23).

[8] Kistemaker, *Psalm Citations*, 38–40.

[9] Similarly Nestle-Aland (26th edition) labels 3:5 a quotation, while I call it a
paraphrase. Like 7:1–2, it is not formally introduced and and the word order has been
completely mixed up.

handling of the text at other times must be for a reason, and we should categorize these latter instances differently. They are not simply bungled or altered citations; they are paraphrases, in which the author wishes to rehearse the biblical episode in his own words.

Based on the aforesaid criteria, I count 31 different scriptural citations in Hebrews. Indeed, the author uses quotations from a variety of biblical books, although these citations are not atypical in terms of early Christian usage.[10] Twelve quotations come from the Pentateuch,[11] seven from the Prophets,[12] and twelve from the Writings, all of the latter coming from the Psalms, with the exception of one from Proverbs.[13]

What is most striking about the scriptural citations in Hebrews—and yet gone unnoticed—is that nearly all of them are quotations of *direct speech*.[14] By direct speech, I mean not only that indirect discourse is avoided, but that narrative texts from scripture are almost never chosen for quotation. Each quotation contains either the literal words of God (although often a character such as Moses is the actual speaker) the oracular utterings of the prophets, or the musings of the psalmist. Given the hermeneutical presuppositions of the time, we can safely assume that, for the author of Hebrews, these are all instances of divine utterance. When a prophet speaks,

---

[10] As E. E. Ellis ("Biblical Interpretation in the New Testament Church," in *Mikra*, 691) notes, almost all NT quotations come from the Pentateuch, Isaiah, and the Psalms.

[11] They are as follows (the numbers in parentheses refer to the their location in Hebrews): Deut 32:43 (1:6b); Gen 2:2 (4:4); Gen 22:17 (6:14); Exo 25:40 (8:5); Exo 24:8 (9:20); Deut 32:35 (10:30a); Deut 32:36 (10:30b); Gen 5:24 (11:5); Gen 21:12 (11:18); Deut 9:19 (12:21); Deut 4:24 (12:29); Deut 31:8 (13:5).

[12] 2 Sam 7:14 (1:5b); Isa 8:17=2 Sam 22:3 (2:13a); Isa 8:18 (2:13b); Jer 31:31–34 (8:8–12; 10:16–17); Isa 26:20 (10:37a); Hab 2:3–4 (10:37b–38); Hag 2:6 (12:26).

[13] Psalms: 2:7 (1:5a; 5:5); 104:4 (1:7); 45:6–7 (1:8–9); 102:25–27 (1:10–12); 110:1 (1:13); 8:4–6 (2:6–8a); 22:23 (2:12); 95:7–11 (3:7–11; the author also repeatedly quotes words and phrases from Psalm 95:7–11 throughout his discussion of it); 110:4 (5:6; 7:17, 21); 40:7–9 (10:5–7); Prov 3:11–12 (12:5–6); Psalm 118:6.(13:6).

[14] There are two exceptions. One is found in 4:4 where the author quotes Gen 2:2 "And God rested on the seventh day from all his works;" these are the words of the impersonal biblical narrator and do not constitute direct speech. However, as Attridge (*Hebrews*, 24) points out, the reason the author quotes this verse is to define the meaning of the term 'rest' by means of a *gezera shawa*. He is in the middle of exegeting a line from Ps 95, which contains the word, when he quotes Gen 2:2. The author's primary concern is the text from Ps 95; the only reason he cites the Genesis text explicitly is for lexical purposes. The other exception occurs in 11:5 where Enoch is "not found because God translated him." A possible explanation for this citation is that because the author follows it with exhortative commentary in v. 6, he wants to have his exhortation resonate with literal biblical words.

for example, he is clearly a mouthpiece for God; and David, as the composer of the psalms, is presumed to be under divine inspiration.

There are several ways that the author makes clear that these are God's words he is quoting. Sometimes quotations occur from the LXX that are the unmediated *ipssissima verba* of God, as in God's promise to Abraham in Genesis 22, "Surely I will bless you and multiply you," quoted in Heb 6:14.

The most common form of direct speech quoted in Hebrews is the saying uttered by a divinely inspired person, such as a prophet or a psalmist (although no reference is made to human agency in Hebrews). Sometimes the fact that God is speaking is made overtly clear by the quotation itself, which explicitly identifies God as the speaker, as in the case of Jer 31:31–34 (LXX: Jer 38:31–34), found in Heb 8:8ff. "The days will come, *says the Lord*, [λέγει κύριος] when I will establish a new covenant with the house of Israel and the house of Judah . . . ."

In other cases, the fact that God is the speaker is self-evident in the use of the first person. As an illustration, we may point to the second citation in the opening catena; it is from Nathan's oracle in 2 Sam 7:14 ("I will be to him a father, and he shall be to me a son"). While Nathan is actually the speaker in 2 Samuel, the use of the first person both in the original biblical context and in Hebrews indicates the direct divine voice. There is no acknowledgment of Nathan as the speaker in Hebrews.[15]

The vast majority of scriptural citations in Hebrews are introduced as quoted speech by employing a typical verb of saying. This is the case in the first group of quotations in the document, "for to what angel did God ever *say*, ..." The epistle in fact begins with a statement about God's verbal communication through the ages: "In many and various ways God spoke (λάλησας) of old to our fathers by the prophets . . . ." Indeed, the most frequent introduction to a piece of scripture is simply 'He says,' referring almost always to God, although sometimes the speaker is Jesus (2:12; 10:5) or the Holy Spirit (3:7).

Indeed, verbs of saying are commonly used in introductory formulae in the Mishnah and Qumran.[16] They appear in other NT writers too, although

---

15 A quotation of this oracle also occcurs in 4QFlor, and Nathan is not named as the speaker there either. However, the way the pronouns are used, as well as the author's interpretaion, indicates that the author clearly has the Davidic context in mind. See my discussion of 4QFlor below.

16 For discussion of introductory formulae in Qumran and the NT, see J. A. Fitzmyer, "The Use of Explicit Old Testament Quotations in Qumran Literature and in the New Testament," *Essays on the Semitic Background of the New Testament* (SBLSBS 5; London: Scholars, 1971) 7–17. Examples given comparatively for the Mishnah and the NT can be

Paul at least prefers verbs of writing. Hebrews contains the standard array of Greek verbs of saying, e.g., λέγω, φήσι, λαλέω, in a variety of tenses, although the present indicative and participle dominate. When the perfect tense is used, it usually indicates that the text has already been quoted earlier in the argument.[17] The passive is uncommon in Hebrews;[18] its use is limited to re-introducing a quotation, or in describing what has been said of a person. These verbal forms themselves do not stand out as unusual in the NT, but serve to reinforce the immediate oral character of the citation.

Typically, the author of Hebrews does not name the human speakers of the biblical words he cites, as in the cases of Nathan and Moses referred to above. Although pentateuchal characters or prophets are the original speakers of most sayings in Hebrews, there are only a few instances where the author will name them by way of introduction. Since I believe that Hebrews intentionally omits the name of the biblical character when introducing the majority of his quotations, it is necessary to analyze the exceptions. In 4:7 David is referred to as the speaker of a quotation from Ps 95:7–8:

> again he sets a certain day, "Today," saying through David so long afterward, in the words already quoted, "Today, when you hear his voice, do not harden your hearts."

There are particular reasons why our author finds it necessary to point out that David is the speaker of these words. He is in the midst of a detailed exegetical discussion of Psalm 95. As the author himself notes here, he has already quoted this text, twice in fact; each time it has been introduced differently.[19] Psalm 95 is important because it refers to the wilderness experience and the rebellious generation notoriously associated with that period in history. The author calls attention to a subtle problem: God swears in Psalm 95 that they, i.e. the Israelites, shall never enter his rest, κατάπαυσις.[20] In the context of the wilderness story, the words "they shall

---

found in B. M. Metzger,"The Formulas Introducing Quotations of Scripture in the N T and the Mishna" *JBL* 70 (1951) 297–307.

[17] The one exception to this occurs in 13:5.

[18] Cf. rabbinic literature, where the most common form of the word אמר is in the niphal. See Metzger, "Formulas Introducing Quotations," 299.

[19] The first time the Holy Spirit is explicitly named as the speaker (3:7); the second time the introduction takes the form of a passive impersonal, ἐν τῳ λέγεσθαι (3:15).

[20] κατάπαυσις is a theologically weighty term in Hebrews, which we can not elaborate on here. It must suffice to say that it is a desirable eschatological and perhaps heavenly state, which the believer attempts to achieve (4:11). See the comprehensive discussion of James W. Thompson, (*The Beginnings of Christian Philosophy: The Epistle to the Hebrews*

never enter my rest" (Ps 95:11) reflect God's frustration with Israel and her less-than-satisfying display of faith in the desert. God *swears* he shall *never* give them rest.

Yet two scriptural points mitigate against God's oath. First, in 4:4 the author cites "And God rested on the seventh day from all his works" from Gen 2:2. Using a *gezera shawa* on the word 'rest,'[21] he wishes to indicate by quoting Gen 2:2 that God and God's creation are in a state of rest. "Therefore," our author reasons, "it remains for some to enter it" (4:6). Second, although historically speaking the people of Israel did stop wandering in the desert, and Joshua did lead them into the promised land, Psalm 95, especially verses 7–8, 11, is *prima facie* evidence for the author of Hebrews that entering the promised land did not count as entering κατάπαυσις. Immediately following his quotation of Ps 95:7–8 ("Today, when you hear his voice, do not harden your hearts."), he says "for if Joshua had given them rest, God would not speak later of another day. So then, there remains a sabbath rest for the people of God."

The reason it was necessary to name David as the one who spoke the words "today, when you hear his voice, do not harden your hearts" is explained by the fact that David lives at a later point in history than Joshua does. The word "today" highlights, and, in a sense, freezes that historical moment—the moment David penned the psalm. If God is exhorting the people at the time of David to turn from their disobedience, the people of Israel have obviously still not achieved κατάπαυσις, despite Joshua's ending their desert wanderings and settling them in the promised land. There remains some greater Sabbath rest than that achieved by land settlement. Thus, David must be named as the speaker of the quotation from Psalm 95, in order for the author to call attention to the fact that these words came *after* the people of Israel settled in the land.

There are two instances where Moses is introduced as the speaker of a quotation. Only the one found in 9:19–20 is significant.[22] Moses says, "This is

---

[CBQMS 13; Washington D.C.: Catholic Biblical Association, 1982] 81–102); and the monograph by O. Hofius (*Katapausis: Die Vorstellung von endzeitlichen Ruheort im Hebräerbrief* [WUNT 2; Tübingen: Mohr, 1970]).

[21] See Thompson, *Beginnings of Christian Philosophy*, 100.

[22] The other instance, found in 12:21, is a minor exception to the author's otherwise consistent avoidance of naming human speakers. It amounts to two words, ἔκφοβός εἰμι. In describing the epiphany at Sinai from Exodus 19, the author of Hebrews says, "Indeed, so terrifying was the sight that Moses said, 'I tremble with fear'." This quotation is unique in Hebrews in that although it is an example of direct speech, it is the one instance which is technically not *divine* speech. Moses is not speaking for God; he is expressing his own

the blood of the covenant which God commanded you" (Exod 24:8). The reason Moses is noted as the speaker is different from the case of David above. Chap. 9 of Hebrews is an exegetical discussion of the sacrificial cult, in which the faulty mode of sacrifice practiced by ancient Israelites is made out as an anti-type of the perfect sacrifice performed by Christ. The old sacrificial system was determined by the first covenant, i.e., the law, which was handed down by Moses. Christ's sacrifice is of a heavenly nature and takes place in a heavenly tent. Christ then has inaugurated a new covenant.

The author preceded his discussion of the tent and sacrifice with a lengthy citation from Jeremiah 31 concerning the new covenant. Prior to this discussion, the typological comparison between Moses and Jesus has been a recurring theme in Hebrews (3:1–6; 8:1–7). The typological argument in chap. 9 is an extension of the Moses/Jesus typology. Thus Moses's pronouncement quoted in 9:21 serves as his sacrificial enactment of the covenant, which is parallel to Jesus' sacrificial enactment.[23] Moses must deliver the words in order to carry through the typology.[24] Therefore, as with the case of David above, naming Moses when introducing the quotation was essential to the author's argument.

Aside from these exceptions, in which the author has some argumentative stake in using the name, all quotations in Hebrews neglect to name the quotation's original speaker or, as we shall see, fail to mention the scriptural origin of the cited text. To highlight the peculiarity of this situation, we need only take a brief look at introductory formulae in the NT and other contemporary literature. When saying verbs are used elsewhere in the NT, the biblical prophet who originally spoke the words being cited is usually named, or at least reference is made to a human prophet. For example,

---

feeling. This quotation is present for no other reason than to make the scene at Sinai more vivid.

[23] As Mary Rose D'Angelo (*Moses in the Letter to the Hebrews* [SBLDS 42; Missoula: Scholars, 1979] 243–9) points out, Heb 9:16–21 is very much a revisionist history of Exod 24:1–8. The way the author of Hebrews tells it, the blood referred to in 9:21 is a sign of purification. But the sprinkling of the blood is a sign of bonding the people to God's covenant in its original context, not a sign of cleansing, as he interprets it (9:22). The author has conflated two events involving blood: the inauguration of the covenant and the inauguration of the temple, of which only the latter is an act of cleansing. This conflation serves the purpose of tightening up the Moses/Jesus typology, since Jesus' crucifixion is at once a sacrificial act and one that initiates a new covenant.

[24] Since Christ himself enacted his covenant, Moses must be the principle actor of his. In typology, even when one is dealing with an anti-type, elements of continuity are as important as elements of discontinuity. For a discussion of this issue see Graham Hughes, *Hebrews and Hermeneutics* (Cambridge: Cambridge University, 1979) 102–5.

Matthew, whether or not he is using the fulfillment formula, generally uses a variation of "as it was spoken by the prophet" (e.g. 3:3; 12:17). This formula 'as it was spoken by the prophet'[25] can be found in all the canonical gospels, in Acts and in Paul—in other words, in all those places in the NT where significant quoting is done.[26] In Hebrews, as we have noted, a prophet is never specifically identified as the speaker of the words of scripture,[27] except when such a prophet must be named, not necessarily to validate a quotation—as would normally be the case—but to locate and contextualize a particular moment in history, when such a moment has a bearing on the argument.

So while Hebrews is in most cases similar to other NT documents in the kinds of biblical texts it quotes (from the Pentateuch, Psalms, and Isaiah), the document is very different in its use of introductory formulae. The author never follows a prophesy and fulfillment formula as in Matthew or John. In fact, the presentation of quoted material in Hebrews does not resemble any of the gospels, in which a biblical verse is quoted as something proclaimed in the past, preserved (in writing), and ultimately comes to fruition in the events recounted by the evangelist.[28]

One of the most striking facts about Hebrews is that the author never uses 'as it is written,' an introduction which we find frequently in nearly all other ancient exegetes, including those who also use saying verbs. Although the use of saying verbs to introduce an OT citation is common among many other ancient exegetes besides the writers of the NT, especially in Qumran and the Mishnah, no other author uses them to the complete exclusion of writing verbs or references to scripture *qua* scripture, i.e., as written text. And again, these works, like NT writers other than the author of Hebrews, frequently include reference to the actual biblical speaker or book when

---

[25] Sometimes the prophet is named, at other times, unnamed.

[26] For a recent analysis see Ellis, "Biblical Interpretation," 691–725.

[27] Attridge (*Hebrews*, 24) believes that Heb 1:1 "In many and various ways God spoke of old to our fathers by the prophets; . . ." indicates that the author recognizes human instrumentality. However, this verse is not an introduction to a specific citation. Furthermore, this acknowledgment of the prophets as divine agents is qualified by the next verse,"but in these last days he has spoken to us by a Son . . ." As I will argue, when biblical speech is genuinely efficacious and revelatory, God, Christ or the Holy Spirit utters the scriptural words immediately, as if no one ever said them before.

[28] The use of fulfillment verbs is, surprisingly, never found at Qumran, see Fitzmyer ("Use of Old Testament Quotations," 13), and very rarely found in the Mishnah, see Metzger ("Formulas Introducing Quotations," 301).

saying verbs are used.[29] Occasionally in rabbinic literature and in the NT we find 'scripture says,'[30] but even in these cases the mention of 'scripture' indicates an identifiable document in which the quotation is preserved. Very commonly in the midrashim, such as the *Mekilta*, one finds simply 'it is said.' In this case, that the quotation's context is scriptural is obvious. Despite the fact that a saying verb is employed, the oral character is hardly emphasized by its use.[31] In marked contrast, Hebrews never uses the word 'scripture,' γραφή, and never uses the word 'written' in any form in connection with biblical material. The author never names a biblical book; he almost never names a human speaker. As already mentioned, the speaker in a Hebrews quotation is usually God, occasionally Christ and sometimes the Holy Spirit. Hence, a citation's physical location in scripture, i.e. whether a text is from the Law, the Prophets, etc., is nearly always absent. Thus, what makes Hebrews unique in its presentation of biblical citations is an unrelenting consistency in the use of saying verbs (while totally avoiding any reference to scripture being written) and the lack of acknowledgment of human speakers or authors.[32]

Having noted that the author does not use verbs of writing, I must, however, also point out that in two places he employs the verb 'to witness' to introduce a quotation: διεμαρτύρατο δέ πού τις λέγων in 2:6 ("It has been

---

[29] See Fitzmyer, "Use of Old Testament Quotations," 11. In cases where the subject is not explicit, it is difficult to tell if the subject is God or the text, e.g., κατὰ τὸ εἰρήμενον (Rom 4:18; Luke 2:24). The problem of the indefinite subject is usually found in connection with passive verbs. When active verbs are used the speaker is named, or is obvious from the context, except in the Epistle to the Hebrews.

[30] Metzger ("Formulas Introducing Quotations," 300) notes that the root כתב occurs in both nominal and verbal forms, involving expressions like "the scripture says . . . ," (*m. Yebamoth* 4:4) "one verse of scripture says . . . and then another . . . ," (*m. Arakin* 8:7) or "that which is written." (*m. Abot* 6:10). Sometimes a passage or division is referred to, "another passage says . . . ," (*m. Sotah* 5:3). NT examples are also listed by Metzger, but are too numerous to list here.

[31] Cf. Danby's translation of the recurrent phrase in the Mishnah, נאמר, "it is written," instead of the more literal, "it is said."

[32] Barth ("Old Testament in Hebrews," 58–9) misses this aspect of Hebrews' citation formulae. He likens Hebrews' use of saying verbs to the rabbis or Philo; he just assumes Hebrews is more radical in its presentation of scripture as the living word. But the lack of specificity in Hebrews about whence and from whom the words of scripture are to be credited is undeniably peculiar. Even at Qumran, in the most eschatological uses of scripture, such as 4Q Flor, the book or speaker is named. As Metzger points out ("Formulas Introducing Quotations," 306), even though the NT and the Mishnah have the highest conception of divine inspiration in the scriptures, they both regularly recognize human instrumentality.

testified somewhere . . .") and μαρτυρεῖται γὰρ ὅτι in 7:17 ("it is witnessed of him . . ."). The stress of this verb is often of an oral nature because of its oath-like character,[33] but at least in the first example the πού seems to indicate that the author is thinking of a written text. Although he lacks precision in specifying the scriptural location,[34] the fact that he is thinking of a *place*—as opposed to a moment in time—points toward writing, rather than speech.[35] In this case, the author is not ignoring or hiding the textual factor underlying the quotation. Indeed, the use of this verb may be a kind of intermediate stage[36] between a saying verb and a writing verb. We could say that the text "speaks" in such cases, in the sense that the text is called as a witness to testify concerning the status of a person. In 2:16 Psalm 8 is used a description of Christ, and in 7:17 Ps 110:4 is used as a testimony about Melchizedek. Significantly, the author also uses μαρτυρέω in the process of paraphrasing, as he does in 11:5, where he says of Enoch, "Now before he was taken he was *attested* as having pleased God." It appears that the author uses this verb specifically to refer what is said about people, whether he quotes a description of them or describes them in his own words. The fact that the author can use this verb both of quotations and retellings may further point to its intermediate character.

There is no doubt that the oral and immediate character of scripture is what is most stressed in Hebrews. Even though the letter typically quotes from the same kinds of texts as other NT documents, our author takes these quotations quite literally to be the words of God—words which are not mediated by a speaker, a body of writing, or even in many cases by the historical context. For him, these divine words flow directly from the mouth of God to the listener. That the quoted text in Hebrews transcends its biblical and/or historical context will become clearer after the retellings

---

[33] The implication is often to speak favorably of someone, or occasionally of something, see examples in BAGD and LSJ. It is interesting to note that Hans Walter Wolff (*Das Zitat im Prophetenspruch* [Evangelische Theologie Beiheft 4; Munich: Chr. Kaiser Verlag, 1937] 36–129) cited by George Savran, *Telling and Retelling: Quotation in Biblical Narrative* [Bloomington: University of Indiana, 1988] 8) believed that prophetic quotation, i.e., where the prophet speaks in the voice of God, thus "quoting" God, originated in the judicial tradition, because of the abundance of prophetic judgment speeches.

[34] Metzger ("Formulas Introducing Quotations," 301) notes that this kind of indefinite expression is unique to Hebrews among the documents of the NT; in the Mishnah there are one or two instances.

[35] Cf. Rom 3:21.

[36] I am grateful to D'Angelo, who initially suggested conceiving of the verb μαρτυρέω in this way.

have been observed. It is enough for now to say that the actual words of the quotation, the lemmata, are treated with great care by the author. In the case of Ps 95:7–8, eleven words are repeated over and over in a lengthy exposition. Nevertheless, the words of scripture and the author's commentary remain distinct.

This method of quoting is an extremely direct and powerful form of using scripture as divine revelation. Therefore scholars correctly point out that Hebrews presents scripture as the word of God.[37] But they are only partially right, because the author devotes a great deal of attention to texts which depend heavily upon scripture but contain virtually no quotations. It is these notable but largely ignored retellings of scripture to which I now turn.

Retellings as Narrative

By retellings I refer to those instances where the author describes an event, institution, or person from scripture using his own words, and for the most part refrains from quoting the text he paraphrases. There are primarily five sections within the text of Hebrews where significant retellings occur:[38] 1) 3:1–6a, where Moses is described as the servant of God; 2) 3:6b–4:11, where the wilderness experience is recounted; 3) chap. 7, where Melchizedek is discussed; 4) 8–10:18 where we find a lengthy discussion of the old covenant (in comparison to the new) and that which it entails, including descriptions of the sanctuary of the Lord, and the nature of law, sacrifice, and other priestly functions; and 5) chap. 11, the list of heroes by which the author recounts a good bit of Israelite history. In all of these— with the exception of the first—there are quotations, but they are mostly from the psalms and the prophets, not from Genesis, Exodus, or Numbers, i.e., books which contain the information that the author recounts. The few quotations that the author does include from the Pentateuchal context are, as we have seen, quotations of direct speech.

---

[37] Barth, ("Old Testament in Hebrews") for example, stresses this hermeneutical orientation for the author. The phrase "ὁ λόγος τοῦ θεοῦ" is used in Hebrews (4:12; 5:12), but I do not think it refers to the whole body of scripture.

[38] The author so often refers to persons, places, and events from scripture, that it is difficult to maintain consistent criteria in identifying biblical 'retellings' without including every biblical allusion. The retellings I have identified here are not exhaustive of retellings in Hebrews; they are rather the most striking examples of retellings. There are some other brief statements that could be called 'retellings,' e.g., 12:16–17 which refers to Esau selling his birthright, or 6:13–15, which although it contains a quotation, is a brief summary statement of the promises to Abraham.

The first case, Heb 3:1–6a, concerns the retelling of only one verse, Num 12:7.

> Therefore, brothers and sisters, holy partners in a heavenly calling, consider that Jesus, the apostle and high priest of our confession, was faithful to the one who appointed him just as Moses also was faithful in all God's house. Yet Jesus is worthy of more glory than Moses, just as the builder of a house has more honor than the house itself. (For every house is built by someone, but the builder of all things is God.) Now Moses was faithful in all God's house as a servant, to testify to the things that would be spoken later. Christ however, was faithful over God's house as a son . . . .

In this miniature retelling the author wishes to re-describe Moses as God's servant, in order to contrast him with Jesus, who is God's son. This first retelling allows me the opportunity to emphasize an important qualification of my description of the quotation/retelling pattern as analyzed thus far. I said at the outset that the tendency to quote directly or to retell depends upon whether or not the *author himself* wants to render the biblical text as speech or narrative. This dependence is only partly related to whether or not the biblical text actually is—or originally was—speech or narrative. What we find in Hebrews, on the one hand, is that the author will almost always resist quoting any narrative texts, i.e., he renarrates biblical narrative. On the other hand, simply because a scriptural text is divine speech does not *necessarily* mean the author is irresistibly compelled to quote it; sometimes he quotes and sometimes he paraphrases. In logical terms, we could say that a text's being divine speech is a necessary but not sufficient condition for a direct quotation.

Indeed, the passage from Num 12:7 which the author of Hebrews has in mind in 3:1–6a is a theophany scene, where God proclaims to Aaron and Miriam—who have questioned Moses' judgment—that Moses has a unique kind of authority. God tells them that Moses has an unmediated connection with divine authority.

> And [the Lord] said, "Hear my words: If there is a prophet among you, I the Lord make myself known to him in a dream. Not so with my servant Moses; he is entrusted with all my house. With him I speak mouth to mouth, clearly, and not in dark speech; and he beholds the form of the Lord. (Num 12:6–8)

The text from Numbers is not only direct, divine speech; the words are spoken during a theophany at the tent of meeting. But a glance at this text makes plain why our author did not quote it. There are no biblical passages I know of that represent a higher "Mosesology." Quoting this text would surely have undermined the author's purpose, which was to make Moses an anti-type, or at least inferior, to Jesus. He does not want to remind his audience of God's verbal and visual closeness to Moses. Moses was a Levite (Num 2:1) and post-biblical Jewish speculation presents him as the "intermediary par excellence between God and humanity."[39]

Quoting the text, even part of a verse, would have reproduced the divine voice speaking to Moses, thereby elevating Moses' intermediary role. The author, therefore, not only avoids quoting the verse, he never lets on to his audience that these words come from a direct divine revelation to Moses. The listeners hear that Moses was God's servant as if it were a commonly known historical fact; they do not hear it as the spoken word of God.

While Heb 3:1–6a remains unpeppered by any quotations, the other retellings do include quotations, but in only one case does the quotation come from the narrative under discussion. A brief look at each of the remaining retellings will illustrate what I mean. The retelling contained in 3:6b–4:11 is sparked by the author's exegesis of Ps 95:7–11 which is quoted in 3:7–11. The line from Psalm 95, "today, if you hear his voice, do not harden your hearts as in the rebellion," leads the author of Hebrews to ask "Now who were they who heard and yet were rebellious?" He then gives a brief and highly rhetorical summation of the wilderness generation's "rebellion" based on material in Numbers 14.[40] His primary motive in describing the wilderness generation (which has already been referred to in our earlier discussion of Psalm 95) is to demonstrate that another verse from the psalm "they shall not enter my rest" applies to the Israelites. The retelling remains subordinate to the author's exegesis of the psalm. Thus, the author quotes verses from the psalm repeatedly and self-consciously interprets them. The narrative material from Numbers, like the earlier retelling in chap. 3, is not introduced or referred to in any way *as text;* it is simply used as assumed tradition.

Unlike the case of the Numbers 14/Psalm 95 exegesis in Heb 3:6b–4:10, the retelling of the Abraham-Melchizedek encounter in Hebrews 7 begins with a paraphrase (of Gen 14:17–20) rather than a quotation. The discussion of Melchizedek proceeds for 17 verses, before we encounter the quotation from Ps 110: "Thou art a priest forever, after the order of Melchizedek." No

---

[39] Attridge (*Hebrews*, 105). See D'Angelo (*Moses in Hebrews*, 102–27) as well as Attridge for references to such traditions.

[40] The actual retelling sections within Heb 3:6b–4:11 are 3:16–19; 4:2,6b,8.

quotations are present from Genesis 14.[41] Although Melchizedek is central to the theology of Hebrews, the document's author is concerned only with scriptural lemmata from Psalm 110, not with lemmata from Genesis. Like the comparison made between Moses and Jesus in Heb 3:1–6a, Hebrews 7 concentrates on comparing Abraham to Melchizedek, and Melchizedek comes out the better man. The real reason the author wants to demonstrate that Abraham is inferior to Melchizedek is because Abraham is the patriarchal ancestor of the Levitical priests, and it is they who the author ultimately wishes to portray as inferior to Melchizedek. The denigration of the levitical priesthood in comparison to the timeless ethereal priesthood of Jesus is a theme fully developed in the fourth retelling I have identified (Exod 25:10–40) in Hebrews 8–10:18.

The retelling of Exod 25:10–40[42] is a case similar to that of Heb 3:1–6a, in which the author's source text is a divine speech, but he does not represent it as such. God begins speaking in Exodus 20 with the ten commandments and continues through the end of chap. 31. Thus, chap. 25, which covers the requirements for the tabernacle, falls in the middle of this lengthy speech. Indeed, it is so much in the middle of such a detailed speech involving numerous laws and instructions, that an exegete could forget that the setting is God speaking to Moses on Mount Sinai. In any case, the author of Hebrews relates enough detail from Exodus so that his reader can form a good mental image of the tabernacle. He narrates a description, while being uninterested in conveying the theophonic setting of these instructions, and ignoring that God's voice spoke these words. The oral component is completely excluded.

Like the relationship between Psalm 95 and Numbers 14, this discussion of the tabernacle is spawned by—and ultimately subordinate to—the lengthy citation of Jeremiah 31 in chap. 8. Since Jeremiah mentions a new covenant,

---

[41] Heb 7:1–2 is often called a quotation by scholars, including Fitzmyer ("Now This Melchizedek . . . [Heb 7:1]," in *Essays on the Semitic Background of the New Testament* [Sources for Biblical Study 5; SBL and Scholars Press, 1974] 222) who calls it an "implicit quotation." But the alterations and omissions are far too great even to be called an "implicit quotation." See my criteria for identifying a quotation at the beginning of this chapter.

[42] Throughout 8–10:18, the author depends on more than Exodus 25 for his information; he sporadically draws information from the surrounding chapters in Exodus as well as prescriptions from Leviticus. The advantage of a retelling is that one is not bound to one place in the text. In addition, much of the information the author uses could be considered common knowledge, such as the priest entering the Holy of Holies once a year; he need not be thinking of a particular text.

the author wishes to explain just what constituted the old covenant and how the new one differs. For our author, the old covenant is dependent upon cultic worship, which has now been made obsolete by the ultimate sacrifice of Christ. Thus, the author's recounting of the tabernacle and other cultic details provides historical or theological information which is interwoven with his commentary on the psalm.

The largest part of Hebrews which relies upon the Bible without much use of quotations is chap. 11.[43] Hebrews 11 represents a special case because it is a hero list. To be sure, most Jewish parallels like Sirach 44–50 or 1 Macc 2:49–64, do not employ quotations in their lists. Nevertheless, what is significant for our purpose is that Hebrews has blocks of text, in addition to chap. 11, which paraphrase events from scripture. Thus, Hebrews 11 is part of a larger pattern within the document of Hebrews.

Indeed, wherever the author of Hebrews paraphrases a story, describes a biblical hero's deeds, or explains the meaning of an ancient biblical institution, the "word of God" element of scripture is not important. To be sure, the author chooses to speak about these things because they are part of scripture, i.e., the traditional collection of writings which preserves the story of God and his people. But he does not introduce his material as scriptural and he almost never quotes from the narrative upon which he depends. Although three retellings are dependent upon the author's interest in a psalm or prophetic text, which is cited as divine speech, all the retellings themselves are simply narrated as historical information. Thus, the author of Hebrews recounts narrative in his own words, while he cites direct, divine speech explicitly and formally.

Quotations and Retellings in Contemporary Texts

Before conclusions can be drawn about the rhetorical importance of the contrast between quoted speech and retold narrative in Hebrews, we first need to peruse briefly the use of quoting and retelling among other ancient Jewish and Christian exegetes. Indeed, we must consider the possibility that the author of Hebrews could be motivated to quote some texts and paraphrase others by the fact that some texts are eminently more quotable, like poetry, for example; while others lend themselves to paraphrase, like

---

[43] There are three very brief citations: 11:5b, which quotes Gen 5:24, "and he was not found, because God translated him;" 11:18, which quotes Gen 21:12, "through Isaac your descendents shall be named;" and 11:21 which quotes Gen 47:31 referring to Joseph, who "bowed down on the tip of his staff."

narrative. After all, Isaiah and the Psalms are poetry—could one really paraphrase Isaiah without butchering the text?

I have two responses to this caveat: First, it is partly true that some incidental linguistic factors encourage the author to choose what to paraphrase and what to quote. Poetic speech from Isaiah or the psalms or the Song of Moses is perhaps more quotable than stories of Genesis. Indeed, poetically patterned speech is more likely to be remembered intact than is written narrative.[44] However—and this is my second point—the reverse does not hold true. In other words, while we do find that most ancient Jewish exegetes quote rather than paraphrase Isaiah, they also quote from the narrative parts of scripture. The rabbis or Philo can take one line of narrative, which they quote, and then go on to explore every single syllable and semantic possibility. Conversely, Josephus, in his *Antiquities*, which is a comprehensive rewriting of biblical history, has no compunction about paraphrasing God's words. Thus, as we shall see further below, the distinction that appears in Hebrews between the treatment of speech and narrative does not occur in Jewish literature with the same consistency.

I have already mentioned that in the NT the majority of quotations are from divine speeches found in the Pentateuch, the Psalms, and the Prophets.[45] In the gospels and Acts quoted speech usually functions as fulfilled prophecy. The preachers in Acts spend a lot of energy interpreting scripture, both quoting and retelling, and these expositions were likely seen as prophetic activity.[46] Although Paul certainly believed in the prophetic power of scripture (e.g., 1 Cor 15: 3–4), he engages in a more subtle and varied use of the biblical text.[47]

---

[44] Walter J. Ong, *Orality and Literacy: The Technologizing of the Word* (London and New York: Methuen, 1982). See esp. 34–36.

[45] It may be that there are hermeneutical dynamics similar to Hebrews operating in those documents, i.e., that a text being a record of direct speech makes it far more attractive for quotation, not just in Hebrews but in several NT texts. As far as I know, no one has explored this possibility. The use of particular biblical quotations in the NT is usually studied with regard to content; the quotations are thought to resonate with the early Christian experience of Jesus as Messiah. I would not deny the contribution of experience to the choice of texts, I would simply argue that the choice seems to have already been limited at a more fundamental level, so that when one wanted to quote, one was more likely to choose from a text that was recorded speech rather than narrative.

[46] E. E. Ellis, *Prophesy and Hermeneutic*, (WUNT 18; Tübingen: Grand Rapids, 1978) 129–44.

[47] He, too, is more likely to quote speech, while recasting narrative in his own words, although not as consistently as is found in other NT texts. The famous line from Romans and Galatians, "it was reckoned to him [Abraham] as righteousness," is a quote from

In early rabbinic hermeneutics, the kind of distinction that Hebrews draws between speech and narrative is not at all present.[48] For the rabbis, biblical books might be hierarchically distinguished, but as far as the component parts of scripture are concerned, every word or phrase has seemingly equal value.[49] Even though the earliest rabbinic commentaries focus on biblical texts that contain numerous divine speeches,[50] they are no more interested in turning their interpretive sights on those verses whose words are literally from the mouth of God, than they are in analyzing narrative verses which merely describe what God has done.[51] Thus the integrity of the scriptural lemmata is always an essential hermeneutical presupposition for the rabbis, a notion which surely underlies the principle that scripture is to be interpreted by scripture. As Daniel Boyarin has pointed out, when two verses that within the biblical text itself have nothing to do with each other are brought together, the point is to create new intertextual relationships between verses,[52] thus once again emphasizing the synchronic whole of scripture.[53]

Similarly, the targums in their highly interpretive translations, show no favoritism toward divine speech. The tendency to paraphrase in order to give greater explanatory power to the biblical text is no less present in verses where God speaks in the first person than in other parts of scripture. Rather, that which motivates the composers of the targums to alter the biblical text—such as the desire to tone down anthropomorphism, or to

---

biblical *narrative*, which Paul believes speaks directly to the current readers and listeners. "The words, 'it was reckoned to him,' were written not for his sake alone, but for ours also" (Rom 4:23).

[48] In so many studies of NT hermeneutics, one finds scholars showing parallel after parallel between the methods of NT authors and the rabbinic methods. But we must remember that techniques of interpretation are to be distinguished from underlying hermeneutical principles.

[49] Daniel Patte, *Early Jewish Hermeneutic in Palestine* (Missoula: Scholars, 1975) 122. Cf. the comment in *b. Sanhedrin 99a*, which says that every single verse has the same divine authority.

[50] Such commentaries include *Sifra, Sifre,* and the *Mekilta.*

[51] Examples abound, see, e.g., *Mekilta's* discussion of Exo 15:22, "And Moses removed Israel from the Red Sea." Problems in the travelogue of the Israelites appear to preoccupy the exegetes of the Mekilta, see Daniel Boyarin, *Intertextuality and the Reading of Midrash* (Bloomington: Indiana University, 1990) 41–5.

[52] Boyarin, *Intertextuality,* 31. See also James Kugel "Two Introductions to Midrash," in *Midrash and Literature,* ed. Geoffrey Hartman and Sanford Budick (New Haven: Yale University, 1986) 93–5.

[53] Patte (*Jewish Hermeneutic,* 123) calls scripture for the rabbis a closed system of signs.

contemporarize biblical places, names and institutions—operates without regard for whose voice lay behind the text.[54]

Philo—as already mentioned—quotes almost exclusively from the Pentateuch and does not appear to distinguish between speech and narrative. Throughout Philo's commentaries on the Bible, one finds numerous septuagintal quotations, many of which consist of narrative. Philo is known for opening a treatise on a given text with a quotation, and these are just as likely to be a piece of narrative as direct speech.[55] Neither does Josephus, in the *Antiquities*, have any compunction to employ citations primarily for speech rather than for narrative. Although actual quotations are rare,[56] Josephus does occasionally quote narrative, while at the same time embellishing the speeches of God to make them more impressive.[57] In marked contrast, when the author of Hebrews chooses to paraphrase the words of God, he never presents them as speech or revelation, but as narrative information.[58] No trace of orality remains in Hebrews' paraphrase. In Josephus, God's words, even if grossly altered, are still presented as God's words.

In contrast to the rabbis, Josephus, and Philo, the apocrypha and pseudepigrapha tend to quote biblical speech while re-narrating narrative, just as we find in Hebrews and other NT literature. However, explicit quotations are extremely rare and almost all of this literature is itself of a narrative genre which precludes the use of citation-plus-commentary.[59] Since so much of this literature is comprised of biblical and apocryphal story-telling, rather than analytic discourse—as Hebrews is—the comparison

---

[54] For a recent treatment of interpretive translation techniques in the targums, see Philip S. Alexander, "Jewish Aramaic Translations of Hebrew Scriptures" in *Mikra*, 226–9. Furthermore, the method of reading Torah in the synagogue liturgy would seem to reinforce that every word, indeed every letter, counted and counted with equal importance within the Pentateuch. The Prophets and the Writings were of course treated differently. "A passage may be skipped in the reading of the prophets, but not in the Torah" (*m. Megilla* 4.4).

[55] See, e.g., the well-known *On the Posterity of Cain and His Exile*, where Philo spends unparalleled energy interpreting the sentence "And Cain went out from the face of God, and dwelt in the land of Naid, over against Eden" (Gen 4:16).

[56] Shaye Cohen (*Josephus in Galilee and Rome: His Vita and Development as a Historian* [Leiden: E.J. Brill, 1979] 29–31) comments that there may have been pressure not to copy the exact language of a source text.

[57] See, e.g., *Ant* 1.8 §100–102.

[58] As we saw in the retelling of Num 12:7 in Heb 3:1–6a or that of Exod 25:10–40 in Heb 8–10:18.

[59] Devorah Dimant, "Use and Interpretation of Mikra in the Apocrypha and Pseudepigrapha," in *Mikra*, 379–419.

is not substantially helpful. When we do find explicit quotation of biblical speech in the intertestamental literature, its purpose is usually to make the characters in the narrative appear pious in their prayer language.[60] Sometimes an author's interest in quoting speech is just as likely to arise from a desire to emulate biblical characters like Moses or Jacob as from the conviction that the quoted speech might be the word of God.

A special case is Qumran, where we find a variety of uses of scripture, and where quoted speech is rendered as direct divine revelation. The majority of citations in the Qumran texts involve divine speech, either from the Pentateuch or the Prophets. While it is true that the pesharim, by the very definition of the genre, are running commentaries concerned with every word of a biblical book, the pesher method was used only for prophetic books or psalms (i.e., divine speech)—there is no pesher for Genesis. Rather, books like Genesis are interpreted in works like the Genesis Apocryphon and the *Book of Jubilees*, which are rewritings or retellings of scripture.

Thus the individual interpretive techniques employed in Hebrews are not unique among ancient exegetes, especially in the apocrypha and pseudepigrapha, Qumran, and other NT documents. Overall, if we were to analyze statistically the citations in all of the contemporary literature, we would probably find that explicitly quoting speech is more common than quoting narrative. However, the reason for this differs in different texts and in different communities. The members of the Qumran community were most interested in eschatological insight, which they found in prophetic speech. The divine speeches in Exodus and Leviticus were attractive to the early rabbis because their project was to interpret the *halacha*. What makes Hebrews stand out is that it has combined two contrasting methods of using the biblical text. As will become clear in the following section, Hebrews' contrasting method serves the author's Christian purpose.

The Rhetoric of Quotation and Retelling

As we have seen, the interpretive techniques employed in Hebrews are not unique among ancient exegetes. The technique of quoting as a prooftext for an argument has many precedents, and the practice of retelling biblical stories is nearly ubiquitous among ancient exegetes. However, these interpretive methods function together in Hebrews in such a way that the presentation of scripture serves a sectarian Christian purpose.

---

[60] E.g., 1 Macc 7:16–17; Cf. Heb 12:21.

The second half of this chapter will be devoted to specifying the rhetorical function of quotations and retellings in Hebrews, so as to illustrate the author's ultimate purpose with regard to the biblical text.

Quotation as Oracle

Although the act of quoting—whether one text cites an earlier one, or a person quotes something s/he heard—is practically a universal phenomenon, biblical quotations are seldom studied in any comparative way. Attention paid to phenomenological issues in quotation can highlight the distinction that we have already determined exists in Hebrews between explicitly cited quotations and rephrased narrative. Therefore, we begin the analysis of the rhetorical function of quotation and retelling in Hebrews with such theoretical discussion.

George Savran's study of quotations in biblical narrative provides a starting point. Influenced by Meir Sternberg, he comments on the distinction between the repetition of originally non-verbal expressions (e.g., actions) and the repetition of direct speech:

> Narration tends to repeat descriptions of events, persons, and states of mind with some variation, because the repetition itself is also another description of the earlier object. Direct speech, however, is not a description of something else, but a more explicitly defined object in and of itself . . . .[61]

In quoted direct speech, a statement that was "formally bound by its own coordinates of time and place,"[62] is inserted into a new situation that creates a contextual conflation between what is quoted and the context in which it now finds itself. In other words, when quotation of direct speech is chosen over indirect discourse or narrative redescription, it speaks directly to and within the new context, with as much immediate impact as it had in its original context. In contradistinction to the immediacy of quoting, when one redescribes a past event in one's own narrative voice, the past and the present are juxtaposed but remain distinct. Direct speech is a re-presentation of prior speech, and as such its function is not limited to evoking the memory of the past.

> When a quotation is examined not simply as a description of the past, but as a re-presentation of a verbal act restated in the spoken form in

---

[61] Savran, *Telling and Retelling*, 11.
[62] Savran, *Telling and Retelling*, 12.

which it originally occurred, then the act of quotation itself must be seen as a speech-act.[63]

Savran's designation of quotation as a speech act is an apt one, and one I wish to explore further. Although speech-act theory has become a complex science,[64] J.L. Austin's tripartite breakdown of performative utterances or speech-acts still holds true.[65] A speech-act is an utterance that not only informs or describes something else but is itself an act. It is comprised of 1) the locution, i.e., what is actually said; 2) the illocution, i.e., what is done or accomplished by the utterance; and 3) the perlocution, or the effect upon the hearer.

Since we are concerned with rhetorical function, our focus here lies with the illocutionary force of the quotations. In one sense, several functions can be seen in Hebrews' quotations that do not differ from those of any author who would quote earlier material. For instance, an air of objectivity is gained by the authority that comes from citing a witness independent of the author's point of view. Citing a quotation which corroborates the author's claims from a recognized authority gives the illusion of external evidence. Another example of the function of quotations is to demonstrate the fulfillment of a past idea in the present, or perhaps to make a comparison between the past and the present. A saying uttered in the past and then re-spoken in a later context draws an analogy, either by similarity or contrast, between the words as they were spoken in the past and the words as spoken in the present.[66] But such functions in the context of the use of OT quotations in the NT are relatively trivial. It is my contention that a distinct illocutionary function of the quotations in Hebrews can be understood by examining their oracular nature.

More often than not, because the author of Hebrews introduces his quotations as spoken in the present, the knowledge that the quotation has previously been spoken depends upon its familiarity to the audience and/or the locution itself, which may hearken back to past events. Explicit comparisons between the past and the present are usually avoided in the introductory formulae. In chap. 3, the first time Psalm 95 is cited, the Holy Spirit speaks in the present tense, and in Heb 8:8 it is Christ who utters the

---

63 Savran, *Telling and Retelling*, 14.

64 The most complete systematic study is J. R. Searle, *Speech Acts* (Cambridge: Cambridge University, 1969).

65 J.L. Austin, *How to do Things with Words* (Cambridge: Harvard, 1975).

66 Savran, (*Telling and Retelling*, 54) cites these and similar functions for the use of direct speech quotations in biblical narrative.

words from Jeremiah 31.[67] Yet the words of Psalm 95 speak of the wilderness generation, while Jeremiah speaks of a former covenant and its intrinsic connection to the exodus experience. The words from these quotations are familiar, but they are being spoken in a new voice. Indeed, the quotations in Hebrews are reused prophetic oracles.

In order to grasp this understanding of the Hebrews' quotations, a word must be said about the use of biblical oracles in general. First, the oral aspect is essential.[68] The prophet—in whatever mode he might have received the divine revelation: aurally, visually or in a dream—must *proclaim* the content of that revelation in order for it to become an oracle. Whether it be a prophecy of doom, judgment, or victory in war, it is an oracle because the prophet publicly proclaimed it. Second, upon the prophet's uttering of the oracle, he not only informed the public (or the king in some cases) of what would occur, his speech was in fact causative.[69] The words ushered in the anticipated event; the people's fate was sealed by the proclamation.

In the gospels, particularly Matthew and John, we find reused prophetic oracles from the Hebrew Bible. However, they no longer possess the illocutionary function of oracles, because, from the point of view of the gospel writer, what the oracle predicted has already happened.[70] The gospel writer cites the biblical text as an oracle that was spoken long ago and has now been fulfilled.[71] The quotation does not prove the truth of the event, i.e., its facticity; rather it proves that the event has a connection to the divine plan.[72]

---

[67] Although Jesus' name does not appear in the introduction of the quotation, it is inferred by the context (see 8:6).

[68] Michael Fishbane, *Biblical Interpretation in Ancient Israel* (Oxford: Clarendon, 1985) 458.

[69] For examples of causative language of the יהוה דבר see Fishbane, *Biblical Interpretation*, 468.

[70] Donald Juel (*Messianic Exegesis: Christological Interpretation of the Old Testament in Early Christianity* [Philadelphia: Fortress, 1988]) argues that many of the earliest core texts used by early Christian interpreters were already considered messianic oracles, and they were applied to Jesus because they understood him to be the messiah at the time of his death. Many texts may have had no previous predictive value at all, such as Isa 40:3 or the words and images from Psalm 22.

[71] As David Aune (*Prophecy in Early Christianity and the Ancient Mediterranean World*, [Grand Rapids: Eerdmans, 1983] 55) says, this is one of the most common functions of Greco-Roman oracles when they appear in literature.

[72] See C. H. Dodd, *According to the Scriptures: The Substructure of New Testament Theology* (New York: Charles Scribner's Sons, 1952).

While Hebrews' quotations are like those in the gospels in the sense that they are oracular, they differ significantly from the gospel usage precisely in terms of illocutionary function. The author of Hebrews employs quotations in order to effect reality in the present, not as fulfillment formulae.[73] Hebrews does not look backward to try to explain what happened earlier. Hebrews is trying to explain and enact what is happening now. The oracles in Hebrews are attempting to transform the present. Jesus *is* not like the angels (1:5–7), he *is* a priest like Melchizedek (5:6; 7:17). Sacrifices are no longer necessary because Christ *is* "the mediator of a new covenant" (9:15). The quotation-oracles in Hebrews point to Christ in the life of the present community and not the Jesus of history.

An oracle uttered for the first time, in its original context, not only has the force of predicting the future, but its very pronouncement helps *create* what will happen in the future. It is as if the utterance compels the future to transpire accordingly. When an oracle is re-cited from the other side of history, i.e., after the event predicted by the oracle has occurred, it has the function we described above, to prove the significance of the event by demonstrating its connection to the divine plan. If, however, an interpreter is situated between the original oracle and the imagined event to which it corresponds, s/he can recycle the oracle *qua* oracle. More commonly, the interpreter who re-cites an oracle believes the events to which the oracle points are *in the process of coming into being.* The oracle can be re-cited with the same illocutionary force of the original divine word.

In other words, the author of Hebrews is not merely interested in giving divine confirmation or sanction to past events; he recycles oracles as dynamic proclamations directed immediately at his audience. One of the most overt examples of such oracular use of quotations is the compound citation in 2:12–13. This is one of the three quotations where Christ is the speaker,[74] and the quotation is set-up to demonstrate the salvific correlation between Christ, the one "who sanctifies," and "those who are sanctified."

---

[73] See Fitzmyer ("Use of Old Testament Quotations," 13) who points out that fulfillment formulae are non-existent at Qumran, while common in the NT. He explains this surprising divergence between the NT and Qumran texts by saying that while the Qumran community is so thoroughly eschatological, so forward-looking in its anticipation of events, the eschatology of the NT writers is mitigated by christology and what has aready happened to Jesus. I do not dispute that this is true of other NT writers, but it is not true of Hebrews.

[74] The others are found in 8:8 and 10:5. In no case is Jesus explicitly named the speaker—only the masculine singular verb appears. That Jesus is the speaker is implicit in the context.

The first part of the quotation is from Ps 22:22:

For he who sanctifies and those who are sanctified have all one origin. That is why he is not ashamed to call them brethren, "I will proclaim thy name to my brethren, in the midst of the congregation I will praise thee."

Early Christian tradition had of course made great use of this psalm in recounting and understanding Jesus' passion. The author of Hebrews, however, has no such interest in the psalm here. Rather, he is trying to demonstrate that Christ's relationship to believers is characterized by a kind of kinship, *which Christ himself now proclaims.*[75]

In fact, the only significant alteration of this verse from the LXX is contained in the word "proclaim;" the author substitutes the word ἀπαγγέλω for the word διηγήσομαι, which, while certainly not a radical alteration, serves to emphasize the enactment value of the words. Christ thereby designates the believers brothers and sisters. Furthermore, Christ praises God from within the midst of the congregation. In the quotations that follow, Christ speaks in a sense both to God and the members of the congregation at once, thus portraying himself in his speech as an intermediary. Following the quotation from Psalm 22 the author quotes Isa 8:17–18: "I will put my trust in him," and "Here am I, and the children God has given me."[76] Christ, through these words, is depicted as being in solidarity with believers. He is at once standing before the congregation and standing before God—declaring his role, not in his own words, but in the words of scripture.[77] The oracle, therefore, effects the realization of Christ's

---

[75] By making this statement I am following Michel (*Der Brief,* 154) and Bruce (*Epistle,* 45) who understand that Christ is speaking now, and these words must therefore be the words of the the exalted Christ. Attridge (*Hebrews,* 90) disagrees with this position, but admits that no time is specified for this proclamation by Jesus.

[76] The Greek of Isa 8:17 is identical to two other passages, 2 Sam 22:3 and Isa 12:2, but since v. 18 follows, it seems most likely that the author had v. 17 in mind here. The two verses are separated by πάλιν but continuous verses are similarly separated in Heb 10:30, wherein Deuteronomy 32 is cited. See Schröger, *Verfasser,* 91 n. 2; and Attridge, *Hebrews,* 90–1.

[77] These words from Psalm 22 and Isaiah 8 declare and display the intermediary role of Christ. They lay a foundation for three distinct points that the author takes up in the chapters that follow: In chapters 3 and 4, in his exegetical discussion of Psalm 95, the listeners are exhorted not to harden their hearts, because they will have a share in Christ (3:14) if they only stand firm. Chapters 5, 6 and 7 concern the priesthood of Christ. The office of priest is by definition an intermediary position. Finally, beginning in chapter 10 and extending through 12, the theme of faith and endurance in the face of persecution is explored. When Christ said "I will put my trust in him," he set the example which the

intermediary role, which at this early stage of Christian history needs to be established or continually re-established in the experience of the community.

However, as directly as the oracles are used in Hebrews, their illocutionary force is still tied to their being scripture, in the sense that scripture is the divine reservoir of traditional material, common to all Jews (and now presumably Christians). As we noted earlier, one of the functions of citing quotations is to draw an analogy between the past and the present. Nevertheless, the primary concern of the speaker of a quotation is the impact it has on the present audience. By returning to the author's discussion of Psalm 95, we can illustrate the impact on present reality which a recycled oracle can evoke. There are three citations of Ps 95:7 in Hebrews. When the author first quotes Ps 95:7–8 (in 3:7–11), the Holy Spirit is named as the speaker and the verb is in the present.

> Therefore, as the Holy Spirit says, "Today, when you hear his voice, do not harden your hearts as in the rebellion, on the day of testing in the wilderness . . . ."

After the author finishes quoting, he returns to the language of exhortation and in 3:13 he says, "But exhort one another every day, as long as it is called 'today,' that none of you may be hardened by the deceitfulness of sin." Thus, before he enters into discussion of the psalm's meaning for the wilderness generation, the author uses the psalm as a direct unmediated exhortation to his listeners. The key issues are the word "today," which means now, in the present, and the encouragement not to "harden one's heart," which for our author means an unbelieving heart.

Because this first citation of Psalm 95:7 is part of the longer citation of Ps 95:7–11, it includes verses which make reference to the wilderness generation's 40 year exile. The past is no doubt evoked and an analogy is indeed set up between the past and the present.[78] "[D]o not harden your hearts *as in the rebellion*." This evocation leads the author to make the second citation of Ps 95:7 in 3:15, after which he comments on its meaning for the wilderness generation. As a result, in this citation of Ps 95:7 in 3:15, he exhorts his audience not to be like the wilderness generation. For the other key verse from the psalm is v. 11, "they shall never enter my rest." Because

---

people are exhorted to follow. He, too, had to have faith or all would have failed.

[78] It was thesis of Ernst Käsemann (*The Wandering People of God: An Investigation of the Letter to the Hebrews* [Minneapolis: Augsburg, 1984] 17–22) that chaps. 3–4 of Hebrews contained the primary motif of the document, because the wandering generation of the wilderness was the definitive state for the Christian community addressed by Hebrews.

they rebelled, the Israelites did not receive 'rest.' As the author says, "So we see that *they* were unable to enter because of unbelief" (3:19). But, he tells his audience, "*we* who have believed entered that rest" (4:3).

That the psalm is an oracle directed at the present Christian community can perhaps best be seen in the third citation of Ps 95:7 in 4:7. We discussed this citation already in our discussion of introductory formulae in Hebrews. When the author re-cites the psalm verse here, David is named as the speaker. The importance of David as the speaker is precisely due to the issue of time. David lives long after the first Israelites. Thus, the exhortation "today, if you hear his voice, do not harden your hearts" means there is another chance to respond to God *after* the rebellion in the wilderness. (The author of Hebrews does not consider the possibility that David is speaking of his own time.) The word "today" leaves open the possibility that someone, other than the Israelites, has the privilege of entering God's 'rest.'

> For if Joshua has given them rest, God would not speak later about another day. So then, a sabbath rest sill remains for the people of God; for those who enter God's rest also cease from their labors as God did from his. Let us therefore make every effort to enter that rest, so that no one may fall through such disobedience as theirs. (4:8–11)

The author's interest in the story of the wilderness lies in contrasting it with the current situation of his community. Thus, the past is evoked by the locution of the psalm itself,[79] and by the author's commentary, but the illocutionary import of the psalm lies in its use as an oracle directed at the author's community.

There are a few significant places, roughly contemporary with Hebrews, where biblical oracles are used in a way similar to that found in Hebrews. One example, from Qumran, will further aid our understanding of the oracles' particular function in Hebrews. Because Qumran texts clearly

---

[79] The role of the past functions at the perlocutionary level as well. The perlocution can perhaps be found in the fact that the audience may know the psalm through liturgical experience, as Kistemaker asserts, or perhaps they simply have a vague familiarity with psalmody or certain scriptural verses. In any case, it is a reasonable assumption that these words have been heard before and that the audience knows they derive from scriptural authority. For those members of the audience who are Jewish, the fact that the author initally exhorts his audience with words from their past is surely a reassuring gesture. When Christ or the Holy Spirit speak, they utter familiar words, not new-fangled teachings. The audience hears words they have heard before, words they have no intention of turning their back on, for there is nothing threatening about scripture; it is a known entity. The author re-cites the oracle, which is familiar, Jewish and a mutually recognized authority, but he does so in order to re-activate the oracle, to demonstrate that its fulfillment transpires in Christian belief and community.

engage in the oracular use of scripture, and because several scholars have perceived a relationship between the Epistle to the Hebrews and the Qumran Texts,[80] they are an appropriate comparison.

Many biblical quotations found in Qumran texts, especially in the pesharim, 4QFlor, and 11QMelch, are employed as oracles. A verse is cited, usually with an introductory formula, and an interpretive statement will follow—one which connects the verse (=oracle) to a current event in the life of the community or to an event anticipated in the near future. A representative example, and one which particularly pertains to Hebrews, can be found in the quotations from 2 Sam 7:11-14 and Amos 9:11 in 4QFlor, fragment 1, lines 10-13:

> "And the Lord declares to you that he will build you a house. And I will raise up your seed after you, and I will establish the throne of his kingdom forever. I will be to him as a father, and he will be to me as a son:" he is the shoot of David who will stand with the Interpreter of the Law, who [will rule] in Zion in the latter days as it is written, "And I will raise up the booth of David which is fallen:" he is the booth (or branch) of David which was fallen, who will take office to save Israel.[81]

Technically speaking, the first citation does not have an introduction. Although a citation without an introductory formula does sometimes occur in the DSS, the reason for it here is partly due to the fact that the quotation itself provides its own introduction, "And the Lord declares to you . . ."[82] Nathan's oracle has been edited in the quotation (much more so than the average Hebrews' quotation) to fit the following interpretation. Although here the word *pesher* is not used to introduce the interpretation, the words "he is" are an interpretive marker.[83] The interpreter's comment unequi-

---

[80] E.g.Yigdal Yadin, "The Dead Sea Scrolls and the Epistle to the Hebrews," in *Aspects of the Dead Sea Scrolls* (Scripta hierosolymitana 4; Jerusalem: Magnes, 1958) 36–55; and J. Fitzmyer, "Now this Melchizedek . . . (Heb 7:1)," 221–43. See Fitzmyer (223 n. 9) for a list of others who have explored the relationship between Hebrews and the DSS.

[81] Translation from G. J. Brooke, *Exegesis at Qumran: 4Q Florilegium in Its Jewish Context* (JSOTSup 29; Sheffield: University of Sheffield) 92.

[82] God and/or Nathan is the speaker of the original quotation, but there is nothing unusual about God referring to himself in the third person. In addition, 2 Sam 7:11a is in a section of 4QFlor, which precedes the excerpt I have taken; Brooke (*Exegesis at Qumran*, 136–7) believes the quotation from 2 Sam 11:c is subordinate to the one from 2 Sam 7:11a, and subordinate quotations often lack introduction.

[83] See Brooke (*Exegesis at Qumran*, 130–3) where he provides an outline of the text, making it easy to see that the word הוה, "he is," is a mark of interpretive identification, i.e., "this equals that." See also Maurya Horgan, *Pesharim: Qumran Interpretation of Biblical Books* (Washington: Catholic Biblical Association, 1979) 258–9.

vocally connects the figure described in the oracle with a contemporary figure, a royal Davidic Messiah, one who will rule with the Interpreter of the Law and be the savior of Israel.[84] Although this figure is not yet present, he is imminently expected.[85]

While this oracle is cited as one for which the community still awaits fulfillment, other quotations in 4QFlor assume the oracle-quotations correspond to on-going events in the community, for example, lines 14 through 17 of the same fragment:

> Midrash of "Happy is the man who does not walk in the counsel of the wicked;" the real interpretation of the matter concerns those who turn aside from the way of [sinners concerning] whom it is written in the book of Isaiah the prophet for the latter days, "And it will be that as with a strong [hand he will cause us to turn away from walking in the way] of his people;" and they are those concerning whom it is written in the book of Ezekiel the prophet that "they shall not [defile themselves any more] with their idols." They are the Sons of Zadok and the m[e]n of their council who keep far[r from evil . . .] and after them [. . . .] a community (or, together).[86]

In this passage, in addition to the more regular introductions and interpretive markers, we can see that these oracles are in the process of being fulfilled. The quotations come from Psalm 1:1, Isa 8:11, and Ezek 37:23. Taken together, the quotations define the community. The psalm verse is not merely a generic ethical proverb, but is an oracle which points toward a certain group of people and the special blessed status they achieve. The oracular interpretation identifies the persons, events or objects referred to in the text with actual people, events, or objects in the contemporary life of the interpreter. These quotations concern the latter days, but the community is in the midst of the latter days.

This text, as well as others that use interpretive techniques like it, is distinct from the way Hebrews engages biblical oracles. First, there are stylistic differences, in the introductory formulae and in the way the interpretation is separated from the scriptural text. Second, and more

---

84 Brooke, *Exegesis at Qumran*, 139.

85 Brooke, *Exegesis at Qumran*, 138.

86 Brooke, *Exegesis at Qumran*, 92. The translation here differs substantially from older editions of 4QFlor, such as one finds in Vermes (*The Dead Sea Scrolls in English* [Middlesex, England: Penguin, 1975] 247–9) where the Sons of Zadok are a hostile party distinct from the community. Brooke relies on the work of Strugnell ("Notes en marge du volume V des Discoveries in the Judean Desert of Jordan," *RQ* [1967–69]) for his reconstruction.

important, there is a fundamental hermeneutical distinction. The author of 4QFlor does not argue his point; he makes assertions of identification, x = y. We know that the Interpreter was considered to have a divinely endowed gift for interpreting biblical texts. Each text contains a mystery, a רז. The Interpreter's reading of the text is charismatically inspired, not based on an analytical study.[87] Conversely, Hebrews presents a deeply engaged analytical argument when confronting the biblical text. The author of Hebrews walks his audience through the text with his exegesis, repeating verses and proceeding step by step in order to build up to an argument, as we saw for example in chaps. 3–4 regarding Psalm 95.

The example from Qumran is illustrative because the oracular nature of the use of the biblical text is so clearly visible. Events that are happening now, or are presumed to happen shortly, correspond to biblical prophecies, some of which were widely recognized to be left unfulfilled, as is the case with 2 Samuel 7, and some of which appear to have never been perceived as having predictive value. Furthermore, texts like 4QFlor do not just point out that the oracles have been fulfilled, the quotation-*cum*-interpretation *create* the connection between the text and the event. If the connection were self-evident apart from the Interpreter's claim, it would not be known as a mystery.

One last example from Hebrews' use of quotations—one which is not as readily evident as an oracle as those previously discussed—will serve as the final proof that their illocutionary function is to serve as oracles directed at on-going religious experience in the community. The opening catena of quotations in Hebrews begins with two well-known verses, one from Psalm 2:7, "thou art my Son, today I have begotten thee," and the other is the same line we saw in the Qumran example, from 2 Sam 7:14, "I will be to him a father, and he shall be to me a son." Several more quotations follow, most are introduced as sayings that God speaks to the Son.[88] The others are sayings that God speaks to the angels. The point is to set up a comparison in which Jesus is portrayed as a figure immeasurably greater than the angels.

---

[87] Frank Moore Cross (*The Ancient Library of Qumran* [London: Duckworth, 1958] 84, 179) makes two points that serve to stress the charismatic nature of biblical interpretation at Qumran: 1) the pesharim are all autographs, copies were not made of them, perhaps pointing to their special status; and 2) for all their fascination with the biblical text, there is no indication that it was systematically studied.

[88] Barth ("Old Testament in Hebrews," 62) makes the poignant observation that for the author of Hebrews, "to listen to the Old Testament means 'to listen in' on a dialogue between God and the Son."

The final quotation in chap. 1 is the well-known Ps 110:1, "Sit at my right hand, till I make thy enemies a stool for thy feet." The interpretive comments that follow do not include statements of correspondence or identification, like x = y. The lack of a one-to-one correspondence may be partly due to the fact that the biblical validity of the historical events surrounding Jesus's life is not under dispute, or least not the concern of the author of Hebrews. The oracles in the gospels, as we discussed earlier, perform the function of connecting prophesies to events in Jesus's life, which have already occurred. In Hebrews the oracle's fulfillment is in the process of being achieved. The biblical oracles in Hebrews do not exactly correspond to a historical event, but rather to a protracted religio-historical era.

That religio-historical era concerns the Lordship of Jesus, which is a position Jesus holds subsequent to his earthly life, but which at this early stage was surely far from clear to many Christians. Indeed, one of the interpretive comments the author of Hebrews makes when reflecting on these quotations concerns the lack of experience Christians have of Jesus as Lord.

> Now in putting everything in subjection to him, he left nothing outside his control. As it is, we do not yet see everything in subjection to him. But we see Jesus, who for a little while was made lower than the angels, crowned with glory and honor because of the suffering of death, ... (2:8–9)[89]

Thus, uttering the words of Ps 110:1 enacts the experience of Jesus as Lord. The oracle accomplishes fulfillment by its being proclaimed. Similarly, the verse from Psalm 2 serves an oracular purpose different from the gospels, where it is tied to the event of Jesus's baptism. In Hebrews the point is that Jesus *is in a state of being God's Son*, not that he was designated such at a certain point in time. His sonship is important now because it distinguishes his status from that of the angels.

---

[89] This translation is from the RSV. In my opinion, the NRSV has bungled the translation of this passage, and that which immediately precedes it. These verses follow a quotation from Psalm 8 which refers to an ἄνθρωπος. The NRSV, in its attempt to make the passage inclusive, translates the word as "human beings," which then means the translators must render the verses that follow (which I have quoted above) in the plural (thus, the NRSV reads, "Now in subjecting all things to *them* . . .). The trouble is the author of Hebrews interprets the Psalm as a forecast of the life of Jesus—the use of the plural makes no sense.

Retelling as Historical Example

If the function of the quotations is to actualize oracles in direct, divine discourse, then surely the function of rephrased narrative must lie somewhere else. Unfortunately, unlike the case of quotations, theoretical discussions of paraphrased material in biblical studies are almost non-existent.

Devorah Dimant is perhaps the first to attempt to articulate a theoretical framework within which we can understand the function of different uses of scripture in intertestamental literature. In her study of the types and functions of biblical interpretation in the apocrypha and pseudepigrapha, she distinguishes between the 'expositional' and 'compositional' functions of scriptural interpretation.[90] The expositional use of scripture usually involves the quotation of text, so as to distinguish between the biblical lemmata and the exegetical statement being made about it. Expositional use usually employs markers (such as an introductory formula) to set off the biblical text from the surrounding text. She names the pesharim, rabbinic midrash, the biblical commentaries of Philo and the fulfillment formulae in Matthew as examples.

"In the compositional use biblical elements are interwoven into the work without external formal markers."[91] The compositional use of scripture is found primarily in works which are modeled on the Bible, i.e., texts known as rewritten Bible, including *Jubilees*, The Genesis Apocryphon, and Pseudo-Philo's *Biblical Antiquities*.[92] Although neither the compositional or expositional type is necessarily determined by the genre, the two types favor certain genres over others.

In general, we can identify the use of retellings in Hebrews as 'compositional,' since the retellings are unmarked and narrated anew by the author (at the same time, we can refer to the quotations in Hebrews as 'expositional,' since the author cites the text and follows it with interpretation). However, Hebrews is itself not of a genre which we expect to favor the compositional use of scripture—it is not a narrative like *Jubilees* or Pseudo Philo's *Biblical Antiquities*. As an exhortatory speech, the biblical text, whether in the form of quotation or paraphrase, is there to augment a larger theological argument. The ultimate goal of Hebrews is not simply to make

---

[90] Devorah Dimant, "Mikra in the Apocrypha and Pseudepigrapha," in *Mikra*, 419.

[91] Dimant, "Mikra," 382.

[92] See George Nickelsburg, "The Bible Rewritten and Expanded," in *Jewish Writings of the Second Temple Period* (CRINT 2.2; Philadelphia: Fortress, 1984) 89–156.

the Bible more understandable or more accessible or even more applicable. Rather, its goal is to demonstrate the superiority of Christ and the theological system that has come into being as a result of his reign. Scripture is only used to make this larger point.[93] Dimant claims that while the function of the expositional use is to explain the biblical text, the function of the compositional method is to create an independent text, to make the biblical text part and parcel of a new work.[94] On one level we could ascribe such a function to any individual retelling in Hebrews. In other words, when the author narrates the story of Melchizedek and Abraham, he does not want his audience to think of what he says as a comment on the story, but as the story itself. However, because Hebrews is not a continuous narrative, but a discourse, we cannot be satisfied with identifying the function of the biblical text within the confines of a single pericope; we must consider how the retellings function within the author's larger discourse. Just as we isolated the illocution of the quotations in their oracular nature, so we must identify the illocution of the retelling.

In retellings, the author's agenda must be teased out of his telling of the story itself. Retellings, those in Hebrews or anywhere else, conflate the text with the interpretation. Like Josephus' *Biblical Antiquities* or the *Book of Jubilees* or the Genesis Apocryphon, the writer rehearses the biblical text in his own words. A retelling is simply an unmarked paraphrase. Since there is no explicit commentary, interpretive elements—whether major or minor—will be contained in the retelling of the biblical episode itself. Unlike a direct quotation (especially one which is direct divine revelation), which is formally introduced and followed by the author's commentary, the reader (or listener) of a retelling cannot easily distinguish between the biblical text and the commentator's interpretation.

Thus, in order to uncover the author's interpretive voice within the narrative, we need to employ two literary-critical concepts in addition to Dimant's categories that will further help categorize and illumine the author's use of the biblical text. First, we need to make use of the now familiar distinction between the rhetoric of a narrative and its informational

---

[93] In other words, Hebrews contains commentary on scripture, but it is not *a commentary*, in the sense that the interpretation of scripture was not the original motive that gave rise to the document called Hebrews. (Buchanan makes this mistake in his commentary [*Hebrews*]. He believes Hebrews should be classified as a midrash on Psalm 110.) That scripture was not the original reason for the writing of Hebrews must be borne in mind when comparing Hebrews to works that do have scripture as their primary *raison d'être*, such as the pesharim, rabbinic midrash, and many examples of rewritten Bible.

[94] Dimant, "Mikra," 383.

content.[95] Simply put, the rhetoric resides in the mode and technique of recounting the narrative, as opposed to the elements that make up the content. The illocutionary function of the author's use of a retold biblical text will be found at the rhetorical level. In other words, the rhetoric of a given retelling in Hebrews will surely serve some larger purpose in the overall discourse of Hebrews.

The second concept I wish to invoke—intertextuality—is a thornier one. In many literary-critical works that are concerned more with questions of theory than with practice, intertextuality refers to the notion that all discourses, indeed all utterances, are in dialogue with previous discourses or other cultural codes.[96] Every text is made up of marked and unmarked inclusions of previous texts. Among biblical scholars, the notion of intertextuality has been taken up in a more pragmatic way;[97] since the primary discourse is Jewish scripture, the currency of the dialogue consists of a specific group of texts which are often explicitly referred to, and which can be studied directly by the critic. What makes the concept of intertextuality useful is that it emphasizes the dialogical aspects of text, whether or not a dialogical format is in evidence. In other words, even though a retelling does not present itself as a dialogue between text and interpreter, it nevertheless is one. The notion of intertextuality implies the need for the deconstruction of the present text into more basic elements, in order to reveal the function and meaning of precursor texts in relation to the present text, i.e., to define the dialogical nature of the text.

Furthermore, intertextuality implies unconscious interpretation. When an author expositionally exegetes a text, s/he self-consciously engages in the act of interpretation. But when someone retells a story, s/he may be self-consciously interpreting it, but more often s/he tells the story as s/he thinks it is. The teller of a story will be influenced by all sorts of contemporary discourses and cultural assumptions in retelling an older story. Indeed, his/her retelling is made up of the dialogue between his/her own cultural codes and those contained in the story. Thus, intertextuality is an accurate

---

95 See Wayne C. Booth, *The Rhetoric of Fiction* (Chicago & London: University of Chicago, 1961).

96 Julia Kristeva (*Semiotiké* [Paris: Seuil, 1969]) is credited with having coined the term. It was further explored by Roland Barthes (*S/Z* [Paris: Seuil, 1970]). See also Jonathon Culler, *The Pursuit of Signs* (Ithaca: Cornell University, 1981) 100–18 and Gérard Genette, *Palimpsestes: La Littérature au second degré* (Paris: Seuil, 1982).

97 Two interesting and successful uses of the concept of intertextuality among biblical scholars are Boyarin, *Intertextuality and the Reading of Midrash* and Richard Hays, *Echoes of Scripture in the Letters of Paul* (New Haven: Yale University, 1989).

designation for the use of the biblical text in the retellings, because it encompasses conscious and unconscious weaving of previous texts and textual traditions into one's own voice. I will apply these literary-critical tools to the retellings in Hebrews in order to uncover the author's purpose in making use of retellings.

Let us begin by looking at the retelling in 3:1–6. While the author evokes many crucial elements of Numbers 12:7—Moses is called a servant by God and he is entrusted (πίστος) with God's house—the presentation (or rhetoric) changes the emphasis of those elements, so as even to alter the semantic meaning of the term 'servant'. While 'servant' in Num 12:7 is a term of high praise which sets Moses apart from other leaders, in Hebrews it refers to the humble stature of Moses. In Numbers, the setting is a direct revelation of God to Miriam and Aaron; it is not a scene recounted by the biblical narrator, but a theophany spoken by God. The author of Hebrews, however, narrates the mini-narrative of Num 12:7 in his own voice; God's perspective[98] has been eliminated. Furthermore, while there is a comparative aspect to Moses's being designated a servant both in Numbers and in Hebrews, the orientation of the comparison is different in each. In Numbers, Moses is compared to other prophets and is unequivocally superior. In Hebrews, not surprisingly, Moses is compared to Jesus and is inferior.

Although the author probably does not attempt to combat a Moses christology,[99] he does denigrate Moses in the process of the comparison.[100] First, the use of the word servant (θεράπων) as a title for Moses is essentially negative in Hebrews; it has an unusually humiliating connotation here, because it is being contrasted with Jesus' sonship.[101] Second, although Moses as well as Jesus is said to be "faithful" (πίστος), Moses is faithful "in" (ἐν) God's house, while Jesus is faithful "over" (ἐπί) God's house.[102]

---

[98] The words of Num 12:7 are ὁ θεράπων μου Μωυσῆς, "*my* servant Moses," while Heb 3:5 is missing the pronoun.

[99] As argued by Spicq, *L'Epître*, 2.62; and Buchanan, *Hebrews*, 54, 255.

[100] Attridge (*Hebrews*, 105) in critiquing the positions of Spicq and Buchanan, claims that there is no particular interest in making Moses look bad on the part of the author. While I think it undeniable that the author's primary interest in this pericope is to exalt Jesus, my point is that in cases of biblical retelling, the author portrays biblical examples such as Moses in a less than flattering way.

[101] Cf. John 8:35 and Gal 4:1–7. Although the word in those passages is δοῦλος, the choice of the term θεράπων in Hebrews was determined by the LXX text of Num 12:7; see Attridge, *Hebrews*, 111.

[102] The wording in the LXX is as follows: ὁ θεράπων μου Μωυσῆς ἐν ὅλῳ τῷ οἴκῳ

Yet Jesus is worthy of more glory than Moses, just as the builder of a house has more honor than the house itself. (For every house is built by someone, but the builder of all things is God.) Now Moses was faithful in all God's house as a servant, to testify to the things that would be spoken later. Christ, however, was faithful over God's house as a son, and we are his house if we hold firm the confidence and the pride that belong to hope. (3:3–6)

The term θεράπων often denotes priestly service.[103] The ultimate status of Moses and Jesus in this text is related to their status "in God's house" (τὸν οἶκον θεοῦ). 'God's house'—referring either to the temple or the tabernacle—indicates the setting is a place of worship. Thus, the servant/son contrast of Moses and Jesus functions as a comparison of two kinds of priests. In this way, the dialogical intersection of the author's contemporary bias and the codes in the story has occurred. The relationship between the two characters is indicative of the author's attitude toward the levitical cult in the rest of the document.

A look at the description of the cult in chap. 9 can further illumine the kind of comparison the author makes in chap. 3 between Moses and Jesus:

[T]he priests go continually into the first tent to carry out their ritual duties; but only the high priest goes into the second, and he but once a year, and not without taking the blood that he offers for himself and for the sins committed unintentionally by the people. By this the Holy Spirit indicates that the way into the sanctuary has not yet been disclosed as long as the first tent is still standing. This is a symbol of the present time, during which gifts and sacrifices are offered that cannot perfect the conscience of the worshipper, but deal only with food and drink and various baptisms, regulations for the body imposed until the time comes to set things straight. But when Christ came as a high priest of the good things that have come, then through the greater and perfect tent (not made with hands, that is, not of this creation), he entered once for all into the Holy Place, not with the blood of goats and calves, but with his own blood, thus obtaining eternal redemption. (9:6–12)

The earthly cult stands as a symbol (παραβολή) for an eschatological reality. This means that the house Jesus serves is not the same as the house Moses serves. Moses lived during the time of the earthly tabernacle; Jesus dwells in

---

μου πιστός ἐστιν. Thus, πίστος in Num 12:7 means trustworthy or the like.

[103] In early Christian literature the word is only used of Moses, but in Greco-Roman literature it means the servant of a divinity. The verb θεραπεύω can also mean to be in the service of a divinity in Jewish Hellenistic Greek. See BAGD, 359; and LSJ, 793.

the heavenly tabernacle. The author of Hebrews sees Moses as an earthly priest because he serves the earthly tabernacle; Jesus is the high priest of a perfect tabernacle, which is not made with hands, but is heaven itself. Thus, the author's understanding of Jesus as the ultimate priest informs his recounting of the incident from Num 12:7.

Furthermore, like the community at Qumran, the author of Hebrews identifies God's house with the Christian community, at least eschatologically:[104] "Christ . . . was faithful over God's house as a son, and *we are his house* if we hold firm the confidence and the pride that belong to hope" (v. 6). This final statement may indicate that the author also has the theme of inheritance on his mind. Though he does not explicitly relate the servant-Moses/son-Jesus contrast to the theme of inheritance, his interest in the bequeathal of the promised inheritance is so pervasive in Hebrews in general,[105] that it may well have influenced him here. Jesus and his Christian believers are the ultimate inheritors of God's heavenly house. Just what happens to Moses and the Israelites is left unspoken at this point.

Moses is surely intended as an example from the past who can help the author better explain who Jesus is. Moses is a model. However, the author's use of this tiny biblical episode reflects his historical dualism. There exists a serious disjuncture between the biblical past and the present which circumscribes his use of biblical examples. Thus, the author is not compelled to stress the similarities between Moses and Jesus, but rather the dissimilarities. As a result, he must denigrate the image of Moses in order to elevate the status of Jesus.

The story of Abraham and Melchizedek recounted in chap. 7 offers another example of the author's interest in comparisons; this one, too, results in the deflation of a biblical character. Although 7:1 begins with a paraphrase of the story in Genesis 14, the author has already quoted from Psalm 110 (5:6)—which contains the one other reference to Melchizedek—and alluded to it twice (5:10; 6:20).[106] While the majority of scholars believe the psalm verse is ultimately what the author is interpreting,[107] Fitzmyer at least understands chap. 7 primarily as a midrash on the relevant verses from

---

[104] Attridge, *Hebrews*, 111. For the identification of the Qumran community with the temple of God, see 1 QS 8.

[105] 6:12; 9:15; 10:36; 11:13, 39–40.

[106] Despite the fact that a quotation of Ps 110:4 has been cited earlier, most scholars see 7:1 as starting a new section, see Albert Vanhoye, *La structure litteraire de l'Epître aux Hébreux* (Desclée De Brouwer, 1976) 125, 281.

[107] E.g., Schröger, *Verfasser*, 152–9; Buchanan, *Hebrews*; Attridge, *Hebrews*, 186.

Genesis 14.[108] While the bulk of chap. 7 concentrates on the Genesis material, the repetitive quoting of Psalm 110:4, which the author believes directly attests to the nature and status of Jesus' priesthood, illustrates the preeminence of the psalm text in general in Hebrews. In terms of the overall discourse of Hebrews, the retelling from Genesis 14 must be seen as subordinate to Psalm 110. As one scholar has noted, the author betrays what could be called an obsession with the psalm verse, while only casually and selectively treating the Genesis material about Melchizedek.[109]

In his recounting of the story of Melchizedek and Abraham, the author indulges in a few scene-setting details which ostensibly do not further his argument. In 7:1 the author refers to the fact that Abraham has just returned from the slaughter of kings, before he mentions that Melchizedek blessed Abraham and subsequently received a tithe of his spoils—which is the key point for the author. This initial observation is hardly necessary for the author's argument, which holds that Abraham must be inferior to Melchizedek, because only an inferior man would receive a blessing from and tithe to a superior. The author of Hebrews could simply have quoted from Gen 14:20, "And [Abram] gave him a tenth of everything," as a good rabbi might have done. Yet he prefers a more cumbersome retelling to a direct citation. He resists the explicit quotation of a narrative text. Furthermore, he omits quoting Melchizedek's blessing, which should have seemed precious, since this is the only occasion where the character of Melchizedek speaks.

The author includes other narrative details that appear unnecessary. He tells us that Melchizedek was the King of Salem, and that he was a priest of the Most High God.[110] That he was a king is not as important as his being a priest, but reminding the audience that he was a king makes him a royal

---

[108] Fitzmyer, "Now this Melchizedek . . . ," 222.

[109] David Hay, *Glory at the Right Hand of God: Psalm 110 in Early Christianity* (SBLMS 18; Nashville and New York: Abingdon, 1972) 146.

[110] Exegetes prior to and contemporary with the author of Hebrews sometimes saw Melchizedek as symbolic of heavenly realities or as a heavenly figure himself. How much of this speculation about Meclchizedek was familiar to our author is unclear, although many modern scholars feel that even if the author of Hebrews did not know of other exegesis directly, he was aware of the general consideration of the importance of Melchizedek. For studies in Melchizedek see Fred L. Horton, *The Melchizedek Tradition: A Critical Examination of the Sources to the Fifth Century A. D. and in the Epistle to the Hebrews* (SNTSMS 30; Cambridge: Cambridge University, 1976); and Paul J. Kobelski, *Melchizedek and Melchiresa'* (CBQMS 10; Washington D.C.: Catholic Biblical Association. 1981).

priest, which is what Jesus is.[111] Furthermore, in the author's first interpretive comments, he explains both Melchizedek's name and the place name Salem through etymology; he says, "he is first, by translation of his name, king of righteousness, and then he is also king of Salem, that is king of peace."[112] While it is true that etymology is a common enough interpretive technique, neither the theme of righteousness, nor the theme of peace have much of a bearing on the argument.[113]

Except for the blessing and the tithing, most commentators think the narrative details play no significant role, since the author does not employ them in his argument. However, a closer reading reveals a more intimate connection between the author's explicit discourse and his selective presentation of the biblical story. The listener/reader is initially presented with two biblical characters, before there is any mention of Jesus. We must keep in mind that the author not only compares Jesus to Melchizedek in this passage, but also, beginning in 7:4, contrasts Melchizedek with Abraham . In 7:1–2 he provides qualifiers for each character: Abraham is said to be returning from the slaughter of the kings. Melchizedek is a priest who is a "king of righteousness" and a "king of peace." The author's purpose of these details is not to evoke the setting of the original story—Abraham's courageous rescue of Lot. Rather, "the slaughter of kings" evokes war, carnage, brutality, and conquest, which stands in sharp contrast to Melchizedek's being a "king of righteousness and peace."

Furthermore, Melchizedek blesses Abraham, and Abraham tithes to Melchizedek. What is clear from interpretive comments that follow in vv. 4–10 is that the author includes the blessing and the tithing to show that Melchizedek is superior to Abraham, since, according to the argument, a superior blesses an inferior and an inferior tithes to a superior. In comparison to Abraham, Melchizedek, the priestly king, the holy man, who does nothing but bless Abraham and presumably accept the tithe, appears serene, peace-loving, spiritual, and heavenly. Thus, the initial contrast between Melchizedek as peace-loving and Abraham as bellicose functions as

---

[111] While Jesus as king is not a developed notion is Hebrews' christology, the author does use royal-messianic psalm quotations (Psalm 2). He also uses the title 'Christ' in connection with his being God's son (3:6).

[112] Both Josephus (*Ant.* 1.10.2 §180; *J.W.* 6.10.1 §438) and Philo (*De legum allegoria* 3.79) reach the same etymological conclusions, although these popular etymologies are probably not based on an accurate understanding of the Hebrew. See the discussion in Fitzmyer, "Melchizedek," 229–32.

[113] Because these themes have such a limited role in Hebrews, Attridge (*Hebrews*, 189) speculates that perhaps they are intended to evoke messianic imagery.

an adumbration of the superior-inferior relationship that is explicitly stated after the description of the tithing scene.

In the Hebrew Bible, Genesis 14 is the story of Abraham's rescue of Lot and the Sodomites, into which the Melchizedek episode is most likely an insertion.[114] In the biblical text itself and in later Jewish interpretations,[115] it is a story of the heroism and generosity of Abraham. Abraham selflessly battles other kings, and the story climaxes when Abraham refuses to keep the spoils from his conquest and gives everything up to the king of Sodom. Even where the Melchizedek episode is omitted in other Jewish retellings, Abraham's generosity toward the king of Sodom is preserved.[116] Indeed, that Abraham is said to be the one that tithes to Melchizedek is itself an interpretive move. Neither the MT nor the LXX names the recipient or the giver; the biblical text says only that "he gave him a tenth of everything," leaving it unclear which character is the subject of the sentence. But Hebrews is not innovative in understanding Abraham as the giver and Melchizedek as the recipient—it was already standard Jewish exegesis to read Abraham as the subject who tithes to Melchizedek.[117] Such action on the part of Abraham was not of course seen to diminish the status of Abraham in relation to Melchizedek. Quite the contrary, the tithing scene was traditionally understood as an illustration of Abraham's generosity. But in Hebrews there is no mention of Abraham's returning of the spoils. The tithing is due to Abraham's recognition of Melchizedek's greatness, and not to Abraham's generosity.

In his interpretation of the tithing in vv. 6–7, the author calls the blessing indisputable proof that Abraham is an inferior. The original text of Genesis contains the blessing that Melchizedek bestowed upon Abraham, and it includes the following: "and blessed be God Most High, who has delivered your enemies into your hand!" In Genesis, Melchizedek not only blesses Abraham but he blesses God Most High at the same time. Presumably God Most High is *not* inferior to Melchizedek, and, given that these words would

---

[114] See J.A. Emerton ("Some False Clues in the Study of Genesis xiv," *VT* 21 [1971] 24–7; and "The Riddle of Genesis xiv, " *VT* 21 [1971] 403–39) for a thorough review and discussion.

[115] See, e.g., Josephus, *Ant.* 1.10.2 §179–82.

[116] There is a lacuna in both the Ethiopic and Syriac texts of *Jubilees* where the Melchizedek episode is expected. However, the Syriac version includes the phrase "and he pursued the kings and he returned everything which they had taken captive from Sodom." See the translation and notes in O.S. Wintermute, "Jubilees," in *OTP* 2.84.

[117] Josephus, *Ant* 1.10.2 §181; 1QapGen.

have disproven the proof that a superior blesses an inferior, the author prudently chose not to quote them. The author's retold version of Gen 14:17–20 worked in his favor; quoting it would not have served his purpose. But more than this observation, we can see that narrative qualifiers or adjectival descriptions of biblical characters focus the listener's attention on the nature of the characters, rather than on the scriptural text. Indeed, the phrases describing Abraham and Melchizedek, while scriptural, are decontextualized, detached from their being words of scripture, and used rather as character associations. The paraphrase has evoked a mood of contrast between the two characters that does not exist in the earlier biblical text and could not have been achieved by quoting from it and following with an interpretation. The result is a subtly unflattering picture of Abraham.

In addition to Hebrews 11, we mentioned two other substantial retellings, one contained in chaps. 3–4 regarding the disobedience in the wilderness, the other a description of the tabernacle and the cult in 8–10:18. In those retellings the author's less-than-enthusiastic attitude toward his subject matter is readily evident and needs no in-depth exegesis. The best the author can say about the tabernacle and the cult is that they are symbolic, they are types—or anti-types—of heavenly realities. As a result the author of Hebrews depends upon a spatial and temporal dualism. The old covenant was created in earthly materials and corresponds to the past; the new covenant is heavenly and corresponds to the eschatological age, which has already begun.

What is self-evident in the retellings about the wilderness and the levitical cult emerges in the other retellings, too. In the pericopes we exegeted on Moses and Abraham, the dualism present in the discourse of Hebrews in general is operative. In both cases, biblical heroes of enormous magnitude undergo some character deflation. Unfortunately for them, Abraham and Moses participate in the old covenant. Whenever the author engages in a retelling of a biblical episode, he is utilizing a historical example, but one which by definition is part of a vanishing, earthly past.

It is my contention that the retellings of the various parts of the biblical text in Hebrews serve to devalue the contents or the objects of biblical narrative. Whatever event, person, or institution the author makes use of, the function of that historical information is to portend the future—i.e., the situation in which the addressees now find themselves, the situation engendered by the new covenant. The elements of the biblical story are signs of what is to come. As a result, their status—even their reality—is compromised because they are only a model or shadow of better things to come. In the words of the author to the Hebrews, "in speaking of a new covenant he treats the first as obsolete. And what is becoming obsolete and growing old is ready to vanish away" (8:13). What needs to be stressed is that the old covenant is not just an abstract idea; it is manifest in Jewish scripture.[118] Thus, those elements that make up biblical history are necessarily diminished, while the biblical text itself stands as a sign pointing to a post-biblical reality. The author displays profound ambivalence toward scripture for this reason. The Bible is *the* primary locus of historical (and theological) information, but its contents refer to people, places, and events that are becoming obsolete.

The past's contrasting relationship with the present is further developed by the author's distance as a narrator or even as a preacher. He does not make use of his personal experience in his arguments, as Paul does, for example. He does not use the first person singular except at the very end and very superficially. Furthermore, he is not a self-conscious interpreter, again, as Paul is.[119]

The distant voice of the author of Hebrews contributes to a historical distancing of the biblical events. While the retellings function as historical examples with which the author teaches and exhorts his followers, they also function as inferior prototypes of Christian people, places, and institutions. Moses is inferior to Jesus, Abraham is inferior to Melchizedek, and by extension, the levitical priests are inferior to Melchizedek and Jesus. Abraham and Moses are both priests who serve the old covenant. And the old covenant and the sacrificial system of worship in the eyes of the author of Hebrews, was bloody, mundane, repetitive, and ineffectual. While the author of Hebrews certainly has an awareness of the historical continuity between the people and places of the Bible and the people who believe in Jesus, his historical continuum has a serious disjuncture because of his dualistic presuppositions. Although he occasionally refers to the community

---

[118] Susanne Lehne (*The New Covenant in Hebrews* [JSNTSS 44; Sheffield: JSOT, 1990] 11) warns against seeing the old covenant in Hebrews as coterminous with Jewish scripture (or the Christian OT). I do not mean to argue that they are one and the same. Jewish Scripture, however, is the record which contains the instructions for the old covenantal relationship between the people and God. As such, when the old covenant became obsolete, so did those instructions.

[119] I can think of two major retellings in the letters of Paul: 2 Cor 3:4–18 and Gal 4:21–31, both of which are hermeneutically self-conscious. In the Galatians example Paul formally introduces the biblical text and calls his reading an allegory. In the example in 2 Corinthians Paul is also discussing how to read scripture.

he addresses as the "descendants of Abraham" (2:16), more commonly he refers to those he currently addresses as in a privileged position vis-à-vis biblical characters. The biblical promises, which the author repeatedly refers to, are not fulfilled in the lives of the biblical characters (11:13, 39), but are about to be fulfilled in the new community of Christ as part of the new covenant.[120] What is so unusual about the presentation of biblical history in Hebrews is that the author is lacking that uninhibited enthusiastic reverence for the past that we normally find in ancient commentators, Jewish, Christian, and pagan.

The Hermeneutical Interaction between Quotations and Retellings

I cannot recall another document where two such starkly different presentations of scripture are juxtaposed. Thus Hebrews appears to have taken an almost accidental hermeneutical fact—the tendency of speech to be quoted and narrative to be rephrased—and turned it into a rhetorical device. For if one quotes scripture as simply a direct divine oracle in one place and in another renders narrative as descriptive information about the past, the two are not assigned the same hermeneutical value. The quotation will inevitably appear to have an authority that the rephrased material will not, precisely because the quotation will stand as testimony external to the author's point of view. An air of objectivity is gained by directly quoting another, without interference from one's own voice. This seeming objectivity is what gives the quoted material a greater authority than material that is paraphrased and presented in indirect discourse. A story from Genesis or the description of an institution such as the priesthood from Leviticus will not have the *presence* that a direct oracle from Psalm 110 or Psalm 95 will have.

Moreover, when the two types of texts are distinguished in this way, one can be used to testify against another. This is completely different from contemporary Jewish hermeneutics. When the rabbis perceive that there is a contradiction in scripture, or any type of interpretive problem, it is resolved by appealing to other scriptural texts so that what appears as a contradiction is made into a non-problem. In Hebrews the author purposely creates contradictions so that God's words can be used as a testimony against historical precedent in the biblical narrative. Thus, the author's bi-level use of scripture is rhetorically self-serving: it enables him to use scriptural

---

[120] See 4:1; 6:12; 8:6; 9:15; 10:36.

prooftexts to argue against the continuation of traditional religious practices contained in scripture.

In chap. 8 the author begins his lengthy discussion of the so-called new covenant. Beginning in v. 7 he writes,

> For if that first covenant had been faultless, there would have been no occasion for a second.

This remark is immediately followed by the well-known quote from Jeremiah 31:

> The days will come says the Lord, when I will establish a new covenant with the house of Israel . . . .

Thus, the new covenant is not merely described; the direct speech of God in Jeremiah is quoted as a divine revelation mandating its realization. To be sure, the author does rely on scripture to describe the old covenant, but that covenant is depicted merely as historical information rather than divine revelation.

In chapter 9, which I discussed earlier, the author embarks upon a detailed description, based primarily on Exodus and Leviticus, of the tabernacle and the ritual duties of the priesthood. Although the biblical passage upon which the author bases his description is actually taken from a divine speech in Exodus, he never quotes from it; instead he chooses to describe it. Having detailed in his own words the biblical institution of the priesthood, the author goes on to argue that Christ is the ultimate priest and mediator of the new covenant, a mediator which renders the old one completely ineffectual. In Hebrews, the law and the priestly institutions are only an earthly shadow of the heavenly pattern, which has now come to fruition in Christ. Then in 10:5–7 the author quotes from Psalm 40:6–8 (LXX: 39:7–9), which speaks of sacrificial ritual in a demeaning way— thereby implicitly demeaning the entire levitical system—and names Christ as the speaker. A few verses later the author again quotes from Jeremiah 31, naming the Holy Spirit as the speaker.

Taken together, these quotations function as a divine mandate that stands in direct contrast to the Bible's own institutions (e.g., the covenant, temple, and sacrifice). The quotations are used in an immediate oracular way, while the description of the institutions in the Old Testament is formulated as a contrasting example and given no scriptural status. A few words from Jeremiah or the psalmist are presented in such a way that they stand as God's testimony against dozens of chapters from the Pentateuch! To realize how unusual this is, we need only compare it to the covenanters at

Qumran, who used the prophetic literature as divine testimony not against *biblical* institutions but rather against *present* institutions perceived to be corrupt and *un*biblical. For the author of Hebrews, it is not that once pristine Jewish institutions became corrupt; on the contrary, his view is that they were always corrupt, made of inferior, earthly material.

Chapters 8 to 10 highlight how the author exploits his two approaches to scripture for rhetorical purposes. In general, when a biblical passage is renarrated by a later author, the distinction between the source text and its interpretation is blurred. The renarrated text is not presented as an 'other' to be confronted; instead it is usurped by the interpreter. When this happens in a work primarily devoted to the expositional use of scripture, as is Hebrews, the biblical text becomes subsumed into the author's argument. In this case, scripture receives no special status *qua* scripture. And when this narrative use of the text is combined with selective quoting, the independent status of that which *is* retold, or renarrated, becomes further reduced.

The author uses the retellings to describe the past, i.e., the state of the world before Christ, while the citations of speech determine the present, i.e., the post-Christ world. As a result, the religious significance of the historical record (narrative) is diminished, while speech that is perceived to transcend history is imbued with increased power. Speech is quoted not simply to edify or inform, but to reveal truths. And scripture as God's word is superior to scripture as mere historical record. Therefore, the word of God quoted in Hebrews can authoritatively contradict anything that might be contained in the historical record, such as the temple and the priesthood. Indeed, that which the author of Hebrews chooses to diminish by the invocation of the divine word is invariably that event or institution connected with the national distinctiveness of Israel. These targeted events and institutions include the temple and the priesthood, as I said, but they also encompass national myths like the exodus story, the wilderness experience and the conquest of the land. As we shall see in the following chapter, Hebrews 11 represents the clearest expression of this emerging Christian hermeneutic.

Chapter Three

HEROES AND HISTORY

ುⓈ ಲ

The Place of Hebrews 11 in Hebrews

Scholars have never agreed on how chap. 11 functions in Hebrews.[1] At one time chap. 11 was thought of merely as an appendage which followed the culminating argument of Jesus as high priest (7:1–10:18).[2] More recently, Barnabas Lindars has argued that the section on faith—which includes chap. 11 (10:19–12:29)—is in fact the apex of the work.[3] Lindars' position is, however, at least partly dependent upon his understanding of Hebrews as a letter[4] (and not as an epideictic oration), a view which we earlier determined was problematic.[5]

Nevertheless, the supposition that Hebrews is an oration hardly diminishes the importance of chap. 11 within the context of the document. Since Hebrews was composed for oral delivery,[6] and since chap. 11 falls near

---

[1] Although 12:1–2 initiates a paraenetical section which has obviously been inspired by chapter 11, I have marked off the pericope under study at 11:40. Because vv. 1 and 40 form an *inclusio*, chapter 11 is a distinct unit.

[2] Albert Vanhoye, *La structure littéraire de l'Epître aux Hébreux* (StudNeot 1; Paris: Desclee de Brouwer, 1963) saw the whole of Hebrews as a chiasm in which this section is central.

[3] Barnabas Lindars, "The Rhetorical Structure of Hebrews," *NTS* 35 (1989) 382–406.

[4] More specifically, Lindars ("Rhetorical Structure," 383) argues that Hebrews is a letter in deliberative style. Although the lines between different species of rhetoric are not always perfectly clear, the deliberative style usually points toward specific action in the future—e.g., should we go to war? Epideictic rhetoric, on the other hand, may exhort the listener to a general kind of future behavior implicitly, but the speech does not require a specific collective response from the audience. Lindars thinks Hebrews is deliberative because he believes the author is trying to change the minds of his audience with regard to a distinct course of action, to implement a change of policy. Those of us who see Hebrews as less tied to a specific situation think epideictic is a more appropriate designation. See the discussion of species of rhetoric in George Kennedy, *New Testament Interpretation Through Rhetorical Criticism* (Chapel Hill: University of North Carolina, 1984) 19–72. Kennedy also regards most Christian preaching in general to be epideictic, unless it has an explicit deliberative purpose.

[5] See the introduction, pp. 10–12.

[6] As all speeches in antiquity were. See Walter Ong, *Orality and Literacy: The Technologizing of the Word* (New York: Metheun, 1982) 110–11 for a discussion of the orality of writing in the ancient world, as well as his bibliography, 180–95.

the end of the text, we may assume that the author intended the hero list to make a lasting impression. Like the large majority of lists surveyed in chapter one, Hebrews 11 stands out as a distinct unit within the larger text. What makes the Hebrews hero list even more distinctive is its anaphoric catch-word structure (much like Wisdom 10 and the Covenant of Damascus),[7] which bonds each member of the list together into an unmistakable whole. Moreover, this tightly structured list has substantial mnemonic and exhortative potential. The rhythmic cadence created by the structure not only assists the speaker in his oral delivery of the speech, but makes the list more memorable for the hearer as well.[8] The exhortative power of the text lies in the very construction of such a large list of heroes. Calling the names of so many great biblical individuals and describing their accomplishments is intended as inspiration as well as argumentation. Indeed, as Attridge says, the chapter includes both paraenetic and expository aims.[9] As we saw in chapter one, many rhetorical theoreticians of antiquity recognized the exhortative potential of examples. Although Aristotle was concerned with identifying the logical mechanics of examples, Quintilian, among others, recognized the value of their emotive power.[10]

Thus, while chap. 11 follows the climax of the author's argument in Hebrews, chap. 11 is not an appendix. In fact, *synkrisis*, the comparison of the subject to something else—as an example series is—is a typical part of epideictic rhetoric.[11] I suspect that modern exegetes' confusion over the place of chap. 11 in Hebrews has more to do with the cultural gap between the text as it was originally intended for oral presentation, and the text in its timeless written form. Modern scholars tend to see the *argument* as the most essential part of analyzing a document such as Hebrews. This is due to the fact that the written text itself is all that remains for study. In antiquity—even in literate antiquity—oral presentation provides the primary context for rhetorical writing.[12] Thus, in the oral world of antiquity, a speech-maker

---

[7] For a discussion of catch-word type lists, see Thomas Lee, *Studies in the Form of Sirach 44–50* (SBLDS 75; Atlanta: Scholars, 1986) 41–48.

[8] The orality of Hebrews 11 has been thoroughly studied by Michael Cosby, *The Rhetorical Composition and Function of Hebrews 11: In Light of Example Lists in Antiquity* (Macon, GA: Mercer, 1988).

[9] Harold Attridge, *The Epistle to the Hebrews* (Hermeneia; Philadelphia: Fortress, 1989) 307.

[10] See my discussion of Quintilian in chapter one.

[11] Kennedy, *Rhetorical Criticism*, 24, 89.

[12] See Kennedy, *The Art of Persuasion in Greece* (Princeton: Princeton University, 1963) 3–7; and Rosalind Thomas, *Literacy and Orality in Ancient Greece* (Cambridge: Cambridge

valued *pathos*—the emotive response of the audience to the speaker—as much as *logos*,[13] and this is especially true of epideictic kinds of speeches.[14] Indeed, in the epideictic variety of rhetoric, the speaker usually follows an "orderly sequence of amplified topics,"[15] the central goal of which is to effect or strengthen certain sentiments among the listeners.[16] Insofar as sentiments act as bonding agents between members of a community,[17] the public delivery of a speech succeeds in this goal far more than privately reading a text. Thus, I strongly suspect that when Hebrews was heard, rather than read, the climax was, in fact, the catalog of heroes.

In any case, the hero catalog follows an exhortative section just prior to it (10:35–39), which includes the well known quotation from Hab 2:4.

Do not, therefore, abandon that confidence [παρρησίαν] of yours; it brings a great reward. For you need endurance [ὑπομονῆς], so that when you have done the will of God, you may receive what was promised. For yet "in a very little while, the one who is coming will come and will not delay; but my righteous one will live by faith [πίστεως]. My soul takes no pleasure in anyone who shrinks back." But we are not among those who shrink back and so are lost, but among those who have faith [πίστεως] and so are saved.

The word faith, πίστις, appears in the quotation from Habakkuk, and its appearance in this citation is at least part of the reason the author chooses the word for his anaphora. The author also describes his audience as "those who have faith and so are saved."[18] πίστις, therefore, not only links chap. 11

University, 1992) 101–127.

[13] *Pathos* and *Logos* are two of the three kinds of rhetorical proof mentioned by Aristotle (*Rhet.* 1.2/1356a); the third is *ethos*. On *pathos*, see Kennedy, *Art of Persuasion*, 63, 69–70; and *Rhetorical Criticism*, 15.

[14] Kennedy, *Art of Persuasion*, 152–53. Kennedy claims that since epideictic is, of all the species of rhetoric, most closely related to poetry, its emphasis on performance is utterly fundamental.

[15] Kennedy, *Rhetorical Criticism*, 24.

[16] In other words, the speaker wants to instill shared values amongst his/her audience; see Kennedy, *Rhetorical Criticism*, 73–75.

[17] 'Sentiments' is a semi-technical term, which I have taken from Bruce Lincoln (*Discourse and the Construction of Society: Comparative Studies of Myth, Ritual, and Classification* [New York: Oxford University, 1989] 9–10) and which is more thoroughly discussed in the following chapter.

[18] A more accurate translation of the Greek, εἰς περιτοίησιν ψυχῆς, is provided by Attridge (*Hebrews*, 305): "preservation of the soul."

to a biblical quotation, but helps establish a connection between the biblical heroes and the members of the author's community.[19] Other words appear in this passage which are perhaps just as important for understanding chap. 11. Some scholars have noted a significant conceptual relationship between πίστις and confidence, παρρησία, and endurance, ὑπομονή.[20] While the latter two words do not appear in Hebrews 11, they could be used to describe the behavior of the heroes. The heroes typically find themselves in adverse circumstances which they willingly endure. Moreover, ὑπομονή becomes prominent immediately following the list of heroes, when the audience is called to follow the example of Jesus (12:1–3).[21]

More than these descriptive qualities which adumbrate the character of the heroes, the mention of receiving a reward and a promise becomes a highly significant motif in chap. 11. Indeed the terms reward, μισθαποδοσία, and promise, ἐπαγγελία, appear repeatedly in the hero catalog, and are applied to the heroes collectively. In some cases it is unclear exactly what the referent is for either word. The term μισθαποδοσία is usually connected with an eschatological, or at least divine reward or, in the case of Heb 2:2, divine punishment.[22] The ἐπαγγελία often refers to some kind of ultimate divine fulfillment,[23] but it can also mean the specific promises God made in the past—and this is an important sense of the word in chap. 11. This meaning of the word would include, for example, the promises God made to Abraham about his descendants and the land they would inherit.[24] But the larger, ultimate or eschatological meaning of ἐπαγγελία also seems to function in some places in the hero catalog.

---

[19] See n. 43 regarding the meaning of 'faith' in Hebrews.

[20] Erich Grässer, *Der Glaube im Hebräerbrief* (Marburg: Elwert, 1965) 42; and Hans Windisch, *Der Hebräerbrief* (HNT 14; Tübingen: Mohr [Siebeck] 1931) 99. As Attridge (*Hebrews,* 300) says, "The words are not synonymous, but in concert define the general attitude that Hebrews is trying to inculcate."

[21] δι' ὑπομονῆς τρέχωμεν τὸν προκείμενον ἡμῖν ἀγῶνα ἀφορῶντες εἰς τὸν τῆς πίστεως ἀρχηγὸν καὶ τελειωτὴν Ἰησοῦν, ὃς ἀντὶ τῆς προκειμένης αὐτῷ χαρᾶς ὑπέμεινεν σταυρὸν...

[22] μισθαποδοσία only occurs in Hebrews in the NT and so its sense comes from these very passages. In addition to 2:2 and 10:36, the word occurs in 11:26 where Moses is said to be "looking ahead to his reward." In 11:6 the related word, μισθαποδότης, occurs, where it describes God who "rewards those who seek him."

[23] 4:1; 6:12,17; 8:6.

[24] As it does in 6:13 and 11:17.

One clue to help us distinguish one meaning from the other is the use of the differing verbs for "receiving" the promises. In 10:36 the verb used is κομίζω: κομίσησθε τὴν ἐπαγγελίαν. Of all the mention of promises in chap. 11 the only time this verb of receiving is used is at the end of the catalog in v. 39, to say that the heroes did *not* receive the promise: ... οὐκ ἐκομίσαντο τὴν ἐπαγγελίαν.[25] Attridge points out that the verb κομίζω, when associated with ἐπαγγελία in other NT literature, is used for the reception of the promise of eschatological salvation.[26] Although our author is not consistent,[27] the verb κομίζω can be a helpful gauge. When the author directly addresses his Christian audience with the verb κομίζω—as he does in 10:36—the promises almost certainly equal eschatological rewards. But when he speaks of figures of the past—as in chap. 11—the issue is more complicated, because the author refers to more than one kind of reception of promises. Sometimes he means the recipients receive the promise itself (11:17) and sometimes he means they receive the object of the promise (11:13). The thematic role of ἐπαγγελία is undoubtedly highly significant, albeit complicated, in our chapter, and therefore will be explored more fully as we progress through the text.

That the author picks up themes from a prophetic quotation which is directly addressed to his audience, and then proceeds to retell a portion of biblical narrative, is a pattern repeated by the author of Hebrews that we identified in the previous chapter. Here, too, we have an oracular quotation from Habakkuk in 10:35–39, followed by a discussion of the biblical past and nearly devoid of quotations in chap. 11. Chapter 11 is such a tightly structured unit, however, that it seems almost like an independent excursus sandwiched between the two paraenetical sections at the end of chap. 10 and the beginning of chap. 12. Nevertheless, the paraenetic themes adumbrated in the adjacent chapters exist as a leitmotif in our chapter. But chap. 11's connection to the rest of Hebrews runs even deeper: many of the same themes we uncovered in the retellings of individual biblical episodes appear also in chap. 11. The great advantage of chap. 11 is that it provides a big picture—it covers so many events in succession that we can identify the author's concept of biblical history writ large.

---

[25] Other verbs of receiving in chap. 11 include λαμβάνω, ἀναδέχομαι, and ἐπιτυγχάνω.

[26] Attridge (*Hebrews*, 301) lists 2 Cor 5:10; Eph 6:8; Col 3:25; 1 Pet 1:9; 5:4.

[27] In 11:13, like 11:39, the author also says the heroes did not receive the promises but the verb is λαμβάνω.

The Principle of Selection

Like all the other lists and summaries, Hebrews 11 displays peculiarities. Rahab, for example, occurs on no other Jewish list. (In fact, women never appear on Jewish lists.) Why is she included here? The traditional answer is that Rahab is an example of faith like all the other members of the list. She risked her own life to protect Joshua's spies. This is partially true, but with so many biblical heroes to choose from, why make the choice of Rahab? Why not Debra? Furthermore, the fact that Rahab appears on the same list as Abraham and Moses makes a statement about her importance in general. Indeed, the analysis of the factors that led the author to choose a particular individual must be kept in a dialectical relationship to the list as a whole. Standard biblical images and common intertestamental traditions inform the author in his choice of each hero, but the peculiarity of his list lies in the particular combination of people and events. Only the *principle(s) of selection* can tell us what Rahab and Abraham have in common.

Usually scholars have taken the principle of selection for granted. The anaphoric use of πίστει has led to the assumption that each hero is an individual who exemplifies faith. Occasionally scholars have noticed that most of those included on the list are not good examples of faith,[28] at least not the best the Bible has to offer. Some scholars attributed the choice of heroes to the author's dependence on a source.[29] The author has then strung together this list with the catchword πίστει. But this is a less-than satisfying analysis. We have already determined that Hebrews 11 is not dependent upon a source, although the author was familiar with, and may even have been imitating those prototypical texts from the LXX.[30] Even if the author had used a source, surely he still would have exercised selection. The precision with which Hebrews in general and chap. 11 in particular is composed indicates that there is little that is arbitrary in this document. Although every list exhibits peculiarities, I intend to demonstrate that the Hebrews list differs markedly from any intertestamental prototypes to which one could point (indicated by inclusions like Rahab, and omissions like Joshua and Phinehas). The comment that any Jew could have written this text (with the exception of vv. 26 and 39)[31] indicates how scholars have

---

[28] Windisch, *Hebräerbrief,* 99; Attridge, *Hebrews,* 306.

[29] Windisch, *Hebräerbrief,* 98–99; and Otto Michel, (*Der Brief an die Hebräer* [Meyer 13; Göttingen: Vandenhoeck & Ruprecht, 1966] 422–23) were influential in disseminating this idea.

[30] See chapter one.

[31] See, e.g., Sidney Sowers, *The Hermeneutics of Philo and Hebrews* (Basel Studies of

failed to perceive the distinctiveness of Hebrews 11. Indeed, the question of the principle behind the selection has remained largely unasked. And, curiously, even those scholars who insightfully point out that the heroes are not the best examples of faith, invariably attempt to isolate that element of faith in each example that is alleged to be in the mind of the author.[32]

Therefore, I have taken a different approach: to start with the cast of characters and what is said about them, while putting πίστις aside, at least initially. The main function of the anaphoric use of πίστει is rhetorical, i.e., to create the effect of an enormous number of possible examples.[33] Thus, I see no reason to assume that πίστις holds the key to the principle of selection. Furthermore, just what the author means by faith in this text is a complicated question that might be more easily answered by starting with the heroes themselves—searching for what they have in common, rather than assuming it. As we will see, this commonality is something more than a vague notion of faith in God.

We have already determined that Hebrews 11 most closely resembles the multi-dimensional lists, especially those found in Sirach 44–50, Wisdom 10, and the Covenant of Damascus 2–3. Multi-dimensionality means that a list possessed a complex agenda in amassing a series of examples, resulting in variety, rather than uniformity, among the figures listed. Hebrews 11, too, has such a complex agenda, which means that the author selected the heroes with more than one motive. In this sense, 'faith' most likely plays some role in the selection of heroes. That is, faith may not be merely a catchword, but might also be a quality that substantively describes the heroes. But we can only come to know what the author means by faith by studying the description of each hero and then abstracting from such study a profile of the hero.

As we shall see, having faith is not in and of itself a foundational principle of selection. Rather, the most striking characteristic of each hero as

---

Theology 1; Zurich: EVZ, 1965) 133; and Windisch, *Hebräerbrief,* 98.

[32] The most striking example of this is Attridge, who explicitly states at the beginning of his commentary on this section that most of the biblical stories referred to do *not* explicitly highlight faith (*Hebrews,* 306). And yet in his otherwise very thoughtful exegesis of each and every hero, he consistently attempts to find the "faith element" that must be present in the author's mind. About Moses he says, "Hebrews is not concerned with extraordinary experiences attributed to Moses in and of themselves, but with his faith" (343). Indeed, the author of Hebrews has not selected arbitrary extraordinary experiences, but neither has he chosen them necessarily because they exemplify a *specific* manifestation of πίστις.

[33] Cosby, *Rhetorical Composition,* 41–55.

portrayed in Hebrews 11 is that they are divorced from Israel and her history as told in scripture. In contrast to a list such as Sirach, where the status of each hero is largely derived from a national office or institution,[34] Hebrews 11 portrays each character as standing apart from Israel as a nation. Indeed, each hero is an outsider who is depicted as living apart from any national body or institution. The precise meaning of the heroes' estrangement will be fleshed out in the detailed analysis of the text that follows. While some of the heroes—like Isaac and Jacob—are mentioned because they are so essential to the tradition they cannot be left out, almost everyone listed can be accounted for by considering their separation from Israel's national history.

In addition, like the lists in Sirach 44–50, Wisdom 10, and Covenant of Damascus, Hebrews 11 partly functions as a retelling of Israelite history. The collective result of the figures' standing outside of Israel creates a new understanding of the essence of biblical history. Traditionally, events in the biblical story are understood to unfold with a view toward the development of the nationhood of Israel. Promises made to the patriarchs, for example, have in mind the later national vicissitudes of Israel.[35] For our author, however, the depiction of the heroes as marginalized means they cannot play a role in that national teleology. Because the heroes of Hebrews are no longer part of Israel's national teleology, they collectively constitute a very different reading of biblical history. Thus, not only is the goal of this study to abstract a profile of the hero, but we must also assess the author's diachronic retelling of biblical history.

In contrast to previous studies, I will approach Hebrews 11 as both a list of heroes and a retelling of the scriptural story. While doing so, I will keep in mind the entire chapter and the relation of the part to the whole. Thus, each hero or event will be discussed with a view toward how they serve the author's comprehensive picture of biblical history.

---

[34] Burton Mack, *Wisdom and the Hebrew Epic: Ben Sira's Hymn in Praise of the Fathers* (Chicago and London: University of Chicago, 1988) 19–36.

[35] For example, the covenant scene between God and Abraham in Genesis 15 anticipates the exodus (v. 13) and the monarchy (v. 18).

Analysis of the Text[36]

A. Introduction

1Faith is the reality of what is hoped for, proof of things not seen. 2For by this the ancestors were attested to. 3By faith we know that the aeons were set in order by the word of God, for, from that which is not visible, what is seen has come to be.[37]

Our pericope opens with a definition of faith. Because faith is such a theologically charged word in the history of Christian tradition, serious dogmatic matters have been at stake in translating this verse. As a result, the verse has frequently suffered from over-translation.[38] But since more recent commentators have observed the sophisticated rhetorical structure of Hebrews in general and this chapter in particular, this verse should be viewed as a *rhetorical* definition, not a dogmatic one.[39] The form of the definition derives from rhetoric and popular philosophy, as indicated by the structure of the opening clause, Ἔστιν δὲ πίστις.[40] B. F. Westcott points out that "the object of the writer is not to give a formal definition of Faith but to bring out characteristics of Faith which bear upon his argument."[41]

While Westcott's remark is no doubt true, two questions are immediately raised by it. First, exactly what characteristics of πίστις are present in the statement "Faith is the reality of what is hoped for, proof of things not seen?" Second, if the function of the anaphoric πίστει is primarily aesthetic, what relationship is there between the definition in v. 1 and the examples on the list? The two questions are of course related in that we must decide to what extent our understanding of πίστις should be informed by the examples, and further decide what notion of πίστις is operative in Hebrews in general.

---

36 The subheadings in this section correspond to my outline of the text in Appendix A.

37 The translation is mine for chapter 11.

38 Some examples are: "Faith is the assurance of things hoped for, the conviction of things not seen" (NRSV); "And what is faith? Faith gives substance to our hopes, and makes us certain of realities we do not see" (John H. Davies, *A Letter to Hebrews* [Cambridge: Cambridge University, 1967] 105); "Only faith can guarantee the blessing that we hope for, or prove the existence of the realities that at present remain unseen" (Jerusalem Bible).

39 See especially Cosby, *Rhetorical Composition*, 25–40, for the formal rhetorical function of this verse.

40 For examples from Plato, Plutarch, and Philo, see Ceslas Spicq, *L'Epître aux Hébreux* (SB; Paris: Gabalda, 1952–53) 2:336.

41 B. F. Westcott, *The Epistle to the Hebrews* (London: Macmillan, 1909) 351.

Given that I have already argued that the author has a multi-faceted agenda in constructing his list and that the heroes display such variety of behaviors, it seems unlikely that the author intended his audience to abstract analogically the true meaning of πίστις from the list. In addition, despite Westcott's comment, Hebrews 11 does not exactly constitute an "argument." Unlike most of the other chapters of Hebrews, the use of scripture in chap. 11 is more compositional than expositional.[42] The tone of the text would therefore indicate that the author has no interest in arguing for a particular understanding of faith as opposed to another.

This observation is consistent with the use of πίστις in Hebrews in general. Most scholars who have tried to discern the meaning of faith in Hebrews see it as conventional. While there is not unanimity about the meaning of faith in Hebrews, the predominant view is that Hebrews is continuous with the Jewish understanding of faith as fidelity, firmness, and trust in God.[43] Beyond this conventional usage in Hebrews, the only characteristic of faith that stands out is its connection with eschatology. The connection between faith and the ultimate future vision of the author is

---

[42] These categories come from Devorah Dimant, "Mikra in the Apocrypha and Pseudepigrapha," in *Mikra*, 419. See my discussion of them on pp. 120–21.

[43] The most thorough study of πίστος was done by Grässer, *Der Glaube im Hebräerbrief*, who by contrasting Hebrews' conception of faith with Paul's, found that faith in Hebrews was not christological, or even Christian in its orientation, but rather was an ethical quality of the typical Hellenistic Jewish variety. Grässer then assumed that Hebrews represented a theological step backwards in Christian thinking about faith. Grässer has been rightly criticized and his thesis almost uniformly rejected. Gerhard Dautzenberg ("Der Glaube im Hebräerbrief," *BZ* 17 [1973] 161–77) for one, pointed out that Paul's notion of faith can hardly be considered normative for early Christianity, nor is Paul's understanding uniformly christological. Still, Dautzenberg conceded that there was nothing uniquely Christian about the notion of faith in Hebrews. Some, e.g., Jean Héring (*The Epistle to the Hebrews* [London: Epworth, 1970] 98) and Hugh Montefiore, (*A Commentary on the Epistle to the Hebrews* [New York: Harper, 1964] 186–7) have argued that the concept of faith in Hebrews is nothing more than the Pauline conception of hope. More recently, Dennis Hamm ("Faith in the Epistle to the Hebrews: The Jesus Factor," *CBQ* 52 [1990] 270–91) believes that faith is "profoundly christological" in Hebrews. (See also Vanhoye, "Jesus 'fidelis ei qui fecit eum,' Heb 3,2," *VD* 45 (1967) 291–305.) But Hamm overstates his case. While Jesus appears in one verse as connected with faith, the use of the term most often falls within conventional Jewish and Hellenistic usages. According to Attridge (*Hebrews*, 311–14), Hebrews is very much in continuity with the Jewish meaning of the term. See also James W. Thompson (*The Beginnings of Christian Philosophy: The Epistle to the Hebrews* [Washington D.C.: Catholic Biblical Association of America, 1982] 53–80) for a balanced account of the term in Hebrews and the general literary environment.

evident from 10:39: "But we are not among those who shrink back and so are lost, but among those who have faith and so are saved."[44]

Recently, Robert Brawley has given this eschatological component some content which bears directly on 11:1.[45] Using discourse analysis, he reasons that Heb 2:5–9 can help provide information about what the "unseen things" are in 11:1. Heb 2:5–9 includes a quotation from Psalm 8 which resonates with Ps 110:1, "you have crowned him with glory and honor, having subjected all things under his feet."[46] The author realizes that his audience might experience some cognitive dissonance upon hearing this statement because Jesus has not yet visibly achieved this lofty status. Thus, he comments, "As it is, we do *not yet see* everything in subjection to him" (2:8b). For the author of Hebrews, the subjection of all things to Jesus is a promise as yet unfulfilled—something not seen, but sure to come. Brawley reasons, therefore, that "faith in 11:1 . . . has to do with the reality of the ultimate subjection of all things to Christ, which is hoped for and *not yet seen*."[47]

I suspect that Brawley is correct although I doubt that this is what the author of Hebrews means exclusively. We must still reckon with the relationship of the definition to the examples. Although I myself argue for minimizing this relationship, we must account for the author's choice of πίστει for his anaphora. It is difficult to imagine that the author or the audience holds the image of the future event of Christ's lordship in mind while reciting the hero list. For example, when the author says in v. 29, "by faith [the people] crossed the Red Sea as if on dry land . . . ," it seems

---

[44] Although scholars have been traditionally divided between those who view Hebrews as Platonic, Philonic and spatial in its dualistic categories, and those who view it as eschatological, apocalyptic, and temporal, George MacRae ("Heavenly Temple and Eschatology in the Letter to the Hebrews," *Semeia* 12 [1978] 179–99) has argued that both are held in tension in Hebrews, because the author represents the former point of view and the audience the latter. He demonstrates this tension primarily by analyzing the author's understanding of temple, which of necessity includes apocalyptic and Hellenistic dimensions. MacRae also believes that the same tension is present with regard to the relationship of faith and hope in 11:1–3: "Hope is the specific goal of the audience (e.g., 6:18–19) in the face of persecution, and faith is introduced to strengthen it (6:11–12, 10:22–23). Heb 11:1–3 shows that faith is understood in Alexandrian terms as 'insight into the heavenly world,' which functions as a support for apocalyptic hope.

[45] Robert Brawley, "Discursive Structure and the Unseen in Hebrews 2:8 and 11:1: A Neglected Aspect of the Context," *CBQ* 55 (1993) 81–98.

[46] Translation mine. The NRSV translates ἄνθρωπος in 2:6 collectively as "human beings" and then must translate all the pronouns that follow in the plural. This creates confusion, because the author uses the psalm christologically; thus, the singular is more appropriate.

[47] Brawley, "Discursive Structure," 85. Emphasis mine.

unlikely that he means that the hope of the lordship of Christ literally caused the people to cross. It is more likely that the generic meaning of trust in God is operative here. Two other aspects of faith contained in the definition in v. 1 resonate with the examples. First, that faith is said to be the "ὑπόστασις of what is hoped for" points to some kind of impersonal essence.[48] The heroes are never said to *have* faith, but rather they act *by* or *through* faith, and sometimes they are the passive recipients of good fortune that is said to happen to them 'by faith.' While our author does not personify faith, as Wisdom 10 personified Sophia, πίστις appears to be a principle or a power that the heroes employ. In other words, πίστις is not simply a quality individuals have, but it is a power external to them in which they participate.

Second, the eschatological component of faith is important for chap. 11, as evidenced by Brawley's insights about the meaning of "things hoped for" in the definition, but also by the fact that the heroes are commended for their ability to anticipate the future. As we will see in more detail in the verses that follow, the heroes demonstrate that they have knowledge of future events, even if they cannot literally see such events because they are beyond their lifetime. In this regard, the definition has a programmatic function for the examples that follow.[49]

Verse 2 straightaway points to the testimony of scripture; it contains a record of the ancestors (πρεσβύτεροι). Although Hebrews 11 has been called an encomium on faith[50]—in which a general statement of faith opens the discussion and is followed by a list of examples illustrating faith—this verse undermines that designation. As I said earlier, many commentators have been baffled because scripture does not literally attest to the faith of the exemplary heroes that follow in Hebrews 11.[51] But v. 2 does not say that *faith* was attested to, but rather that *the ancestors were attested to by faith,* ἐν ταύτῃ

---

[48] See Helmut Koester, ὑπόστασις, *TDNT* 8. 585–88. As Attridge (*Hebrews*, 308–14) makes clear, the translation of the word ὑπόστασις is also best understood in a popular-philosophical context and without psychological (the most common interpretation, see the NRSV translation in n. 37) or legal connotations (as in Michel, *Der Brief*, 373; and Thomas Hewitt, *The Epistle to the Hebrews* [Tyndale NT Commentaries 15; Grand Rapids: Eerdmans, 1960]). ὑπόστασις refers to the underlying reality of the things in the world, temporal (future) or spatial (things above), which are "not seen," as the second clause describes.

[49] Attridge, *Hebrews*, 308.

[50] Attridge, *Hebrews*, 305; Burton Mack, *Rhetoric in the New Testament* (Minneapolis: Fortress, 1990) 75.

[51] E.g., Davies, *Letter*, 107; Montefiore, *Commentary*, 187.

γὰρ ἐμαρτυρήθησαν οἱ πρεσβύτεροι. Given what follows in the chapter, this means that scripture—that which constitutes the record of the ancestors' lives—was provided by faith. What is attested to are the ancestors themselves: their personalities, their deeds, their history.[52] In other words, what follows is not a series of examples illustrating what faith is, but a series of examples of scripture which illustrate who the πρεσβύτεροι are.[53]

Some scholars do not place v. 3 in the introduction.[54] Since v. 3 initiates the anaphoric structure of πίστει, they believe this verse opens the catalog of examples. The primary reason that this verse properly belongs to the introduction is the word νοοῦμεν, "we know." Following this verse every example occurs, as expected, in the third person, until the conclusion in v. 40 where the first person plural is resumed. Therefore, these first person plurals fence off the pericope by forming an *inclusio*.

Furthermore, because the author will list his biblical examples in chronological order, it may appear that the natural place to start would be with creation.[55] This description of creation, however, sounds more like philosophical doctrine than a biblical example. It is not so much a fact of biblical history that is being cited here, but the understanding of the world possessed by the present community to which Hebrews is addressed. Indeed, this verse resonates better with the first verse than with the verses that follow. Faith is directed at unseen things; similarly, visible things are created from unseen things.

B. Primeval Figures

4By faith Abel offered a better sacrifice to God than Cain, because of which he was attested to be righteous; God himself attested to the gifts, and because of this, although he is dead, he still speaks. 5By faith Enoch was translated so that

---

[52] This understanding is supported by the typical use of μαρτυρέω in Hebrews; see my discussion of this verb in chapter two.

[53] In this sense Hebrews 11 bears some resemblance to the rabbinic enumeration of scriptural examples; see Wayne Sibley Towner, *The Rabbinic "Enumeration of Scriptural Examples": A Study of a Rabbinic Pattern of Discourse with Special Reference to the Mekilta D'R. Ishamael* (Studia Post Biblica; Leiden: E. J. Brill, 1973). Ultimately Hebrews 11 is a different pattern of discourse than appears in the texts collected by Towner. Those are always literally enumerated with very specific parameters, e.g., men who never saw death.

[54] E.g., Montefiore, *Commentary,* 187; Cosby, *Rhetorical Composition,* 25

[55] None of the Hellenistic hero lists begin with creation as the first item, although chapter 43 of Sirach, which precedes the Hymn to the Ancestors, is a praise of God's creation. Psalms 135 and 136 begin their recounting of God's acts in history with creation.

he did not see death, and he was not found because God translated him. For, before translation he was attested to as having pleased God. ⁶Apart from faith it is impossible to be pleasing. For it is necessary that the one who approaches God has faith that he exists and that he is one who rewards those who seek him. ⁷By faith Noah received an oracle concerning things not yet seen, and fearing God, he constructed an ark for the salvation of his household, through which he condemned the world, and became an heir of the righteousness according to faith.

The first hero is Abel, a figure nowhere traditionally known as a man of faith. There is one other example list which begins with Abel (4 Macc 18:11–19), but it does little to help us understand why our author chose to start with him. First, the list in 4 Maccabees 18 appears within a larger discussion on martyrdom; the mention of Abel is natural there.[56] Hebrews 11, however, is not a list of martyrs.[57] To be sure, the theological role of suffering is very important in Hebrews, but many of the heroes who are listed are not mentioned for their suffering (e.g., Enoch, Noah, Joseph).[58] Second, no one would argue that this list underlies the one in Hebrews. Several names appear which do not appear in Hebrews.[59] In addition, many of the names appear merely as the authors of scripture, not as the subjects of scripture, as is the case with Hebrews.

Most likely—and this is true of each figure individually in Hebrews 11—a confluence of factors has given rise to the author's choice. First, the author does not begin with the murder of Abel by Cain. He begins with the enigmatic biblical fact that Abel's sacrifice was accepted, while Cain's was not. Although speculation already abounded as to why this was so,[60] the author of Hebrews makes no attempt to explain this fact. But he does add to the biblical text when he says that Abel "was attested to be righteous" (ἐμαρτυρήθη εἶναι δίκαιος). Perhaps the author wanted to integrate the hero list with what came before, since in Heb 10:38, just prior to our pericope, he quotes Hab 2:3–4, "my righteous one shall live by faith." More important, though, are extra-biblical traditions about Abel. Although he

---

[56] The main topic in 4 Maccabees is reason, but a large section of the work concentrates on the reasonableness of suffering.

[57] As for example, Héring (*Epistle*, 100), among others, asserts.

[58] Note that while 4 Maccabees 18 begins by listing martyrs, the author moves to a listing of general figures from scripture. But this is not paralleled in Hebrews either. The two names that *immediately* follow after Abel's, Enoch and Noah, are not martyrs.

[59] Phinehas, Hananiah, Azariah, Mishael, and Daniel (although the author of Hebrews may have the Danielic figures in mind in vv. 33–34), Solomon and Ezekiel.

[60] Philo, *Sac. A.C.* 52,76; Josephus *Ant.* 1.2.2 §54.

bears no reputation as faithful, he is said to be righteous,[61] Thus, this tradition appears to have been familiar to the author.

That Abel is the first person in biblical history to have been murdered must have had an impact on the author's imagination. Strangely, the author does not call attention to Abel's violent death; he says only that Abel "died," and does not portray him as a victim here. (Again, this description points away from understanding the list of heroes as a list of martyrs.) In Heb 12:24, however, the author compares the spilled blood of Jesus with that of Abel's. Because Gen 4:10 says that Abel's blood cried out to the Lord, the author in 11:4 understands this to mean that although Abel died, his blood is capable of being a living testimony (ἀποθανὼν ἔτι λαλεῖ).[62] The fact that Abel's blood speaks implies that he in some sense lives. In 12:24 the author subordinates this testimony to that of Jesus' testimony through the new covenant, but in chap. 11 the author does not exploit any typological relation between the blood of Abel and that of Jesus.

One element that commentators overlook is that by virtue of his being killed by Cain, Abel was removed from the earth and the downward spiral of human history that followed (Genesis 6–11). It is the posterity of Cain (and Seth) who will populate the primeval earth. In 1 *Enoch* 22:7ff and *T. Abr* 13, Abel resides in heaven and is portrayed as a judge who distinguishes the righteous from the wicked. Since Abel as the righteous one is connected to the image of Abel as judge,[63] it is likely that our author knows the latter tradition as well as the former. In the *Enoch* passage the souls of the righteous are taken up while the wicked are left behind, buried in the earth—at Abel's discretion. The true home of the righteous is the divine

---

[61] Cf. 1 Enoch 22:7; *T. Abr*. 13:2–3; Matt 23:35; and 1 John 3:12.

[62] There are two views among scholars concerning the meaning of "although he is dead, he still speaks (λαλεῖ)." Spicq (*L'Epître*, 2.342) and Attridge (*Hebrews*, 317) believe that it is to be understood as the voice of a martyr crying out for vindication, while James Moffat (*A Critical and Exegetical Commentary on the Epistle to the Hebrews* [New York: Scribner's, 1924] 165) citing patristic interpreters, believes the author means he still speaks in the record, i.e., scripture. The latter interpretation is more likely because of the way the author has formed his dual covenant theology. In 1:1–2 he opens his speech by asserting that formerly God spoke to our fathers by the prophets, but now he speaks by a Son (the verb λαλέω is used both times). The former refers to scripture, the latter to the event of Christ—both are revelation. Similarly, in 12:24, the blood of Jesus speaks better than the blood of Abel, which is a specific scriptural example, and therefore does indeed have revelatory import, but nevertheless not as much as the import of Christ. In light of these two passages, 11:4 should be interpreted as referring to the testimony of scripture, and not the martyr's cry of vindication.

[63] Attridge, *Hebrews*, 316 n. 136.

realm, while that of the unrighteous is in the earth in its material sense. Abel therefore initiates the process of *separating* the righteous from the wicked, and at the same time becomes the first righteous one to reach the divine realm.

What the author says of Enoch closely follows the rendering in the LXX (Gen 5:24). The prolific intertestamental traditions about Enoch do not play a major role here in Hebrews or elsewhere in the NT.[64] The author simply has in mind the biblical image of Enoch's translation to heaven. Why does this image inspire our author to include Enoch on his hero list?

One clue may be found on some of the other Hellenistic hero lists. Enoch appears as the first name in Sirach's Hymn to the Ancestors:[65] "Enoch pleased the Lord, and was taken up; he was an example of repentance to all generations" (44:16). For Philo (*Abr.* 17–9) Enoch is also known as an example of repentance, because "translation" (μεταθέσεως) implies a turning from a worse life to a better one.[66] The underlying presumption is that during this time, the time of "the ten generations," the earth was in a state of irredeemable wickedness.[67]

Although Enoch is not included in the list in Wisdom 10, there is a rather lengthy commentary in Wis 4:10–16 on Enoch's exaltation that might begin to fill out the meaning of Enoch's being an "example of repentance" in Sirach: It reads:

> There was one who pleased God and was loved by him, and while living among sinners he was taken up. He was caught up lest evil change his understanding or guile deceive his soul. For the fascination of wickedness obscures what is good, and roving desire perverts the innocent mind. Being perfected in a short time, he fulfilled long years; for his soul was pleasing to the Lord, therefore he took him quickly from the midst of wickedness. Yet the peoples saw and did not understand, or take such a thing to heart, that God's grace and mercy are with his elect, and that he watches over his holy ones. The righteous man who has died will condemn the ungodly who are living,

---

[64] Cf. L. Ginzberg, (*Legends of the Jews* [7 vols.; Philadelphia: Jewish Publication Society, 1937] 5.156, n. 58) who says, "In the entire Tannaitic literature and in both Talmudim no mention is made of Enoch."

[65] Although the reference to Enoch is almost surely secondary, see Mack (*Wisdom and Hebrew Epic*, 199–200).

[66] See also Dieter Lührmann, "Henoch und die Metanoia," *ZNW* 66 (1975) 103–16.

[67] For an overview of the ubiquitous and multifarious traditions about the depraved state of the earth during this time see Ginzberg, *Legends of the Jews*, 1.103–41.

and youth that is quickly perfected will condemn the prolonged old age of the unrighteous man.

First, the text describes a state where the one who has pleased God must be separated from the sinners in order not to be contaminated by wickedness, "for the fascination of wickedness obscures what is good and roving desire perverts the innocent mind . . . therefore God took him quickly from the midst of wickedness." The theme of the separation between the righteous and the wicked is well-developed here.[68] Enoch is removed from the world of sinners for his own protection, "lest evil change his understanding or guile deceive his soul." Second, his example condemns the ungodly. Here is a clear point of contact with Sirach's "example of repentance." By virtue of the fact that he is taken up, or perfected, he condemns others.[69]

Although our writer stays close to the biblical text in terms of what explicit comments he makes about Enoch's career, this intertestamental understanding of Enoch as protectively removed from the sinful generation of the flood, in order further to be an exemplary figure of righteousness for others is widespread enough[70] (Wisdom 4 and Philo explicitly; Sirach implicitly) for it to be informing the author's choice of Enoch. Furthermore, this understanding of Enoch fits within the same framework behind the author's depiction of Abel. Although Abel underwent a violent death, while Enoch did not suffer one at all, both end up in a heavenly realm where they condemn the unrighteous of the earth. In fact, there exists an additional link between these first two heroes: each is positively attested to (ἐμαρτυρήθη,[71] in the words of the author of Hebrews) prior to death. Abel is attested to as righteous, and Enoch is acknowledged as having pleased God.

---

[68] Herbert Braun (*An die Hebräer* [HNT 14; Tubingen: Mohr [Siebeck], 1984] 349) calls attention to a statement in 3 *Enoch* 6:3 because it mentions Enoch as faithful (which is very rare): "So I have taken up my Sekinah from their midst and brought it up to the height. And this one [Enoch] whom I have removed from them is the choicest of them all and worth them all in faith, righteousness, and fitting conduct." This reference may be important in terms of identifying Enoch among a group ("them all") of righteous ones who are removed from sinful humanity; c.f. Attridge (*Hebrews*, 318) who tangentially mentions this.

[69] Of course Enoch is also known to have actually preached repentance, see 1 *Enoch* 1:9, which is also quoted in Jude 14, and 1 *Enoch* 12–16.

[70] See Lührmann, "Henoch und die Metanoia."

[71] For Enoch, the verb occurs in the middle voice: μεμαρτύρηται (v. 5).

The author takes a brief break from hagiology in v. 6. This verse functions as an exhortative commentary on v. 5.[72] The author states a general rule, apparently derived from the example of Enoch. Since what is said about Enoch in v. 5 is nearly a quotation of the LXX,[73] perhaps the author felt compelled to comment more explicitly.[74] He does not take it for granted that his audience will understand what is meant by Enoch's having pleased God. But in v. 6 he does not tell them how Enoch pleased God, but how anyone is able to please God: by believing that God exists and that he rewards those who seek him.

Noah completes the first series of heroes. The first part of what is said, that Noah received an oracle concerning things not yet seen (περὶ τῶν μηδέπω βλεπομένων), is clearly an allusion back to v. 1 (οὐ βλεπομένων). Since Noah concludes the primeval heroes on the list, the allusion back to the introduction creates a summarizing effect, and thus helps to mark off the primeval section from the upcoming section on the patriarchs.

The second part of the verse is the more interesting. Noah is said to have condemned the world and become an heir of righteousness (κατέκρινεν τὸν κόσμον, καὶ τῆς κατὰ πίστιν δικαιοσύνης ἐγένετο κληρονόμος). The author of Hebrews refers to Noah's righteousness, and once again, this points backward to the quotation from Habakkuk in 10:38 and Abel in v. 4. But we must take note of what is not said in Hebrews.[75] The LXX translation of Gen 6:9 says "Noah was a righteous man (δίκαιος), being perfect (τέλειος) in his generation, Noah was pleasing (εὐηρέστησεν) to God." Neither Noah's being perfect, nor his being pleasing are mentioned in Hebrews, although Enoch was said to have pleased God. And our author found being "pleasing to God" important enough in Enoch's case that he took the time to elaborate upon it. Perhaps he is trying to avoid muddying the rhetorical catchword πίστει by avoiding the repetition of other words. Neither does he mention that Noah was perfect, although perfection is a

---

[72] Not until the entire resume is finished does the author again engage in exhortative commentary (12:1).

[73] The LXX text reads: καὶ εὐαρέστησεν Ἐνωχ τῷ θεῷ καὶ οὐχ ηὑρίσκετο ὅτι μετέθηκέ αὐτον ὁ θεός (Gen 5:8). Verse 5 of our text reads . . . καὶ οὐχ ηὑρίσκετο διότι μετέθηκεν αὐτὸν ὁ θεός.

[74] Usually the author does not want to replicate biblical language in a retelling; rather, he uses his own rhetorically astute syntactical constructions to narrate biblical events. Perhaps because the wording was too biblical in v. 5, he breaks his rhythm in v. 6 in order to claim what was said as his own.

[75] Attridge (*Hebrews*, 319 n. 169) notes this and attributes it to the author's striving for variety.

major theme in the epistle.[76] The conclusion of this pericope, 11:40, does mention perfection: "Apart from us they should not be made perfect." In this comment "us" refers to the Christian community addressed in Hebrews and "they" refers to the heroes who have just been eulogized. Apparently, in 11:7, the author consciously avoids making reference to Noah's perfection because perfection cannot be achieved apart from Christ. Thus, none of Israel's pre-Christian heroes can be said to be perfect in their own time.

That Noah is said to have "condemned the world" is probably dependent upon the widespread legend that Noah was commissioned to preach repentance.[77] In any case, the author concludes this section by saying that the world was condemned, and thereby destroyed, while Noah was designated an heir of righteousness. Noah is not simply said to be righteous, as was Abel, but an heir of righteousness. This implies that he has become a member of an elect people who are set apart from the rest of the world,[78] and that the world, κόσμος, both here and in v. 38, should be understood as referring to sinful humanity.[79] Although Noah is the only one who explicitly "condemns the world" in Hebrews, we identified widespread traditions about both Abel and Enoch that also describe them as condemning unrighteous humanity.

The author begins his hagiology at a point where Jewish tradition reckoned humanity was in its most depraved state, the ten generations preceding and including the generation of the flood. Abel, Enoch, and Noah stand apart from an otherwise all pervasive wickedness. Our primary principle of selection is already beginning to emerge. Each hero so far is *removed* from his generation. Abel is murdered, Enoch is taken up, and Noah is saved upon his ark while the world drowned. And each one, by his example, condemns his contemporaries. Now the author moves into a period when the heroes are not just distinguished from generic humanity, but from the would-be nation of Israel.

---

[76] See the study by David Peterson, *Hebrews and Perfection* (Cambridge: Cambridge University, 1982).

[77] *Sib. Or.* 1.125–36; *Sifre* 43; *Mek. Shirah* 5 (38b); *1 Clem.* 7.6; Clement of Alexandria *Strom.* 1.2.1; cited by Attridge (*Hebrews*, 319 n.182). However, although Noah is mentioned both in the list in Wisdom (10:4) and in Sirach (44:17–18), this tradition is not mentioned in either place.

[78] Cf. Sirach 44:17b and CD 3:1.

[79] Moffat, *Commentary*, 168; cf. 2 Pet 2:5.

C. *Pilgrim's Promise: Abraham and the Patriarchs*

1. Abraham

i) Part 1: A Wanderer and a Father

8By faith Abraham obeyed when he was called to go out to a place which he was about to receive for an inheritance, and he went out not knowing where he was going. 9By faith he sojourned in the land of promise as in a foreign land, dwelling in tents with Isaac and Jacob, who were joint heirs of the same promise. 10For he was awaiting the city which has the foundation of which God is the builder and maker. 11By faith Sarah herself received the power to produce offspring, though she was beyond the appropriate age, since she considered the one who had made the promise faithful. 12Therefore, from one individual, and him as good as dead, descendants were produced like the stars of heaven in a multitude and as innumerable as the sand at the seashore.

The popularity of Abraham is difficult to overestimate, so it is no surprise that he shows up on anybody's list. He is included in Wisdom 10 and Sirach 44–50, but their mention of him does not begin with God's calling him out from Chaldea and into the land of the promise, as here in Hebrews. The same is true of 1 Maccabees 2 and 4 Maccabees 16, both of which mention only the binding of Isaac. The historical résumé in Nehemiah 9 and Stephen's speech in Acts 7, on the other hand, begin with the migration of Abraham.[80]

In the text of Hebrews, the discussion of Abraham falls into three distinct sections: Abraham's migration to the nation of the promise (vv. 8–12), a commentary on the true homeland (vv. 13–16), and the offering of Isaac (vv. 20–21). The author chooses to begin where the Genesis story itself does, with the hero leaving his home for an undisclosed destination. Similar to the case of Abel, Enoch, and Noah, Abraham is removed from the people to which he would naturally belong. Because the story of Abraham's migration immediately follows the Tower of Babel story in Genesis, extra-biblical tradition understood Abraham to have been present at Babel (Babel being the climax of the sinful humanity epoch of history). Thus Wis 10:5 reads,

Wisdom also, when the nations in wicked agreement had been confounded, recognized the righteous man and preserved him blameless before God, . . .

In the Covenant of Damascus list (2:16–3:4), where the concern is very much to distinguish a righteous remnant over and against sinful Israel (as opposed

---

[80] See fig. 2, p. 53 for a comparison of Abraham traditions on hero lists.

to righteous Israel against idolatrous nations as in Wisdom 10) Abraham is separated from virtually all of humanity that has come before:

> For many wandered off for these matters; brave heroes yielded on account of them, from ancient times until now. For having walked in the stubbornness of their hearts the Watchers of the heavens fell; on account of it they were caught, for they did not follow the precepts of God. And their sons, whose height was like that of cedars and whose bodies were like mountains, fell. All flesh which there was in the dry earth decayed and became as if it had never been, for having realized their desires and failing to keep their creator's precepts, until his wrath flared up against them. Through it, the sons of Noah and their families strayed, through it they were cut off. *Abraham did not walk in it, and was counted as a friend for keeping God's precepts and not following the desire of his spirit.* And he passed (them) on to Isaac and to Jacob, and they kept (them) and were written up as friends of God and as members of the covenant for ever.[81]

In this text Abraham appears as the first true hero; preceded only by anti-heroes, the Watchers and the Giants. One other example, from *Pirqe Abot* 5:3, will illustrate how common this theme is:

> Ten generations were there from Noah to Abraham, to show how great was His longsuffering; for all the generations were provoking Him, till Abraham our father came and received the reward of all.

None of these texts recite the biblical story of Abraham's migration. They simply tell of Abraham's righteous distinction from the rest of humanity.

In contrast, the author of Hebrews is compelled to recount the migration. While he surely knew the widespread tradition of Abraham as the favored righteous one, he wishes to stress the experience of migration explicitly. Perhaps he does so because the call of Abraham highlights the separation and even alienation that accompanied Abraham's being chosen by God. Although God promises Abraham much, the fact that he is about to be separated from home is evident in God's initial words in Gen 12:1: "Go from your country (τῆς γῆς σου) and your kindred (τῆς συγγενείς σου) and your father's house (τοῦ οἴκου τοῦ πατρός σου), to a land that I will show you." As the author of Hebrews says, Abraham went "not knowing where he

---

[81] Translation from Florentino García Martínez, *The Dead Sea Scrolls Translated* (Leiden: E. J. Brill, 1994) 34. Cf. the outline of this text on p. 47–48. The text goes on to say, "Jacob's sons strayed because of them and were punished in accordance with their mistakes." From the point of view of the author of the Covenant of Damascus, most of Israel's history is just as reprehensible as the rest of humankind's.

was going," since God did not tell him the destination until Abraham had already arrived. Furthermore, although God says he will give him the land (as Hebrews says in 11:8: εἰς κληρονομίαν) Abraham finds other people living there, so he ends up living in the promised land as a resident alien (Heb 11:9: παρῴκησεν εἰς γῆν τῆς ἐπαγγελίας).

Although Abraham's obedience when called by God can indeed serve as a good example of Abraham's faith, and may be based on a traditional interpretation,[82] obedience *per se* does not play a very big role among the other heroes listed.[83] Furthermore, nowhere in his discussion of Abraham as an example of faith does the author cite the popular proof text of Gen 15:6, "And [Abraham] believed the Lord; and he reckoned it to him as righteousness."[84] Since Abraham is one of the few genuine scriptural examples of faith on the author's list, the fact that the author does not exploit the full potential of his own example should make us suspicious that he is not as interested in Abraham's faith as it at first seems.

Rather, the author chooses to emphasize Abraham's special chosenness[85] (represented by the call) and his subsequent isolation from home, nation, and—as we will see in the following verses—world. The word Hebrews uses to describe the land of the promise, "a foreign land" (γῆν ... ἀλλοτρίαν), while not an inaccurate description of the biblical account, emphasizes Abraham's alien status in the land[86] in a way that stands quite apart from contemporary Jewish exegesis. To begin with, the two biblical résumés which mention the call of Abraham, Nehemiah 9 and Psalm 105, never even allude to Abraham's alien status in the land. Indeed, Jewish exegetical traditions avoid or ignore the fact that Abraham is not truly an Israelite.[87] Because Abraham is fundamentally seen as the *father* of the nation, the biblical

---

82 Cf. Philo, *Migr. Abr.* 43; *Abr.* 60ff.

83 The word ὑπακούω is not used of any other hero on the list.

84 Cf. Rom 4; Gal 3:6–9; Philo, too (*Migr. Abr.* 43), cites this text precisely in his discussion of Abraham's obedience to God concerning his migration, even though its Genesis context is the covenant ceremony and not the migration. The omission of this proof text is one of the primary reasons that Windisch thinks the author must be dependent upon a source.

85 Together with Isaac and Jacob, who are the fellow heirs of the promise (συγκληρονόμων τῆς ἐπαγγελίας) in v. 9.

86 The LXX says that Abraham lived in the land as a sojourner, τὴν γῆν ἥν παροικεῖς (Gen 17:8), but never uses the word ἀλλοτρίαν to refer to the promised land.

87 See the survey of early Jewish traditions about Abraham in Jeffery Siker, *Disinheriting the Jews: Abraham in Early Christian Controversy* (Louisville, KY: Westminster/John Knox, 1991) 17–27, 202, n. 16; and Geza Vermes, *Scripture and Tradition in Judaism* (Leiden: E. J. Brill, 1973) 67–126.

description of Abraham's resident alien status is understandably not a focal point. When exegetes narrate the call of Abraham, they take pains to make Abraham's transition smoother than it is in the biblical account.[88] Furthermore, they often portray him as the quintessential Jew. In *Jubilees* (12:25–29), for example, not only is Abraham an observant Jew, but he magically learns Hebrew before he arrives in Canaan. For Josephus,[89] Abraham is a Hebrew because of his biblical ancestry, no matter where he lived. The only reason he left Chaldea and ended up in Canaan is because the Chaldeans became hostile to his high-minded ideas, while Canaan was more hospitable.

In contrast to his exegetical predecessors, the author of Hebrews stresses Abraham's lack of connection to Israel—even though it is the land of the promise—and this is what is unique about his recounting the episode of Abraham's migration. While some Jewish exegetes discuss Abraham's alienation from his country of origin, Abraham is always portrayed as 'at home' when he arrives in Canaan. In the words of Philo:

> Under the force of an oracle which bade him leave his country and kinsfolk and seek a new home, thinking that quickness in executing the command was as good as full accomplishment, he hastened eagerly to obey, not as though he were leaving home for a strange land but rather as returning from amid strangers to his home. (*Abr.* 62)

The lack of connection in Hebrews to either where he came from or where he ends up, indicates Abraham's isolation from *any people* and *any land*. He stands apart from all his contemporaries, and this aspect of Abraham's life is consistent with what we saw earlier among the primeval figures.

The switch to the subject of Sarah in v. 11, however, is unusual, and has been problematic for commentators. The Greek text as we now have it reads: πίστει καὶ αὐτὴ Σάρρα στεῖρα δύναμιν εἰς καταβολὴν σπέρματος ἔλαβεν. The use of σπέρματος with regard to a woman is somewhat surprising.[90] Many have emended the text so that Abraham functions as the subject.[91]

---

[88] Philo, in the *Migration of Abraham* and *On Abraham*, is somewhat exceptional, because he interprets Abraham's migration metaphorically to represent the evolution of the soul's knowledge from the material to the immaterial. Thus, he gives some attention to Abraham's wandering. Still, Philo considers Abraham the father of the nation and thinks of Israel as his true homeland.

[89] *Ant.* 1.7.2 §148–60

[90] As the language of biology would have it, many argue, a woman cannot be said to have received the δύναμιν εἰς καταβολήν σπέρματος; see Attridge (*Hebrews*, 325) for a list of examples of the common use of the phrase.

[91] Because of the awkwardness of the phrase, some have seen the reference to Sarah as a gloss; e.g., Windisch (*Hebräerbrief*, 101). But since the phrase καὶ αυτὴ Σάρρα is well-

While this description of Sarah's twilight fertility is, to be sure, unusual, it is not impossible to conceive of our author using this expression. In 11:18, where the author quotes Gen 21:12, ἐκ Ἰσαὰκ κληθήσεταί σοι σπέρμα, σπέρμα means descendants in general. Since this part of the list is especially concerned with the heirs to the promise, I strongly suspect that the emphasis lies with creating a line of descent, and not with biology.[92]

Many commentators cannot understand how the author could have considered Sarah an example of faith, because she laughed when she was given the news of Isaac.[93] But since it is my contention that none of the examples are good examples of faith, Sarah in no way stands out as an exception. Furthermore, Abraham does not display unshakable faith concerning the upcoming conception of Isaac anymore than Sarah (Gen 17:17). Sarah also serves to balance the example of Rahab in v. 31. Thereby the author mentions a woman's role once in the "Abraham and the Patriarchs" section and once in the "Moses and the Israelites" section.[94]

No particulars about Sarah's role in the Genesis story are retold here. Verse 11 simply says that Sarah considered God trustworthy concerning his

---

attested, the favored solution lately has been to read the reference to Sarah as a simple dative, αὐτεῖ Σάρραι; e.g. Michel (*Der Brief*, 262) and Attridge (*Hebrews*, 321, 325). This solution also rejects στεῖρα as secondary against the opinions of Metzger (*TCGNT*, 672f) and Nestle Aland. More recently Cosby (*Rhetorical Composition*, 43) has argued that scholars should be cognizant of the rhetorical value of Σάρρα στεῖρα, which, he cleverly points out, is an instance of paronomasia similar in English to "Sterile Cheryl."

[92] I am primarily persuaded by the argument of Sowers (*Hermeneutics of Philo and Hebrews*, 134–5) which seems to be unknown to commentators. He quotes from a passage in Philo where Sarah, understood allegorically as sophia, brings the seeds of correct instruction to Abraham: "For in the bodily marriage the male sows the seed and the female receives it; on the other had in the matings within the soul, though virtue seemingly ranks as wife (ἡ μὲν ἀρετὴ τάξιν γύναικός), her natural function is to sow (σπείρειν) good counsels and excellent words and to inculcate tenets truly profitable to life, while thought, though held to take the place of the husband, receives the holy and divine sowings." (*Abr.* 100). Thus, sometimes a woman can be said to produce seed.

[93] E.g., J. R. Harris, "The mention of Sarah with Abraham is an astonishment to the expositor," quoted in F.F. Bruce (*The Epistle to the Hebrews* [New International Commentary on the NT; Grand Rapids: Eerdmans, 1990] 294). C.f. Montefiore (*Commentary*, 194) who accepts Sarah as the subject but says, "according to Gen xviii,12, Sarah laughed at the promise of a child, just as Abraham had earlier laughed at the same prospect (Gen xvii.17). Possibly our author understood Sarah's mood to have changed from incredulity to faith; but more probably he had forgotten these two biblical incidents when he wrote this verse."

[94] See my outline in Appendix A. Several commentators take note of the parallelism that occurs between the discussion of Abraham and that of Moses, see Vanhoye (*La structure litteraire*, 189–91).

promise. The fact that Sarah is the subject implies that the promise refers to the birth of Isaac. But v. 12 refers to God's promise to make Abraham a great nation, with a plethora of descendants.[95] The mention of this greater promise is not without irony. From the point of view of Hebrews, what was important about the promise of Isaac was not merely that Isaac would be born, but that a whole nation would be born. And this is in fact what the author of Hebrews states in v. 12, "from one man . . . were born descendants as many as the stars of heaven . . . ." Abraham, of course, never lives to see the fulfillment of this promise.

That Abraham is said to be "as good as dead"[96] at the time of the birth of Isaac, places him at the same relative point of life as at least two of the previous heroes: Abel and Enoch. We may include Noah if we consider the flood a near-death experience for Noah. Death and near-death experiences seem to be a recurring characteristic applied to the heroes so far,[97] and, as we shall see, continues to describe the upcoming heroes.

If there is any doubt about whether or not our author thinks the promises to Abraham were fulfilled, he tells us in v. 13, "these all died according to faith, not having received what was promised, ..." Therefore, vv. 11–12 should not be understood as the author's reckoning of Abraham's well-deserved blessings; on the contrary, they emphasize how little Abraham actually received from God during his life. Abraham himself does not receive the fulfillment of what God promised: the land and many descendants. These promises pertain to the birth of the nation Israel. Since our author is not interested in portraying the patriarch in his usual role as father of the nation, Abraham, like the earlier figures on the list, remains unconnected to the national promises.

ii) The Heavenly Homeland, a Commentary

13All these people died according to faith, not having received the promises, but saw and greeted them from afar, and having confessed that they were strangers and exiles on the earth. 14For those who say such things make it clear that they

---

95 This promise is already made, in Gen 12:2, at the time of Abraham's call to relocate (although not with all the hyperbolic language of descendants as numerous as the stars). Indeed, it is reiterated throughout the Genesis story.

96 The author's description of the birth of Isaac closely resembles Paul's description of the same event in Rom 4:19; both use the expression "as good as dead," νενεκρωμένου, which means it was probably traditional (Attridge, *Hebrews*, 326).

97 This has been observed by James Swetnam, *Jesus and Isaac: A Study of the Epistle to the Hebrews in the Light of the Aqedah* (Rome: Biblical Institute, 1981) 89.

are seeking a homeland. [15]*And if they had in mind that from which they departed, they would have had occasion to return.* [16]*But as it is they desire something better, that is a heavenly place. Therefore God is not ashamed to be called their God, for he has prepared a city for them.*

The extended commentary of vv. 13–16 on Abraham's experience as an alien and pilgrim[98] indicate how important this is for the author and his audience. First, as I stated above, the heroes are seen to have died without having their promises fulfilled. Most scholars understand the "all these" (οὗτοι πάντες) of v. 13 to refer only to the patriarchs on the grounds that Enoch in fact did not die and the "strangers and exiles" theme refers only to Abraham and company.[99] But "all these" seems too much like a summary phrase to cover only figures in vv. 8–12. The other patriarchs, Isaac, Jacob, and Joseph have not yet appeared as heroes themselves; they are only referred to in passing. The only true subjects of vv. 8–12 are Abraham and Sarah. Thus, it is more likely that the author is commenting generally on all the heroes thus far mentioned.

Whether or not Enoch actually died is not the author's concern. He simply expired in his earthly existence before any of God's promises for his people could be fulfilled. While v. 13 follows on the heels of vv. 8–12, where the promises refer to land and nationhood and these are traditionally associated with the patriarchs, Abel, Enoch, and Noah are part of the same historical trajectory as Abraham.[100] As we discussed earlier, ἐπαγγελία carries overlapping meanings and refers to the promise of ultimate salvation in addition to the national promises. And none of the heroes can be said to have achieved that promise (indeed—that is the point of v. 39!).[101]

---

[98] On the theme of pilgrimage in Hebrews, see W G. Johnson, ("The Pilgrimage Motif in the Book of Hebrews, " *JBL* 97 [1978] 239–51) who critiques and systematizes the work of previous scholars. The theme of the "wandering people of God" developed by Käsemann (*The Wandering People of God: An Investigation of the Letter to the Hebrews* [Minneapolis: Augsburg, 1984]) is prominent in Hebrews. I use the term 'pilgrim' loosely, as many since Käsemann have, to highlight the depiction of alienation in Hebrews 11.

[99] E.g., Attridge, *Hebrews*, 329; Bruce, *Epistle*, 298.

[100] Of course it is also true that the primeval heroes did not receive the national promises either. That the author would refer to them in his statement that "all these died without receiving the promises" should not surprise us. In addition, the description applies to the later heroes on the list. The phase "greeting from afar" (v. 13) already looks ahead to Moses' experience with Canaan.

[101] Cf. Philo (*Mgr. Abr.* 176–189) where Abraham's migration from Babylonia to Haran represents the move from pantheism—since the Babylonians are astronomers their knowledge of what drives the world remains with material bodies—to monotheism, which

Thus, the author has in mind more than the immediate family of the patriarchs, most of whom have yet to be discussed anyway (see vv. 20–22). I suspect that the reason the author chooses to make a general comment here is because Abraham best exemplifies what the author wants to convey: separation and marginalization. With Abraham the Genesis story itself provides the scriptural language of alienation. The heroes are said to have confessed (ὁμολογήσαντες) that they were strangers (ξένοι) and exiles (παρεπίδημοι), the tone of which is an intensification of the expression in Genesis.[102] They declare themselves unrelated to the world in which they live. More importantly, they are alienated from the πατρία from which they come as well as the land of the divine promise. As we now know, being "strangers and exiles" applies to the earlier heroes, too. Abel, Enoch, and Noah were alienated from their contemporaries by their righteousness. Therefore, the author felt this was an appropriate point in his epitome to comment more extensively on the very theme that strings together the heroes on the list.

The confession that they are strangers implies that their homeland must be elsewhere. The contra-factual of v. 15 proves that their yearning for a πατρία is not a nostalgic longing for their old home, but rather for a better one, the heavenly one, as is stated in v. 16.[103] They could have gone back but they never did. By constructing this particular hero list, the author creates a historical trajectory of individuals who are isolated from the rest of society by divine election. The heroes even die in a state of isolation. They never retreated from it. The audience is part of this trajectory by implication (vv.39–40). Christians, too, must therefore abide.

iii) Part 2: The Offering of Isaac

17By faith Abraham, when tested, offered Isaac; he who received the promise offered up his only-begotten, 18to whom it was said "through Isaac your

---

recognizes an invisible pilot who guides the celestial bodies.

102 In Gen 23:4, Abraham says he is a πάροικος and παρεπίδημος. Cf. Gen 47:4,9 and Ps 39:13. The author of Hebrews has substituted the stronger ξένοι for πάροικος. Cf. Eph 2:19, ξένοι καὶ πάροικοι; and 1 Pet 2:11 which uses both septuagintal terms.

103 See Attridge (*Hebrews*, 330–32) for discussion of the heavenly homeland and a list of references to the Greek idea of the soul's true home being in heaven both in pagan and Hellenistic Jewish sources (e.g., Philo, *Conf. Ling.*, 76–77). Cf. George W. Buchanan (*To the Hebrews: Translation, Comment, and Conclusions* [AB 36; Garden City, NY: Doubleday, 1972] 191–94) who stands alone in arguing that the ultimate πατρία of Hebrews is in fact the earthly Israel.

descendants shall be named." *¹⁹He reasoned that God had the power even to raise from the dead; for this reason, he received him back in a figurative sense.*

As we noted earlier, the theme of Abraham offering up Isaac is popular on the other lists.[104] Indeed, those texts also use the language of testing (which comes from Gen 22:1 itself) for Abraham's situation and the language of "faithfulness" to describe his response.[105] Although patristic commentators will make much of this story as a type for Jesus,[106] such an interpretation was not yet formed in the mind of any NT writer,[107] including the author of Hebrews. The term μονογενῆ "only-begotten" is substituted for the LXX word ἀγαπητόν (Gen 22:2), but since there is a tradition for the use of this term,[108] μονογενῆ should not be interpreted christologically.[109]

The pain of a father sacrificing his own son is not what has captured the imagination of our author.[110] What is important about Isaac is that he must be able to deliver progeny; God promised that he would, as the author reminds us when he quotes Gen 21:12. The test that Abraham faces is to believe God even when asked to perform an act that will deliberately flout the divine promise. But the author of Hebrews does not portray Abraham as irredeemably gullible where God is concerned. Abraham figures out God's trick. He reasons that there must be such a thing as resurrection from the dead. This is one of the few places in Hebrews 11 where a personal belief is literally ascribed to the hero. As the author says in v. 19, λογισάμενος ὅτι καὶ ἐκ νεκρῶν ἐγείρειν δυνατὸς ὁ θεός ὅθεν αὐτὸν καὶ ἐν παραβολῇ ἐκομίσατο. Because of Abraham's belief in resurrection, God grants Isaac back to him.[111] Thus, another hero undergoes a near-death experience.

The phrase ἐν παραβολῇ should not be over-interpreted. Since the author nowhere else in the pericope seems interested in typological exegesis, the phrase should not be understood symbolically to refer to the

---

[104] See fig. 2, p. 53.

[105] Sir 44:20; 1 Macc 2:52; 4 Macc 16:20; see also the miniature retelling in James 5.

[106] Among the earliest writers to construe the story this way is *Barn.* 7:3.

[107] Although some have argued that Paul alludes to Gen 22:16 in Rom 8:32, the typological connection between Isaac and Jesus remains an improbable suggestion. See Joseph Fitzmyer, *Romans* (AB; New York: Doubleday, 1993) 531–32.

[108] Aquila's translation as well as Josephus (*Ant.* 1.13.1 §222) use it.

[109] Attridge, *Hebrews*, 334.

[110] As, for example, in Wis 10:5: "[Wisdom] . . . kept him strong in the face of compassion for his child."

[111] When Abraham is said to "receive him back," the verb used is ἐκομίσατο, which as we mentioned earlier, is the verb especially used to refer to the reception of the ultimate promise of salvation.

resurrection of Jesus[112] or even necessarily to refer to the resurrection of the believer.[113] It simply means that Abraham's experience of receiving back Isaac is similar to resurrection because given the command of God, Isaac was "as good as dead."[114] What is stressed is that from one who was almost never born, and who after being born was almost killed, the descendants of Abraham, the descendants of God's faithful ones, are born.

James Swetnam argues that σπέρμα should be interpreted spiritually in Hebrews.[115] That is, the author does not refer to Abraham's physical descendants by this word, but spiritual descendants who have demonstrated faith. While Swetnam's argument is too dependent upon Pauline arguments about the true descendants of Abraham, the author of Hebrews is no doubt concerned to construct a genealogy of those who have been distinguished by divine election. But he perceives a precariousness in this genealogical trajectory through history that makes every step forward rest upon a tiny thread that barely connects it to what came before. This is very different from the glorious and bigger-than-life role in history that Abraham has in Sirach 44:19–21, where he is not just the stalwart patriarch of Israel but the founder of a multitude of nations (Gen 17:4). For the author of Hebrews, Abraham has a delicate and exclusive role in history.

2. The Patriarchs

20By faith Isaac blessed Jacob and Esau, even concerning what was to come.
21By faith Jacob, when dying, blessed each of the sons of Joseph and "bowed down on the tip of his staff."[116] 22By faith Joseph, at the end of his life, made mention of the exodus of the Israelites and gave instructions regarding his bones.

The theme of the precariousness of history is brought out clearly in this brief section on Abraham's successors. The mention of each hero highlights

---

[112] As in BAGD, 612.

[113] As Attridge, *Hebrews*, 335. But cf. Swetnam (*Jesus and Isaac,* 128) who says, "But looking back on the sacrifice from the vantage point of Christ, the author of Hebrews sees that Abraham's offering of Isaac in sacrifice and his receiving him back was a mysterious foreshadowing of the sacrificial death and resurrection of Jesus." See also his discussion in 122–23.

[114] Montefiore, *Commentary,* 199.

[115] Swetnam, *Jesus and Isaac,* 90–127.

[116] The meaning of this quotation from the LXX is discussed by Attridge (*Hebrews,* 336) who thinks it has no special symbolic value in Hebrews but serves to illustrate that Jacob was old and frail and that perhaps the author is accentuating Jacob's faith by quoting a verse that portrays him as worshipping God (cf. Braun, *Die Hebräer,* 374).

a deathbed scene, two of which describe a situation that almost turned out differently. In the author's mention of Isaac he finds the story from Gen 27:27–40 worthy of his attention.[117] The phrase "what was to come," (περὶ μελλόντων) refers to the fact that Isaac's blessings predict the future for each of his sons. This is certainly in harmony with the author's understanding of faith as a future hope. But one should not overlook the fact that the author mentions Isaac's blessing *both* Jacob and Esau. The inclusion of Esau evokes the whole story of Isaac's being duped by Jacob. What kind of faith is this? By Isaac's faith—literally, *blind* faith—he unwittingly blesses the wrong son, the younger son.

The mention of Esau also breaks up the more conventional successionist view of Israelite history.[118] God's blessing usually passes from Abraham to Isaac and from Isaac to Jacob and from Jacob to the twelve patriarchs (cf. Acts 7:8). Even though Esau is not singled out as a character of faith, the author's inclusion of the blessing of Esau disturbs the sequence. In Sirach history moves from the beginnings of humankind, to the establishment of nations, to the founding of Israel, from which point the teleological development of Israel's history is that author's sole concern.[119] The author of Hebrews, on the other hand, does not have in mind either the etiology of Israel as a nation or her teleological direction.

Verse 21 evokes a similar scene and consequently has a similar effect.[120] In Genesis Jacob blesses his younger grandson, Ephraim, rather than the older one, Manasseh (Gen 48:8–22). Although this time it is not done naively, for Jacob explains to Joseph that he is blessing the younger one because he will be the greater in the future. Since the expected course of history is for the older son to receive the inheritance, the history of these

---

[117] It seems Isaac often had little hermeneutical appeal outside of his participation in the Aqedah. He is mentioned in Sirach only because he belongs to Abraham (44:22) and he is completely left out of Wisdom 10. See also 4 Macc 16:20 and 18:11.

[118] Mack (*Wisdom and Hebrew Epic*, 45) points out that in Sirach, the sequence of the heroes becomes succession when "certain notions of continuity are perceived." This is very important in those passages that move from father to son. See Sirach 44:22–3.

[119] Mack, *Wisdom and Hebrew Epic*, 42–3.

[120] See Cosby (*Rhetorical Composition*, 22) who demonstrates that the cadence of these two verses is so similar that it significantly enhances the similarity of content.

heroes is unique.[121] This deviation in the natural course of history implies God's intervention.[122]

Once again the interest in the future and the hero's ability to predict the future operate in the author's selection of Jacob and the mention of this particular deed. His blessing indicates a prediction of the greatness of Ephraim. The same is true of Joseph in v. 22. At the end of the book of Genesis, Joseph predicts the exodus and requests that his bones be removed from Egypt at that time. The theme of Joseph's bones was extraordinarily popular in post-biblical interpretive traditions.[123]

The fact that Isaac, Jacob, and Joseph are depicted on their deathbeds and that they all make predictions was no doubt important in the author's decision to include them here. These characteristics distinguish them as a subset on the author's list,[124] but these heroes also fit in with the death/near-death circumstances which we have already determined characterizes most of the heroes.

So far I have argued that the theme of separation or marginalization is the key to the list. That theme is less explicit in this section, but it is subtly evoked by this particular grouping of heroes. The patriarchs participate in a particular genealogy, having been chosen by a previous hero, and, by extension, God. Isaac, who himself barely makes it as Abraham's heir, blesses Jacob, who never should have been blessed at all. He in turn blesses Ephraim and Manasseh in a most unconventional way. The author does not mention Jacob's blessing of the 12 patriarchs, as one might expect, because unlike other Hellenistic Jewish authors, he is not interested in the founding of Israel as a nation. He is interested in the selection of elites within Israel. The history of this select group can be distinguished from Israel's history in general by the super-normal way history progresses for them. Younger sons

---

[121] The author of Hebrews may be disturbed by the theme in Israelite history of the younger son usurping the rights of the older one. See 12:23 where he calls his fellow Christians "the assembly of the first born."

[122] Swetnam (*Jesus and Isaac*, 95) takes this as further evidence that 'seed' should be interpreted spiritually. He sees the use of the patriarchal blessings of unexpected sons as signs of faith in trusting God to establish a genealogy based on faith, not on biological inheritance.

[123] J. Kugel, *In Potiphar's House: The Interpretive Life of Biblical Texts* (San Francisco: Harper, 1990) 125–56. See also chapter one, pp. 54–55.

[124] Cf. Mack (*Wisdom and Hebrew Epic*, 42), who describes what he calls "serialization" in Sirach. He observes that certain groups of figures have mini-themes that link them together as subsets within the larger structure.

rise above older ones, and those who have had everything against them, such as Isaac, turn out to be the heir.

That these biblical characters, as seen by our author, are not part of the trajectory that founds the nation of Israel will be further proved later by the fact that just when Israel's history becomes truly national, i.e., with the conquest of the land, the establishment of the monarchy, the building of the temple, etc., our author loses interest. The real body of our text ends with Rahab. Like the epitome from Covenant of Damascus discussed earlier, this version of history reflects the sectarianism of the writer. Abraham, Isaac, and Jacob are not the founding fathers of Israel, they are the ancestors of an elite group. They are distinct from Israel, rather than representative of Israel. It is in this sense that they are separate from others. The author has chosen scenes that gingerly connect them one to another without connecting them to the people Israel. The heroes are linked to one another without being linked to the nation.

D. Exodus and Entropy

1. Moses

i) Part 1: An Orphan and a Defector &
ii) The Disgrace of Christ, a Commentary

> *23By faith, Moses, when he was born, was hidden for three months by his parents because they saw that the child was beautiful, and they were not afraid of the king's decree. 24By faith, Moses, when he grew up, refused to be called a son of Pharaoh's daughter; 25he chose to suffer with the people of God rather than have the fleeting pleasure of sin, 26since he considered the reproach of Christ greater wealth than the treasures of Egypt; for he looked off to his reward.*

The section on Moses begins with the early life of Moses. Verse 23 does not stray far from the LXX version of Exod 2:2,[125] even though there was no shortage of popular legendary material about the infant Moses.[126] The significance of the author's mention of Moses' infancy has two aspects. First, most commentators perceive an awkwardness in the verse, because it is not

---

[125] The MT credits only Moses' mother with hiding the child but the LXX mentions both parents. The LXX text of Exod 2:2: ἰδόντες δὲ αὐτὸ ἀστεῖον ἐσκέπασαν αὐτὸ μῆνας τρεῖς; Heb 11:23 describes the event as follows: πίστει Μωϋσῆς γεννηθεὶς ἐκρύβη τρίμηνον ὑπὸ τῶν πατέρων αὐτοῦ, διότι εἶδον ἀστεῖον τὸ παιδίον...; Hebrews goes on to say that the parents were not afraid of the decree of the king, and this is an embellishment of the LXX.

[126] Cf. Josephus, *Ant.* 2.9.4ff §218ff and Philo, *Vit. Mos.* 1.

the faith of Moses that causes him to be hidden, but rather that of his parents.[127] Commentators almost always point this out and explain that the author was merely keeping to the rhythm of the basic structure; he must therefore mention the name of the hero immediately after πίστει. Verse 30 presents a similar problem, "By faith the walls of Jericho fell . . . ." Since walls are not capable of having faith, the faith of the people or perhaps Joshua are the ones to whom the reader should credit the faith. This problem of whom to ascribe the faith to in any given instance is easily soluble if the concept of faith is depersonalized. The πίστις that each exemplar exemplifies is not necessarily demonstrated by something they do, or think, as vv. 23 and 30 show, but by something God does for/with/to them. πίστις is something which the heroes participate in. The anaphoric πίστει thus represents a salvation-historical principle more than a virtue cultivated by individuals.

Second, with the exception of Stephen's speech in Acts 7, Moses' early life does not play a role in Jewish hero lists or historical résumés. Rather, because Moses single-handedly leads the exodus, Jewish texts tend to emphasize Moses as the leader *par excellence* of the Israelite people. In all the biblical summaries, and in Wis 10:15–21 and Sir 45:1–5, Moses' deeds pertain exclusively to the exodus event, e.g., doing signs before Pharaoh, splitting the sea, and giving the commandment. Acts 7 treats Moses' early life in detail but its emphasis is very different from Hebrews. The story of Moses' early life in Stephen's speech helps knit together the stories of Joseph and Moses:

> But as the time of the promise drew near, which God had granted to Abraham, the people grew and multiplied in Egypt till there arose over Egypt another king who had not known Joseph. He dealt craftily with our race and forced our fathers to expose their infants, that they might not be kept alive. At this time Moses was born, and was beautiful before God. (Acts 7:17–20a)

Moses' birth as told in Acts 7 is set firmly within the history of Israel. In fact, no particular heroism on the part of Moses' parents is indicated; everyone in Israel was hiding their children. By contrast, Hebrews 11 highlights the event as unique, or at least unconnected to any events in the history of Israel.[128] In v. 25 Moses chooses to suffer with "the people of God" (τῷ λαῷ τοῦ θεοῦ). In the comparable LXX passage, Exod 2:11, Moses becomes part of the "children of Israel" (τοὺς υἱοὺς Ισραηλ).

---

[127] E.g., Moffat, *Commentary*, 179; Attridge, *Hebrews*, 339; Bruce, *Epistle*, 309.

[128] The only time the name Israel is mentioned in the catalog is in v. 22.

Moses is singled out in Hebrews because he consciously chooses to withdraw from his community. In v. 24 he refuses to remain a member of the royal Egyptian family and gives up all that that may have afforded him[129] to suffer with the people of God.[130] Like Abraham, Moses leaves his nation of origin, only neither hero does so in order to become part of Israel. Verse 26 is a very brief commentary inserted into otherwise traditional material, functioning like vv. 13–16 in the section on Abraham. In both cases the author delves into the motivations of the heroes. In vv. 13–16 the heroes confess (ὁμολογήσαντες) that they are strangers and exiles, and Moses considers (ἡγησάμενος) the reproach of Christ a greater gain than the treasures of Egypt. For both heroes the author describes a situation of emotional pain. Yet, he lets his listeners know that there are still rewards that await these heroes, even if they did not experience them in their own lifetime.

There are various understandings of the "reproach of Christ" (ὀνειδισμὸν τοῦ Χριστοῦ),[131] but all that we need note here is that even though Moses is now one of the people of God, he remains in an infelicitous state. Similarly, Abraham, after migrating to Canaan, had to live there as a resident alien; he had not arrived at his true home to live a life of peace and contentment. Moreover, there is no compelling reason to understand v. 26 as a case of typological exegesis, in which Moses' life prefigures Jesus'.[132] At best Moses'

---

[129] Cf. Josephus, *Ant.* 2.10.1–2 §238–53 and Philo, *Vit. Mos.* 1.32, whose accounts elaborate on what exactly Moses was giving up.

[130] Because Moses is said to choose suffering, Moses' faithful role is sometimes seen to be that of a martyr, and that the role of the martyr is what is being advocated for the community. This is most fully developed by Mary Rose D'Angelo, (*Moses in the Letter to the Hebrews* [SBLDS 42; Missoula: Scholars, 1979] 27ff). Her judgment is based only on a study of the figure of Moses and not of the whole list of characters. She notes that the very language of v. 25, especially the words πρόσκαιρον and ἀπόλαυσιν, are reminiscent of the martyrological language used of other biblical figures, notably Joseph, when he forgoes the "fleeting pleasure" of Mrs. Potiphar and must suffer for it. While the language regarding Moses' actions may in fact resemble what is said of Joseph elsewhere, the point is that what is mentioned about Joseph here in Hebrews is the request about his bones. If the author was emphasizing the role of the martyr in general, he would have chosen those aspects of Joseph's life that traditionally represented his suffering.

[131] See Attridge (*Hebrews*, 341–2) for a systematic analysis of the differing opinions. Some scholars (e.g., Westcott, *Epistle*, 374) have argued that χριστός should be understood generically as the 'annointed one,' so that the ὀνειδισμὸν τοῦ Χριστοῦ means simply to suffer with the people of God, but the clause that follows "for he looked off to his reward" implies a directed future vision. Furthermore, there is no evidence in the rest of Hebrews for the generic use of the word χριστός.

[132] As Montefiore, *Commentary*, 203.

situation is analogous to the life of Christ—or, for that matter, any suffering Christian—not typological.[133] This verse does, however, imply that Moses has prophetic power to see into the future.[134] We observed that other heroes, namely Isaac, Jacob, and Joseph were explicitly said to be able to anticipate the future.

iii) Part 2: Departure from Egypt and the Passover

> [27]*By faith, not being afraid of the king's anger, he left Egypt. For he endured as one who sees the unseen.* [28]*By faith he performed the Passover sacrifice and the pouring of the blood, so that the destroyer of the first born would not strike them.*

Scholars debate whether v. 27 refers to Moses' departure for Midian (Exod 2:11–15)[135] or his leading the people at the time of the exodus.[136] If the verse refers to the departure for Midian the difficulty lies in the phrase "not being afraid of the king's anger," because Exod 2:14 explicitly states that Moses left because he was afraid. If, on the other hand, the verse refers to the exodus, the problem lies with chronology. The exodus of the people happens *after* the Passover sacrifice (v. 28), and up until now the author has not deviated from following biblical chronology. Those who argue in favor of Midian point out that there is already a tradition of minimizing and even contradicting Moses' fear, which our author inherits.[137] Those who argue for the exodus claim that such a deviation in chronology is not a problem because the author will deviate from biblical chronology just a few verses ahead.[138]

---

[133] Interestingly, Chrysostom (quoted in Moffat [*Commentary*, 181]) understood vv. 25–6 to mean that Moses suffered abuse from his own so-called people of God. In Exod 2:11–15, Moses is reprimanded by the Hebrew who had seen him kill the Egyptian when Moses tries to prevent him from fighting. This incident leads to his flight to Midian, which is in fact referred to in the next verse in Hebrews. Thus, just as Christ was tormented by his own people, so was Moses. Indeed, the portrait of Moses being tormented by the wilderness generation is mentioned earlier in Hebrews (3:16–17).

[134] Traditions about Moses as a visionary may also lie behind Hebrews understanding of Moses in this verse; see D'Angelo, *Moses in Hebrews*, 95–140.

[135] Moffat, *Commentary*, 187; Braun, *Die Hebräer*, 382; Bruce, *Epistle*, 312–3; Attridge, *Hebrews*, 342.

[136] Westcott, *Epistle*; Héring, *Epistle*, 105; Montefiore, *Commentary*, 204.

[137] Josephus, *Ant.* 2.11.1 §254–5; Philo, *Leg. All.* 3.14; Artapanus in Eusebius, *Praep. Ev.* 9.27.

[138] Verses. 30 and 31 transpose the events of the walls of Jericho falling down and Rahab's welcoming the spies. Also, the names listed in v. 32 are out of order.

Mary Rose D'Angelo makes a convincing case that the author may have a conflated exegetical view of the meaning of the two events, the retreat to Midian and the exodus.[139] She points to Philo, who keeps each event distinct, since they are distinct events in the biblical narrative, but understands them to have the same meaning.[140] Moses' retreat to Midian indicates his voluntary renunciation of his royal Egyptian life, which in turn realizes his virtuous capacities and moves him toward becoming the leader of the people in their departure from Egypt. As D'Angelo says,

> Thus the flight of Moses from Egypt is an extension of his encounter on Sinai as his encounter with Pharaoh and the leadership of the exodus are its sequel. Moses flees *to* the retreat on Sinai and *to* the oracles given him at the bush, *to* his return to Egypt and *to* his final desolating departure from it.[141]

What is significant about D'Angelo's analysis is that even if the author of Hebrews has in mind the exodus in this part of Moses' biographical sketch, the emphasis of the story is on *Moses'* departure and what this meant for *his* life. This is consistent with the author's portrayal of Moses' early life and with the author's general interests. The biographical events our author included so far portray Moses as an orphan, a defector, and a fugitive. He is not, however, in any way conceived as the leader of the exodus.

Moses is motivated by the "unseen" (ἀόρατον)—this refers of course to the first of Moses' revelations, which occurs at Midian, the burning bush (Exod 3–4:17), but again, the author probably thinks of Moses as a visionary in general.[142] Indeed, because Moses' character traits are so prominent in the tradition and important for the author, the events of his life are seen as examples illustrating his personality. The particularities of those events are not made to stand out. Our author does follow the biblical text closely, and it is fair to assume that he has specific events in mind for Moses just as he did for the others. The emphasis on Moses' personality, however, deflates Moses' role as a savior of the people of Israel. Instead of being depicted as a man who leads the people of Israel out of bondage, he is a man who makes wise choices for himself.[143]

---

[139] D'Angelo, *Moses in Hebrews*, 59–62.

[140] See *Vit. Mos.* 1.148–162.

[141] D'Angelo, *Moses in Hebrews*, 59.

[142] Exod 33:11, 20–23; Num 12:8; cf. Exod 19:9–25 where Moses is permitted to go up on Mt Sinai when God's presence is there but the people are forbidden. See D'Angelo (*Moses in Hebrews*, 95–149) for a full analysis of Moses as a visionary of God.

[143] Alan Culpepper, "A Superior Faith: Hebrews 10:19–12:2," *RevExp* 82 (1985) 386.

Verse 28 is the only place where Moses is portrayed as having done something on behalf of the people. He engages in a sacrificial act, just as Abraham did in vv. 17–19.[144] Once again, no typological significance should be imputed.[145] The symbolism of the Passover is not employed in the service of prefiguring the death of Jesus. Rather, the biblical scene is described by focusing on the sacrificial act of Passover.[146] The sacrifice is efficacious in that it distinguishes the first born who shall live from those who shall be destroyed, and it is in this sense that the people benefit from Moses' actions.

In summary, Moses is not a national hero in Hebrews. His divine commission to lead the people, his intercessory role between the people and God, and the covenant at Sinai are all ignored in Hebrews. A brief look at Sirach 45:4–5 will highlight how significant this omission is. In Sirach, even Moses' mystical reputation as the one who sees God is put to the service of the people:

> He sanctified him through faithfulness and meekness; he chose him out of all mankind. He made him hear his voice, and led him into the thick darkness, and gave him the commandments face to face, the law of life and knowledge, *to teach Jacob the covenant, and Israel his judgments.*

If Hebrews 11 were all the information we had about Moses, we would not know he was a leader of the people or their lawgiver, or that he was even associated with Israel. In his mention of the one explicit event related to the exodus, the crossing of the Red Sea (v. 29), the author does not refer to Moses' leadership. Moses is no more of an Israelite than he is an Egyptian.

2. The Israelites

29By faith they crossed the Red Sea as if on dry land; when the Egyptians attempted this they were swallowed up. 30By faith the walls of Jericho fell after they had been encircled for seven days. 31By faith Rahab the prostitute did not perish with those who disbelieved, because she received the spies with peace.

These verses, which enumerate three brief examples of faith following the discussion of Moses, are parallel to the three brief instances of faith among the patriarchs which followed the section on Abraham. Verse 29 switches the subject from Moses to the people, who are now offered as a virtuous

---

[144] Attridge, *Hebrews*, 343.

[145] Attridge (*Hebrews*, 343) agrees that this verse has no typological significance even though he thinks the Aqedah in vv. 17–19 is typological.

[146] The expression πεποίηκεν τὸ πάσχα is a common way to refer to observing the ritual; see Attridge (*Hebrews*, 343 n. 83) for examples.

example of faith.[147] They are contrasted with the Egyptians, but they remain unnamed; the author simply uses an anonymous "they" (πίστει διέβησαν ...). Similarly, the walls of Jericho fall, allowing the Israelites to be victors and the people of Jericho to be destroyed, although in Hebrews the event is not mentioned as an example of *Israel's* victory in conquest. Both of these events are prominent miracles in the tradition. The story of Rahab is really a part of the Jericho miracle. God spectacularly intervenes to allow history to be favorable for some and disastrous for others. Indeed, it is not just in form, but also in content that these verses are parallel to the mention of Isaac, Jacob, and Joseph (vv. 20–22). There, at least in the first two verses, God chooses a younger son over an older one—the natural social progression of inheritance is thwarted by God. In vv. 29–30, too, nature is contravened by God in order to favor some individuals over others.

As the reader of Hebrews knows from earlier in the document, the author has a low regard for the generation of the wilderness (chaps. 3–4).[148] Moses' faith is contrasted with the faithlessness of the Israelites. It has been suggested that this explains why certain key figures, such as Aaron, are omitted from the Hebrews 11 list—because of their association with the wilderness generation.[149] The absence of Joshua in chap. 11 is especially glaring. Both Aaron and Joshua are, however, mentioned earlier in Hebrews.[150] In 4:8 Joshua is named as the one who was unable to give the people a permanent rest. Psalm 95:11 is quoted there (4:3,5) to prove that the conquest of Canaan did not achieve that for which it was intended. Joshua led the people into the land because Moses could not; this is his claim to fame as well as the probable reason for his exclusion from Hebrews 11. Joshua as hero is irredeemably tied up with his being a national leader. Conversely, the fact that Moses never entered the promised land made him a good candidate for the Hebrews hero list.

Aaron is mentioned in Heb 5:4 and 7:11 in connection with the priesthood. His claim to fame is that he is the founder of the order of levitical priests. The priesthood and the temple are by definition national

---

147 *Mek. Beshallah* 4 (35b–36) ascribes the people's crossing the Red Sea to faith.

148 The wilderness generation is known as notorious. This attitude comes out in some other historical resumes such as 4 Ezra 7:106–11 and CD 2:16ff. But cf. Wis 10:15–12:11 where the righteousness of the people of Israel is contrasted with the wickedness and idolatry of Egypt and Canaan.

149 Moffat, *Commentary*, 183; Montefiore, *Commentary*, 205.

150 Aaron plays a big role in Sirach 45:6–22 because of that author's priestly interests. He is only briefly mentioned in Acts 7:40. Joshua is also mentioned in Sirach 46:1–7 and Acts 7:45 as well as 4 Ezra 7:107.

institutions, which is one reason why Jesus is not genealogically related to Aaron (7:11,14), but rather to Melchizedek (6:20–7:3), who is of a transcendent order. For our author, there is no individualized portrait of someone like Aaron or Joshua in the tradition that would allow him to ascribe them to the supra-national salvation-historical line that he has developed in this list. Their heroic role derives from their national role, and thus does not suit the author's denationalized vision.

The list culminates with Rahab, a woman saved by her hospitality.[151] The verses that follow are a denouement. Although Jewish tradition did come to look on Rahab as a special individual, and Christian tradition accords her an honored place (Matt 1:5, Jam 2:25) her inclusion on the Hebrews hero list is no less surprising. She is included on none of the Jewish hero lists I have studied for comparison with Hebrews 11.[152] She is female, Gentile, and a woman of ill-repute. Furthermore, the author goes out of his way to make the list culminate with Rahab. If he had stayed with the chronological order, the fall of the walls of Jericho would have come after the story of Rahab.

Rahab is an outsider where Israel as a nation is concerned. But she should not be seen merely as the author's attempt to *extend* "the boundaries of the people of the old covenant."[153] She is part of a trajectory the author has been following throughout the list. The true heroes of biblical history are not Israel's national leaders; they are those who are *separate* from national affiliation, distinguished by πίστις. *All* the heroes are outsiders; they stand apart from their generation, from their nation, and from the world.

E. Summary Allusions to Remaining History

32And what more shall I say? For time would fail me if I recounted things concerning Gideon, Barak, Samson, Jephthah, David, and Samuel and the prophets. 33Those who through faith conquered kingdoms, practiced justice, attained promises, shut the mouths of lions, 34quenched the power of fire, escaped the edge of the sword, gained power over weakness, were made strong in battle, broke foreign armies. 35Women received their dead by resurrection, but others who were tortured did not accept release, in order that they might gain a better resurrection. 36And others underwent mocking and scourging, still others bonds and imprisonment; 37they were stoned, sawn asunder, murdered by the

---

151 Cf. the paraenetic demand to practice hospitality in 13:2.

152 She is listed in *1 Clement*, but *1 Clement* is dependent upon Hebrews.

153 Attridge, *Hebrews*, 344.

sword, they went about in the skins of sheep and goats, they were deprived, oppressed, and maltreated—³⁸the world was not worthy of these; they wandered over deserts and mountains and caves and the crevices of the earth.

Verse 32 terminates the anaphoric use of πίστει. Instead the author presents a rhetorical question[154] and says that he could not list all conceivable examples in any reasonable amount of time. Rhetorically, the point is to give the impression that examples could be listed *ad infinitum*; the quick listing of a series of names enhances that impression.[155] Verses 33ff continue the quick vigorous style through the use of asyndeton. Although asyndeton is a very common device generally used to create this rhetorical effect, Cosby points out that it occurs only once among the twenty-five comparative example lists he has studied.[156]

Furthermore, chronology is now completely abandoned. The correct order would have been Barak (Judg 4:6ff), Gideon (Judg 6:11ff), Jephthah (Judg 11:1ff), Samson (Judg 13:2ff), Samuel (1 Sam 1:20ff), and David (1 Sam 16:12ff). The author obviously no longer regards chronology as important. As Attridge says, "This verse serves as a transition from emphasizing individuals to the generically depicted later history of Israel."[157]

Nevertheless, a few points need to be addressed regarding the selection of names. None of the judges listed appear on any other list.[158] Samuel appears in Sirach, and David of course, is a very popular figure who appears on several lists. Occasionally commentators note that some of these individuals, notably Barak and Jephthah,[159] seem like particularly bad examples.[160] Although the list as a whole is not a "best of" where faith is

---

[154] Spicq (*L'Épître*, 2.362) and Moffat (*Commentary*, 184) provide several parallels of this rhetorical technique.

[155] Cosby, *Rhetorical Composition*, 58–9. I have wondered though, why the author cites so many names from one particular period, if he wants to give the impression of innumerable examples. Could not this impression have been more successfully achieved by citing examples from a variety of biblical periods?

[156] Cosby, *Rhetorical Composition*, 58.

[157] Attridge, *Hebrews*, 348.

[158] Although Sirach 46:11–12 does mention the judges generically. In striking contrast, several judges play a disproportionately large role in the *Biblical Antiquities* of Pseudo-Philo. In Pseudo-Philo every hero is primarily depicted in relation to the nation. See G. Nickelsburg, "Good and Bad Leaders in Pseudo-Philo's *Liber Antiquitatum Biblicarum, Ideal Figures in Ancient Judaism: Profiles and Paradigms* (eds. J.J. Collins and G. Nickelsburg; SBLSCS 12; Ann Arbor: Edwards Brothers, 1980) 49–65.

[159] Barak was a coward without the help of Deborah (Judg 4:8) and Jephthah is remembered for a vow he sorely regretted (Judg 11:30ff).

[160] Attridge (*Hebrews*, 348) hypothesizes that the author must be using some traditional

concerned, to end the list with these individuals seems almost an insult to the heroes so far cataloged.

David and Samuel are normally appropriate heroes of faith, since David is the first monarch and author of the psalms, while Samuel is seen to initiate the institution of prophecy, but the very fact that two such prominent figures are part of the string of examples for which the author does not have time, also seems to be implicitly insulting to the memory of those figures. David is just another example. If it seems far-fetched that our author would intentionally offer heroes whom he does not regard as particularly heroic,[161] one should consider the fact that even Moses, whose heroic status is incomparable in Jewish tradition, has been relativized by Jesus (3:1–6). If Moses and the angels pale in comparison to Jesus, every Jewish hero which the author lists, is of an implicitly inferior status.

The disorganized chronology combined with the listing of several mediocre names is an allusion to what our author sees as the dissolution of biblical history. The movement from chronological order to a haphazard order, from a list of heroes and their deeds to a list of disassociated names,[162] and then to a list of events whose referent is not always clear, creates a chaotic reading of history. Israel's history is no longer teleologically directed. The conquest of the land, the establishment of the monarchy, the building of the temple—none of the national glories of the history of Israel receive attention on the Hebrews hero list. This is strikingly different than the usual presentation of Jewish history. But since the author has tried to

---

summary of the judges. Bruce (*Epistle,* 320) attempts to explain this mini-list by pointing out that the spirit of the Lord is said to have come upon three of the four, Gideon (Judg 6:34), Jephthah (Judg 11:29), and Samson (Judg 13:25). He also notes that in Samuel's speech to the people in 1 Sam 12:11 he mentions four deliverers, Jerubbaal, Bedan, Jephthah, and Samuel. Jerubbaal is another name for Gideon and Bedan is probably a corruption of Barak.

[161] There is a brief list in *Lev.R.* 3 where the heroes mentioned are explicitly those who are not the best examples of the virtues they are named for: "The nations of the world, when they dwell in peace, eating and drinking, and becoming drunk, and engaging in lewd converse, what do they say?—'Who is as wise as Balaam? Who is as rich as Haman? Who is as strong as Goliath?' Then do The house of Israel come to them and say: 'Was not Ahitophel wise? Was not Korah rich? Was not Samson strong?'" The effect is meant to be humorous, since the setting is a peaceful drunken exchange between Jews and Gentiles. Presumably the Jews do not want to show off too much in front of the Gentiles who have such poor heroes. But the inadequacy of this list was felt by some—the parallel list in *Num.R.* 10.30 adds Solomon among the wise and rich and David among the strong. I am grateful to Burt Vizotsky for pointing out this list to me.

[162] We should also note that two other lists end with generic "others:" CD 2–3 and 4 Ezra 7:105–111. See Appendix B.

develop a non-national salvation-historical line, the exclusion of these national highlights is not surprising.

The events listed in vv. 33–38 also corroborate the author's interest in this theme: they refer to events in the lives of the prophets and Maccabean martyrs;[163] there are no kings or priests. In addition, this section moves the list from the positive to the negative, leaving the audience on the downbeat of biblical history.[164] Verses 33–4 focus on political and military accomplishments, including scenes from the book of Daniel.[165] Verse 35a shifts to more specific biblical events, the women who "receive their dead" are Zarephat, "whose son was restored by Elijah, and the Shunammite woman aided by Elisha."[166] Verse 35b then initiates a list of sufferings endured by a variety of figures, including Eleazar the martyr (2 Macc 6:18–31), Jeremiah (Jer 29:26, 37:15), and Isaiah (*Mart. Isa.* 5:1–14). The sheep and goat skins recall the garb of Elijah and Elisha (2 Kgs 1:8).

Finally, the list winds down on a note of despair, without making any specific allusions, they were "deprived, oppressed, and maltreated." Verse 38a interrupts the list of hardships with a general remark, "the world was not worthy of these."[167] Such a comment brings into focus the theme of the heroes' alienation from society and the world. Like vv. 13–16, v. 38a partly functions as a commentary on all the heroes' wanderings. Because it is a statement of a proverbial and categorical nature,[168] this verse is more than a commentary on the prophets and martyrs alluded to immediately before it. It anticipates the conclusion.

---

[163] Bruce (*Epistle*, 319–28) provides the most detailed tracing of the biblical events alluded to in this section.

[164] Cf. Nehemiah 9, which, as we noted in chapter one, also ends on a pessimistic note. However, Nehemiah 9 is intended as a penitential retelling of Israelite history, which is followed by a statement of repentance and a renewal of the covenant.

[165] Cf. the lists in 1 Macc 2; 4 Macc 16 and 18, where Daniel and friends also appear.

[166] Attridge, *Hebrews*, 349; See 1 Kgs 17:17–24 and 2 Kgs 4:18–37.

[167] Verse 38b continues with images that again allude to Elijah and Elisha, although the phrase "crevices of the earth" is drawn from elsewhere; see Eccl 12:3; Zech 14:12; Cant 5:4; Ezek 8:7; listed in Attridge, *Hebrews*, 351.

[168] Cf. Wis 3:5.

F. Conclusion

³⁹And all these, although attested to through faith, did not receive the promise, ⁴⁰since God foresaw something better for us, so that they would not be perfected apart from us.

The conclusion leaves no doubt that the heroes are lacking something. Recalling the beginning of the pericope, the author reminds his audience that these individuals are attested to (μαρτυρηθέντες) in scripture. Nevertheless, as great a testimony as this is, they did not receive the promise. Presumably the promise here (the word ἐπαγγελία occurs here for the first time in the singular) means salvation effected Christ.[169]

In the last verse the author speaks of his present community, which he perceives to be in a more advantageous position than the heroes he has just eulogized, "God foresaw something better for *us*." Nevertheless, the phrase "so that they would not be perfected apart from us" implies an intimate connection between the heroes of the past and the present community. The force of this connection works in two ways. First, the conclusion highlights the suffering of the heroes, who are presumably meant to reflect the predicament of the community. Second, when the author says that the heroes "would not be perfected apart from us," he places his audience on the same historical continuum as those on the list.

For the author of Hebrews, biblical history insofar as it is part of the Old Covenant is an unfinished story. The summary allusions to the rest of history in vv. 32–8 leave the events of biblical history in a state of suffering and chaos. Thus, biblical history needs to have imposed upon it a teleological direction. When v. 40 says that "they would not be perfected apart from us," the implication is that the *telos* of history is only being realized in the present community, in the Christian community. Just two verses ahead in 12:2, Jesus is called the perfecter of faith. David Peterson, in his study of the concept of perfection in Hebrews,[170] has shown that perfection should not be understood as a Greek virtue, but as a sense of completion or fulfillment. If

---

[169] The author has referred to receiving promises four times in this text and each time he has used a different verb for "receive." Twice the author says that they heroes did not receive what was promised, here in the conclusion (ἐκομίσαντο) and in v. 13 (λαβόντες) referring to the patriarchs. In v. 17 he calls Abraham the one who had received (ἀναδεξάμενος) the promises, and in v. 33 he also refers to the heroes in general as having received (ἐπέτυχον) promises.

[170] David Peterson, *Hebrews and Perfection.*

this notion is applied to the author's recounting of biblical history, Jesus Christ (and the era ushered in by him) is the *telos* of biblical history.

Profile of the Hebrews Hero

By identifying characteristics that the heroes share, we can form a portrait of the Hebrews hero. To be sure, some heroes reflect the portrait better than others because of more explicit descriptions, but if we keep in mind the relation of the part to the whole, all the heroes fit the profile reasonably well.

Early in this chapter I spoke of isolating the principle of selection, by which we would determine why the author chooses these heroes and presents them the way he does. While at one level the author has made use of multiple characteristics—and thus, more than one principle of selection—these characteristics all serve one greater purpose: the heroes are marginalized individuals who are portrayed as standing outside the nation of Israel. This principle, moreover, also functions in the diachronic aspect of this text. That is, the list adds up to a denationalized reading of biblical history.

Characteristics

Death or Near-Death Experience

The first two heroes die. Even if Enoch did not literally die, he passed from his earthly existence to a divine one. Noah does not die, but the rest of the world does. His survival of the flood certainly counts as a near-death experience, which is succeeded by a new beginning. Abraham and Sarah are practically dead when a new life—that is, Isaac—is given to them. Isaac comes as close to death as anyone on the list without actually dying. The fact that he is so close to death but saved at the last minute is, in the words of our author, like the experience of resurrection itself. As we noted earlier, the patriarchs, Isaac, Jacob, and Joseph are all depicted in Hebrews at the time of their death. The connection with death in the description of Moses is more vague, but nevertheless present in two different instances. In the birth story, the child Moses is miraculously saved from death. Later, the mature Moses, when he flees Egypt for Midian, believes his life is in danger. The mention of the people crossing the Red Sea and the walls of Jericho falling down are vague, although clearly the people are in danger when they cross the Red Sea. Rahab, if she had not assisted the spies would surely have perished with the people of Jericho. Thus, all the heroes die or almost die, but the event is followed by a new beginning.[171] The author does not always describe this aspect explicitly, but he always pinpoints the end of life/new life moment in the career of the hero.

Ability to see into the Future—The Meaning of the Heroes' Faith

Most of the heroes on the list have the ability to anticipate the future. Thus, in the midst of adverse circumstances they are confident because they foresee something better. Given the definition of faith ("faith is the realization of what is hoped for, proof of things not seen"), by which the author introduced the hero catalog, this characteristic is the closest we come to seeing the heroes as examples of faith. Although often the 'faith' characteristic is only indirect.

In the case of Abel and Enoch nothing specific is said about their ability to know what lies in the future. However, both are said to have received divine approval during their earthly life. To be sure, divine approval is something which by definition applies to all the heroes on this list as well as on other Jewish lists. But the approval of Abel and Enoch earns them post-mortem rewards. Indeed, following Enoch's mention on the list, the author makes an exhortative aside: "For it is necessary that one who approaches God has faith that he exists and that he is one who rewards those who seek him" (v. 6). We may therefore assume that Abel and Enoch's approval stems from their faith in the reality of God and in future rewards.

For the other heroes, the faith-as-knowledge-of-the-future element is more direct. Noah receives an oracle, by which he knows what the future will bring and so he builds the ark. Abraham follows the instructions of God, even if they do not appear to lead to the fulfillment of the promises. Though he lives in the land of promise as in a "foreign land," he ultimately knows that a heavenly homeland awaits (vv. 14–16). We already noted that the author twice mentions Moses' ability to see the future. Rahab may not be literally credited with this ability but it is implicit in her actions. By helping the spies in advance of the battle, she saved herself and her family.

While the heroes have faith in, or knowledge of, future rewards, their present life is without reward or recognition for their faithfulness. Some scholars have emphasized the suffering which some heroes on the list are said to have endured.[172] In my estimation these scholars have been overly

---

171 Cf. Brawley ("Discoursive Structure," 95–96) who argues that events like the flood and the splitting of the Red Sea are proto-apocalyptic events in the author's eyes.

172 Héring, *Epistle,* 100; D'Angelo, *Moses in Hebrews,* 27.

influenced by the concluding verses,[173] which, as we already noted, are present primarily for rhetorical effect and not part of the body of the main list. The fact that the heroes are connected somehow with death may also influence scholars to assume suffering plays a key role in the selection of heroes. In my view, while death appears as a theme on the list, it is not necessarily connected with suffering. Of the heroes on the main list, Moses is the only one said to have suffered (v. 25). At the same time, none of the heroes have an easy time of life—Abraham wanders, Isaac is almost sacrificed, and so forth.

Another way of looking at the presence of this so-called theme of suffering is to understand it in relation to the theme of the heroes' ability to see the future. In order for the heroes to focus on future rewards, their present circumstances must be less than ideal. If they were satisfied with an earthly life filled with material niceties, they would not need to look to *future* rewards. The heroes' earthly life is filled with adverse circumstances, so as to contrast the poverty of their current existence with their future rewards.

Alteration of Status

In the previous chapter, we uncovered the author's agenda in his 'retellings' of scripture. He devalued the objects of biblical narrative, such as the temple and the priesthood. We also saw how biblical figures like Moses and Abraham could suffer character deflation at the hands of our author, because the status of these greats from the biblical past has been altered in light of the pre-eminence of Jesus. This same hermeneutic is present in chap. 11, and it helps to explain that nagging mystery: why the heroes are not very good examples of faith.

Hebrews 11 participates in the attitude toward the biblical past which is typical of the document as a whole. The author consistently engages in a hermeneutic of continuity and discontinuity.[174] The national realities of Israel, the tabernacle, the Torah, and the priesthood, are only shadows of perfect divine realities (Heb 8:5). They are both models for, as well as models in contrast to. For example, on the one hand, the author makes a strong case for the inferiority of the levitical priesthood, while Christ, on the other hand, is the perfect priest. Christ is shown to be perfect by fulfilling

---

[173] That is, vv. 33–38, which indeed cover a number of trials and tribulations. Verses 33–34, however, emphasize not the suffering created by trials, but the overcoming of them. These verses conclude the list for the purpose of drama.

[174] This idea comes from the work of Graham Hughes, *Hebrews and Hermeneutics* (Cambridge: Cambridge University, 1979).

the same needs that the levitical system was trying to fulfill, only he fulfills them perfectly and self-sufficiently. Thus the author allows the ancient Jewish system to set the standard: blood must be shed to expiate sin, the victim must be unblemished, and so forth. But Christ has achieved the perfect version of the standard. Therefore, Christ as priest is both continuous and discontinuous with the tradition. He is a superlative priest who is judged to be superlative by the ancient (and, presumably, inferior) standard of measure. He is unlike the former priests because he is infinitely better, and he is like them because he achieves their priestly goals.

This hermeneutic is also at work in the Hebrews hero list. The heroes of biblical history may set a standard for what determines virtuous activity in the Christian community, but they are relatively inferior. Like the sophists on Cicero's example list, the heroes of the old world can function only as partial models. The world of the biblical heroes predates the advent of Christ, the perfecter of faith. That is why some of the best examples are missing; there is no Phinehas[175] or Josiah named here. In the first place the heroism of such men is too much connected to the national peculiarity of Israel. Phinehas's role in history is tied up with the priesthood and Josiah is, of course, a king. In the second, Phinehas's zeal for God and Josiah's reinstitution of Torah might have been too perfect an example. By means of their faith, they achieved this-worldly goals and were consequently recognized in their own lifetime.

So much of the argument of Hebrews is devoted to distinguishing Jesus from others that the author cannot risk the heroes' status being confused with Jesus'. If Jesus is the perfect example of faith (12:2), the heroes must be something less. Furthermore, Jesus was not simply the Son of God, but he also had to suffer humiliation and shame (2:9; 4:15–5:8). Since the heroes of the old covenant cannot possess more glory than Jesus, the author's portrayal of them must somehow diminish their grand stature. In addition, because the author describes the heroes as humble in their own time, their image more closely matches the image of Jesus.

The alteration-of-status characteristic can also help us explain the author's waffling on the position of the heroes' reception of promises. Let us first review the author's varying statements about the promises: On the one hand, the author of Hebrews says that the heroes received neither earthly promises (vv. 13, 33)—meaning biblical promises like land and

---

[175] Phinehas is a very popular figure on lists. He occurs in the Sirach list as well as in 1 Macc 2 and 4 Macc 18. In Sirach and I Maccabees 2, the covenant of the priesthood is mentioned. All three texts mention Phinehas' zeal.

nationhood—nor did they receive the ultimate promise given in Christ (v. 39). On the other hand, sometimes the author says they did receive the biblical promises (v. 17),[176] and he certainly implies that they will receive the eschatological promise ultimately (v. 40). We can sum up the author's position as follows: The heroes were promised earthly rewards, but never actually received them. Conversely, God never directly promised them an eschatological reward, but they will presumably receive it.

Nevertheless, it is an insult to the heroes to say that they never obtained the earthly promises God made to them.[177] In the Hellenistic lists which we discussed earlier, earthly rewards and honor consistently play a major role. In 1 Macc 2:51–60, the list was structured by the rewards accorded each member of the list. Joseph is rewarded with becoming lord of Egypt, Phinehas is given the covenant of the priesthood, etc. In Wisdom 10 Sophia rewards the righteous and punishes the wicked in their own lifetime. In the Sirach list rewards also play a crucial role in describing each hero, and these rewards usually involve a position of honor.[178] In fact, the introduction to Sirach 44–50 generically captures the high position in society which the heroes are assumed to enjoy:

> The Lord apportioned to them great glory, his majesty from the beginning. There were those who ruled in their kingdoms, and made a name for themselves by their valor; those who gave counsel because they were intelligent; those who spoke in prophetic oracles; those who led the people by their counsels and by their knowledge of the people's lore; they were wise in their words of instruction; those who composed musical tunes, or put verses to writing; rich men endowed with resources, living peacefully in their homes—*all these were honored in their generations, and were the pride of their times.* (44:2–7)

The heroes of Hebrews could not be farther removed from this image. They certainly do not receive honor or reward or even recognition in their own lifetime. Furthermore, the heroes are not depicted in the prime of their lives, but rather receive mention in connection with death. In addition, the heroes of Hebrews are not recorded for their impressive accomplishments and talents.

---

176 Cf. Heb 6:15: "When God made a promise to Abraham, because he had no one greater by whom to swear, he swore by himself, saying, 'I will surely bless you and multiply you.' And thus Abraham, having patiently endured, obtained the promise."

177 Cf. Paul, in Rom 9:1–6.

178 Mack, *Wisdom and Hebrew Epic,* named the reception of honor/rewards one of the seven characteristics of the heroes on Sirach's list.

For example, when the author of Hebrews describes Moses as a hero, Moses' heroic qualities appear circumscribed, situation-specific. He chooses suffering with the people of God *rather than* the fleshpots of Egypt. He was not afraid of the anger of the king, but no praise is heaped on him as inherently brave. He was able to leave Egypt because he was not afraid, but no mention is made of his many confrontations with the king (avoiding the rivaling magic tricks). The final act Moses performs in Hebrews 11 is keeping "the Passover" and sprinkling the blood. While the sprinkling of the blood may or may not be meant to evoke the blood Moses sprinkled on the people during the covenant ceremony referred to in 9:21, its mention is more evocative of the blood theme in the document overall than of any special qualities of Moses. In fact, the reason provided for Moses' keeping the Passover is "so that the Destroyer of the first-born might not touch them"—a reason that seems more typical and expected than heroic.

Furthermore, not only is the covenant at Sinai absent in Hebrews, but, as we already noted, Moses is not even depicted as the leader of the people during the exodus. When the crossing at the Red Sea is mentioned in 11:29, we read "By faith *the people* crossed the Red Sea . . . ." And yet Moses' leadership is mentioned earlier in Hebrews in connection with the people's rebelliousness in the wilderness: "Was it not all those who left Egypt under the leadership of Moses?" (3:16). By any Jewish standard of the time, this amounts to a grossly understated and inadequate picture of Moses as hero.

What is missing in Hebrews' retelling of the Moses story are all of Moses' accomplishments, which on other hero lists and in other retellings, are co-extensive with the rewards. Because in the author's version the rewards are delayed until some time which lies outside of biblical history, the saga of Moses not only seems incomplete, but Moses himself lacks honor, prestige, and achievement, as do all the heroes in Hebrews. It is not that the author of Hebrews is not paying Moses compliments, but his descriptions of Moses are restrained. While the tendency of hero lists is to be over-the-top, this author holds back.

This holding back is due to the fact that the heroes live in a time prior to the Christ event. Their heroism is not attributable to their achievements in their own time, but to their ability to anticipate a better time (that is the essence of their faith). The heroes of Hebrews function as seers who portend the future, but whose own heroic image is mitigated by their being part of the old world order. Like the levitical system of worship, the tabernacle, the temple, the priests, or other biblical institutions, the author uses the heroes as historical examples for teaching, but at the same time devalues them because they are what make the old covenant old.

Marginalization

Throughout the analysis of the text I repeatedly made the point that the heroes are portrayed as outsiders. Although this trait is conveyed in different ways, it is the most fundamental characteristic of the heroes of Hebrews. It is closely related to the characteristic mentioned above, the alteration of the heroes' status. Because the heroes' status is traditionally derived from a position of leadership or connection with a national institution, and since the heroes' station must be altered so as not to outshine Jesus, the author's avoidance of mentioning national accomplishments serves both purposes.

The language of separation is self-evident in Abraham's case. Moses, too, voluntarily gives up his status within a nation or society. But we also saw how common intertestamental traditions about the primeval heroes were most likely informing the author of Hebrews. Abel, Enoch, and Noah stand apart from their generations. Rahab also stands apart from her community of origin. The heroes are not distinguished *by* their comrades, as is the case in the Sirach list, they are distinguished *from* them, and are eventually removed from life with them by God.

Perhaps the best way to measure how far the heroes stand from their traditional place within Israel is to consider what the author avoids saying in his descriptions of the heroes. For example, three of the men named constitute a special class of heroes. Noah, Abraham, and Moses each made a covenant with God. Yet, the author does not acknowledge the covenants made with any of them. Covenant, like the rewards, played a major role in the Hellenistic hero lists, but in Hebrews it is absent.

Surely at least part of the reason the author avoids the mention of covenants is because they are inherently tied up with Israel's national identity. The defining characteristic of Israel's relationship with God is the covenant. Since the author wishes to stay clear of national accomplishments, it makes sense that he would not mention covenants. The covenants are also a sign of status for the heroes. They imply theophonic contact between the deity and the individual. Thus, it is natural for the author to avoid mention of them.

Perhaps the author wished to avoid references to God's covenant with Israel because he thought it would not be well received by a Gentile, or partially Gentile, audience. Josephus downplays the covenant in the *Antiquities*, while stressing that Israel is a virtuous people deserving of God's special attention.[179] But Moses in Hebrews does not possess those characteristics that would typically appeal to a non-Jewish audience either. Among Gentiles Moses was known either as a legislator or as a magician.[180] Neither is referred to in Hebrews 11.

If we use Moses as an example once again, we can further illustrate Hebrews' unique portrayal of the hero. Compared to those in Hebrews, depictions of the great leader in other texts—even NT texts—look completely different. For example, while Stephen's speech in Acts is not a hero list, it does rehearse the great events of biblical history while highlighting the works of heroes. In Acts 7 we find everything said of Moses that we expect to find: God speaks to him on Mt. Sinai and he leads the people through the Red Sea. Stephen even says (Acts 7:38) "[Moses] received living oracles to give to us." Thus a note is made of the revelation given to Moses and the fact that this revelation is to be handed down. In fact, several direct quotations of God speaking to Moses appear in Acts 7, while in Hebrews 11 Moses is not the recipient of any revelation.[181] Clearly, the author of Hebrews does not want to allude either to Moses' closeness to God or to his legislative leadership over the people Israel.

The fact that Moses was orphaned and came to be raised by Pharaoh's daughter is an event in the biblical story of Moses that loomed large in Jewish and Christian imagination. The story was told and retold. What makes its presence in Hebrews 11 unusual is that it is found on a hero list,[182] where Moses' heroic qualities are expected to be emphasized. That this element should be listed at the expense of other qualities, like his being the leader of the exodus, is what is so striking.

Transvaluation

In the words of Gérard Genette, the author has "transvalued" the heroes of Jewish scripture.[183] "Transvaluing occurs when the characters in the

---

179 Attridge, (*The Interpretation of Biblical History in the Antiquitates Judaicae of Flavius Josephus* [Missoula, MT: Scholars, 1976] 148), speculates that the theme of covenant is diminished in any setting where Gentiles are included.

180 John Gager, *Moses in Greco-Roman Paganism* (SBLMS 16; Nashville: Abingdon, 1972).

181 Moses does receive a direct revelation in 8:5.

182 Although the birth story of Moses is told in Acts 7, it does not appear in Sirach 44–50 or in Wisdom 10.

183 Gérard Genette, *Palimpsestes: La Littérature au second degré* (Paris: Editions du Seuil, 1982). I am grateful to Dennis MacDonald for introducing me to Genette's work. MacDonald's own work (*Christianizing Homer: The Odyssey, Plato, and the Acts of Andrew* [New York and Oxford: Oxford University, 1994) is indebted to Genette.

hypertext (viz. the derivative text) acquire roles and attributes derived from a system of values not found in the hypotext (the targeted text)."[184] In other words, when the author of Hebrews composed his miniature re-writing of biblical history in chap. 11, the primary objects of his narrative, i.e., the heroes, were transformed by the values of the author. An implicit part of transvaluing is the intentional *devaluing* of the system of values perceived to be originally present in the hypertext. Transvaluing would not be successful if the new values were just added to the text; they must replace the old ones—hence the old ones are devalued so that the audience will reject them. Thus, the author diminishes the heroes' national status in order to highlight aspects of their careers that better reflect his Christian perspective.

The author's understanding of christology and the new covenant as well as his personal experience of being a Christian caused him to value the heroes of the Jewish Bible for reasons different from those that had traditionally been employed. Hence, he 'transvalued' them. National leaders become marginal individuals. A man like Abraham, famous for his power and wealth, is transformed into a wanderer who never received his rightful inheritance. Moses, the hero of the exodus and Israel's lawgiver, is included in Hebrews not for any of those reasons, but because he suffered as an outsider.

The heroes in Hebrews 11 are not primarily examples of virtuous behavior, except in the most general way. The sheer variety of actions ascribed to the heroes makes it difficult to see what behavior is being prescribed or praised. Each hero or event is listed as part of the ancient history of the Hebrews community, existing in an inferior world without the benefit of Christ. Yet, even in this world heroes emerged and heroic events happened through faith. This being established, how much easier is it for the Christian community, which has the benefit of Christ, to have the confidence to abide in faith—that is, to stay the divine course on which they presently travel. Thus, the heroes of the Hebrew Bible are an inspiration to the Christian audience because they did so well with so little.

These images of the biblical heroes have both positive and negative functions as examples or models. On the one hand, the author's hermeneutic of discontinuity is evident in the devaluing of the heroes' actual heroism. They lack achievement, high status, and reward. Like the examples from Greco-Roman lists, the heroes of Hebrews are more human than those typically found on Jewish lists. On this level the heroes function

---

[184] MacDonald, *Christianizing Homer*, 6.

as models of contrast with Christ and life in the new covenant. On the other hand, the author's hermeneutic of continuity functions in that the heroes are models for the new Christian community. Obedience in suffering since the advent of Christ is valued as a sign of high station and not humility, and being an outsider among one's own people need not be a source of shame. Indeed, as we shall see in the following chapter, the catalog of heroes in Hebrews reflects a Christian writer who saw the heroes of Jewish scripture as quintessentially Christian, rather than Jewish.

The Denationalization of Biblical History

By now it should be clear that Hebrews 11 carries a diachronic as well as a synchronic dimension. Indeed, we determined that Hebrews 11 was a retelling of Israelite history in the form of a list when we compared it to cognate texts in chapter one. The 'multi-dimensional' nature—that is, the variety of persons and events—of the text indicates that the author was striving for broad coverage of biblical events, so as to better convey the 'story.' What is most important about the author's diachronic interest, however, is that the text amounts to a narrative genealogy that functions to legitimate the community addressed by the text.

Because the author concludes the list the way he does ("And all these, although attested to through faith, did not receive the promise, *since God foresaw something better for us, so that they would not be perfected apart from us*") the heroes are the heritage of the community. "These"—meaning the heroes, and "us" meaning the community, are part of the same story. Like Wisdom 10 and the Covenant of Damascus, Hebrews 11 implicitly functions as a genealogy which legitimates the Christian audience by providing them with a biblical ancestry. At the same time this ancestry is not identified with the nation of Israel, but forms a trajectory independent of it. That is why the list does not include any priests or kings.[185] All the heroes are outsiders. They stand apart from the national history of Israel while at the same time being recorded in scripture, which is the collection of documents traditionally assumed to contain the story of Israel.[186] The heroes derive their status from πίστις, not from any national role or office. πίστις allows the author to establish a non-national, salvation-historical trajectory which includes the Hebrews community.

---

[185] David is only mentioned (11:32) in the summary allusions, and not as part of the main list.

[186] James A. Sanders (*Torah and Canon* [Philadelphia: Fortress, 1972]) makes the point that scripture was primarily thought of as *story* by the ancients.

As I have noted repeatedly, the author's purpose is to denationalize the history of Israel. To accomplish this, his task was necessarily two-fold. First, he had to show that the heroes were superior individuals because of non-national accomplishments. Those who are typically thought of as national leaders, like Abraham and Moses, are not depicted in their leadership roles. Furthermore, Abraham and Moses, like the others listed, are treated as distinct from the people or nation. Second, he implicitly engages in a polemic against those who would see scripture as a national history by ending the bulk of his summary just before the establishment of the nation, and by giving the impression that Israel's history dissipates—i.e., has no teleological direction—just as she enters what is truly her national phase. Thus, God's promises, which in biblical history are traditionally nationalistic—promises for land, temple, monarchy—are depicted as not having been fulfilled, in order that a new ending might be grafted onto the story: the heavenly rest now attainable because of Christ (Heb 4:6–11). Indeed, Abraham and Moses are the paradigmatic heroes in Hebrews 11 precisely because they do not receive the fulfillment of those national promises. It is difficult to imagine an ancient Jewish writer making this remark, because it represents a perspective so far removed from the traditional laudatory view of the biblical figures.[187] But from the author's transvalued conception, it is a compliment to the heroes, because they will receive a greater promise.

---

[187] What I mean by this statement is that while there may have been a variety of Jewish beliefs and practices in the first century, most Jews would acknowledge the biblical heroes as the recipients of fulfilled promises. I simply want to draw attention to the unusual perspective of the writer of Hebrews. Cf. Windisch (*Hebräerbrief*, 98) who, like many other commentators, misses the radical (and rather "unJewish") reading of Jewish heroes and history in Hebrews 11: "Bis auf den ὀνειδισμὸς Χριστοῦ und die Schlußbemerkung 39f könnte der ganze Abschnitt von einem Juden entworfen sein. Zum mindesten liegt eine jüdische oder judenchristliche Schultradition zugrunde."

Chapter Four
HEBREWS AND HISTORIOGRAPHY
ော ௸

Thus far this study has been concerned with enhancing our understanding of one piece of the ancient document known as the Epistle to the Hebrews. We have discussed cognate texts, analyzed the hermeneutical context of the document, and engaged in an exegesis of the text itself. Now I wish to address the role of Hebrews 11 in early Christianity—specifically its denationalized reading of biblical history. Since we now know that Hebrews 11 is not derived from a Jewish source and is not simply a neutral Jewish recounting of heroes and history, we can inquire whether the perspective contained in this particular discourse played any significant role in the intellectual development of early Christianity.

Bruce Lincoln, a theorist in the study of religion, has produced a body of work devoted to the question of change (social, political, and religious) through discourse.[1] Scholars of religion have always been challenged to explain the mechanics of change, since societal structures, institutions, and patterns so often reinforce the status quo.[2] Except in the event of a violent revolution, radical change usually involves complex and subtle forces. Lincoln attempts to explain these forces by analyzing the uses of discourse. Besides the obvious requirement that a subversive or disruptive discourse needs access to channels of communication, Lincoln argues that a subversive discourse's power of persuasion does not lie in its logical coherence, but rather in its ability to evoke 'sentiments.' A sentiment may be defined as any feeling that aids in the construction or reconstruction of societal borders. As Lincoln says,

---

[1] Lincoln himself (*Discourse and the Construction of Society : Comparative Studies of Myth, Ritual, and Classification* [New York: Oxford University, 1989]) does not define discourse, and his use of it is not explicitly technical. It is, in plain English, the orderly exchange of information. I would only add that discourse is not exclusively verbal (although that is our concern here); it includes modes of communication contained in such things as rituals and symbols.

[2] On this question in general, see the essays in *Innovation in Religious Traditions: Essays in the Interpretation of Religious Change*, ed. Michael A. Williams, Collett Cox, and Martin S. Jaffe (Berlin: Mouton de Gruyter, 1992).

That is, as groups and individuals note similarities and dissimilarities of whatever sort between themselves and others, they can employ these as instruments with which to evoke the specific sentiments out of which social borders are constructed. These I refer to as affinity and estrangement, meaning to include under the general rubric of these terms, on the one hand, all feelings of likeness, common belonging, mutual attachment, and solidarity—whatever their intensity, affective tone and degree of consciousness—and, on the other hand, those corresponding feelings of distance, separation, otherness, and alienation. Although in practice the capacity of discourse to evoke such sentiments is closely conjoined with its capacity to persuade, analytically the two are separate.[3]

The primary means by which sentiments are "aroused, manipulated, and rendered dormant is discourse."[4]

The fact that sentiments can be constructive rather than simply reflective of social borders is useful for understanding Hebrews 11. For example, we observed in chapter three that the heroes are all portrayed as outsiders. A commonplace interpretation of this observation might be to assert that the audience to which Hebrews is directed is composed of people who are alienated from their community of origin. This is most likely true—but we can say more than that. If we suppose that members of the audience feel empathy toward the heroes and identify with them, this means that the audience members then share the same affinity between themselves.[5] Such an affinity then becomes a bonding sentiment out of which a new community can be constructed.

One of the most powerful types of discourse is the recounting of the past. And re-narrating the past always evokes sentiments. Lincoln himself has constructed a taxonomy of narratives about the past.[6] There are four types: fable, legend, history, and myth. A fable makes no truth claims; it is unambiguously fiction. A legend makes truth claims but lacks credibility in the opinion of the intended audience. History also makes truth-claims, of course, and has credibility. Myth is an account of the past that not only possesses credibility but also *authority*. By authority Lincoln means that the

---

[3] Lincoln, *Discourse and Society*, 9–10.

[4] Lincoln, *Discourse and Society*, 11.

[5] This phenomenon is comparable to the experience of spectator sports. The spectators' support for and identification with their team also creates a kinship between the spectators.

[6] *Discourse and Society*, 23–26.

truth-claims possess "paradigmatic truth, . . . akin to that of charters, models, templates and blueprints . . . ."[7] Jewish scripture no doubt held this kind of mythic status for Jews of the ancient world as well as for the first Christian Jews.[8] But the perplexing question has always been how Gentile Christians came to regard Jewish scripture as myth. (The legal prescriptions of course lost their ability to be a model of behavior, but scripture as an ancestral story did retain its power as myth.) After all, some Christians of the second and third centuries, notably marcionites and some gnostics, rejected what was by then the Old Testament. It was by no means a foregone conclusion that the Old Testament would retain its scriptural status after the church became predominantly Gentile and the New Testament became canonical. To be sure, claims to antiquity were important to Christians in their debates with the Romans, and this provided an incentive for Christians to retain the OT as proof of that antiquity. Nevertheless, it was not necessary for Jewish scripture to retain its *mythic* status in order for Christians to claim that their origins were rooted in antiquity. Christians could have incorporated certain Jewish traditions into their own scripture, and given the 'Old Testament' a non-canonical, secondary status.[9]

We have already seen that Hebrews 11 is a recounting of the scriptural story with an agenda. Now I wish to argue that that agenda—the denationalization of Jewish scripture—marks a turning point in the early Christian appropriation of biblical history. While it is true that there is little direct dependence of early Christian authors on Hebrews 11, we can document

---

[7] Lincoln, *Discourse and Society*,24. Lincoln is influenced here by Clifford Geertz, *The Interpretation of Cultures* (New York: Basic Books, 1973) 93–94.

[8] For an excellent discussion of the mythic status of the exodus event (which is of course the nucleus of the biblical story) as well as how the meaning of the story evolved while still being paradigmatic, see Michael Fishbane, "The Exodus Motif/Paradigm of Historical Renewal," *Text and Texture: Close Readings of Selected Biblical Texts* (New York: Schocken Books, 1979) 121–40.

[9] It is instructive to compare the Islamic view of Jewish scripture to the Christian one. Jewish scripture informed parts of the Qur'an, and was indeed viewed as containing historical information about the pre-Muslim world, but it was not retained as scripture. Thus, in Islam, Jewish—or for that matter Christian—scripture is not mythic in the sense we are using it here. On the relationship between the Qur'an and the Bible, see F. E. Peters, *Children of Abraham* (Princeton: Princeton University, 1982). William Graham (*Beyond the Written Word: Oral Aspects of Scripture in the History of Religion* [Cambridge: Cambridge University, 1987] 57) points out that while Muslims call Jews and Christians the 'people of the book' (*kitab*) the Qur'an is called 'the book' (*al-kitab*). The books of Christians and Jews are understood to be faulty.

that the perspective on Israelite history conveyed by the author of Hebrews becomes typical for later authors, whereas before Hebrews, a less radical perspective prevailed. Furthermore, the turning point that Hebrews 11 represents can help us explain how Jewish scripture achieved its mythic status for Gentile Christians.

Lincoln lists three ways in which a mythic past can be used as an agent of change—even to the point of constructing new and unfamiliar social formations. Those advocating change can: 1) contest the authority and/or credibility of a myth, thereby reducing its status to that of history or legend; 2) elevate history or legend to the status of myth by investing it with authority and credibility; and 3) "advance novel lines of interpretation for an established myth or modify details in its narration and thereby change the nature of the sentiments (and the society) it evokes."[10] Hebrews 11 is clearly an example of the third option.

It is my contention that the Hebrews hero list is a distinctly Christian interpretation of Jewish scripture *as a whole*. It is often remarked that what distinguishes Christian hermeneutics in the earliest days of the nascent sect is that a Christian interpreter read any given text through the lens of the death and resurrection of Jesus.[11] This assertion is true, but it fails to address scripture *in toto*, that is, as containing the comprehensive history of the people of Israel and how Christians viewed that history. While the hermeneutical interests of Jews in antiquity—whatever their sectarian orientation—mostly resulted in the interpretations of individual verses or groups of verses, there are occasional texts, like Hebrews 11, which view scripture in a comprehensive way.

Hebrews 11 represents a significant point in the evolution that led from the understanding of Jewish scripture as the ethnic history of the Jews to the theological history of Christians. In order to demonstrate that Hebrews 11 constitutes such a reading of biblical history, we must first briefly consider what the prevailing view of scripture was whenever it was presented as a comprehensive account of Israelite history. We must also consider the two other places in the NT where scripture is treated this way: Romans 9–11 and

---

[10] Lincoln, *Discourse and Society*, 25.

[11] The statement by E. Earl Ellis ("Biblical Interpretation in the New Testament Church," *Mikra*, 691) is typical: "Jesus and his apostles and prophets, as they are represented by the NT, make their contribution to first-century Jewish exposition by their thorough-going *reinterpretation of the biblical writings to the person, ministry, death, and resurrection of Jesus the Messiah*."

Acts 7. After these considerations, early Christian texts that post-date Hebrews will be explored.

The Bible as History in Ancient Judaism

Arnaldo Momigliano has been the most articulate voice in commenting on history and historiography in Jewish antiquity. In his discussion of the differences between Jewish and Greek historiography in the ancient world, he points out that Greek historians never claim to be comprehensive in their accounts of history. History in the Greek sense is always the *historia* of one monumental event or series of events written from a self-conscious point of view.[12] Thus, several versions can be composed, and these are often conflicting. In contrast, Hebrew historians as represented in the Bible composed one exclusive continuous story starting from the origin of the world. Despite the fact that modern biblical scholarship has perceived the existence of several different documents with divergent versions of the same story, the Hebrew Bible was understood in antiquity to be one all-inclusive story. As one scholar has said, "The basic structure of the Pentateuch is not that of a law code but rather that of a narrative. The Torah is essentially a story of the origins of ancient Israel."[13] Indeed, Josephus argues that Greek history is unreliable because there exist so many different—and differing—accounts of any given event, while Jews recognize the Bible as the one true account of their past.[14]

Furthermore, for the Jews history and religious meaning are coextensive; the Bible is a foundational document for the culture. History in the Greek sense never had this status. History might be used for political ends, but for ultimate meaning the Greeks looked to philosophy, education, or cults.[15] The fact that at times of covenant renewal antiquarian history was recited is direct evidence for the foundational status of Hebrew history.[16]

---

[12] Arnaldo Momigliano, T*he Classical Foundations of Modern Historiography* (Berkeley: University of California, 1990) 16–19.

[13] James A. Sanders, *Torah and Canon* (Philadelphia: Fortress, 1972) 4.

[14] *Ag. Ap.* 1.15–27. See also the discussion in Shaye Cohen, "History and Historiography in the *Against Apion* of Josephus," *Essays in Jewish Historiography*, ed. Ada Rapoport-Albert (Wesleyan University, 1988) 5–7.

[15] Momigliano, *Classical Foundations*, 20.

[16] See Karlheinz Müller, "Geschichte, Heilsgeschichte und Gesetz," *Literatur und Religion des Frühjudentums*, ed. Johann Maier und Josef Schreiner (Würzburg: Echter, 1973) 73–105.

Although it is a necessary oversimplification, two strains of ancient Jewish antiquarian[17] historiography can be identified. The first reinterpreted earlier biblical history in order to keep biblical history vital during times of change and internal debate. The primary audience here is usually the domestic Jewish community. Therefore, I shall call this the 'Palestinian' strain. The second originates in the Hellenistic period and is deeply influenced by the literary canons of Greek authors. The audience in this case is usually the Gentile community or the oikoumene in general. These writings I will refer to as the 'Hellenistic strain.'[18] Both strains of historiography exhibit a kind of nationalism, but that nationalism takes on a different character in the Palestinian perspective than it does in the Hellenistic one. Each strain played up certain sentiments in its telling of the biblical story, while ignoring others. The Palestinian perspective emphasizes the institutions peculiar to Israel, while the Hellenistic perspective emphasizes the universal significance of Israelite history.

The Palestinian Strain

The first trajectory includes works like *Jubilees*, the *Biblical Antiquities* of Pseudo-Philo, and the Genesis Apocryphon.[19] These works each represent an attempt to make the biblical text relevant to the writer's current situation, especially when the understanding of that situation is not taken for granted

---

[17] I use the term antiquarian here to distinguish the use of biblical history from the writing of contemporary history. In the Persian and Hellenistic periods Jewish authors, such as those who wrote Ezra-Nehemiah and 1 Maccabees, composed historiographic works of the events of their own times. I am not concerned with those histories, but rather with the use of biblical or antiquarian history.

[18] I use the terms Palestinian and Hellenistic for convenience; they do not necessarily correspond to the geographic origins of the writings.

[19] Because we only possess a fragment of the Genesis Apocryphon—which covers the story of Abraham—we are uncertain of the historical scope of the text, and it is thereby difficult to judge its overall agenda. However, because the Genesis Apocryphon is likely dependent on *Jubilees* and is found only at Qumran, it probably reflects a sectarian point of view, even if nothing seems particularly sectarian about its retelling of the Abraham story. In any case it is properly a retelling, and not a commentary on Genesis or a targum, and it shares many of the same sentiments as *Jubilees* or Pseudo-Philo. See the discussion of Joseph A. Fitzmyer, *The Genesis Apocryphon of Qumran Cave I* (Rome: Biblical Institute, 1971) 6–19. We could also include here the "revealed histories" found in apocalyptic literature, which take a (sometimes world) historical perspective usually for the purpose of gaining eschatological insight. The works are too varied to discuss here, but see Robert G. Hall, (*Revealed Histories: Techniques for Ancient Jewish and Christian Historiography* [JSPSup 6; Sheffield: JSOT, 1991]) who includes many non-apocalyptic works which he rightly points out make claims to inspiration; these include *Jubilees* and Josephus' *Jewish War*.

by the general community. In a sense, this desire to highlight one's own needs in the retelling of the biblical story is not much different from what we observed in the biblical historical summaries or the hero lists in chapter two. For example, the summary in Nehemiah 9 reflects the interest of the returnees in reconstituting the community in the land. Part of this reconstitution involves a covenant renewal that stresses the keeping of the commandments, particularly those that solidify Jewish identity, like the Sabbath and possessing the promised land.

Although it is a fairly commonplace assumption—that these texts of history betray the author's or a community's interest in the current state of affairs[20]—it is worth making a brief exploration into their agendas in order to highlight some recurring interests. For instance, Nehemiah 9's interest in the purity of the land and the keeping of the commandments adumbrates the interests of *Jubilees*. The book of *Jubilees* is concerned with the religious calendar and a comprehensive chronological picture of events. It is no surprise that the culmination of that chronology is the entrance into the land, which takes place in the jubilee of jubilees.[21]

But it is the halakhic interests that most consistently color the author of Jubilees' reading of biblical history. Since the literary setting for *Jubilees* is a revelation to Moses on Mount Sinai,[22] the text begins with an address to Moses, but the recounting of history starts with the six days of creation. After this, a lengthy discussion of the Sabbath ensues in which the connection between God's rest on the seventh day and the observance of the Sabbath is made explicit. The observance of the Sabbath is seen as the identifying mark of the Jews at this stage of history.[23]

The author of *Jubilees* is concerned with the observance of all the feasts because of his calendrical concerns, but the Sabbath is the most important

---

20 Though this statement may seem ubiquitously true, in a variation of historiographical writing known as chronography, the interest was primarily directed at exclusively historical questions (usually about dating) without much didacticism for the contemporary reader. One example of this is *Seder Olam*. See Chaim Joseph Milikowsky, "Seder Olam: A Rabbinic Chronography," Ph.D. Diss., Yale University, 1981, esp. p. 5.

21 *Jubilees* 50; George Nickelsburg, "The Bible Rewritten and Expanded," *Jewish Writings*, 97.

22 See the discussion of Hall on *Jubilees* (*Revealed Histories*, 31–47). He designates *Jubilees* an "inspired prophetic history."

23 See 2:17 where God says "Behold I shall separate for myself a people from among all the nations. And they will also keep the Sabbath;" and 2:31, "The Creator of all blessed [the Sabbath] but he did not sanctify any people or nations to keep the Sabbath thereon with the sole exception of Israel." Translations for Jubilees are from O. S. Wintermute, "Jubilees," *OTP*, 35–142.

feast.[24] The author does not stop at simply proclaiming the need to observe the Sabbath because of historical precedent; he provides legal details about what it means not to work. Furthermore the revelatory character of *Jubilees* allows for some embellishments of the biblical account so as to establish the divine origins of the Sabbath: the Sabbath is a feast celebrated by the angelic host for eternity; only Israel, of all the nations on earth, is allowed the privilege of observing it.[25] Defilement of the Sabbath carries a very serious penalty:

> And you, command the children of Israel, and let them guard this day so that they might sanctify it and not do any work therein, and not defile it because it is more holy than any day. And everyone who pollutes it let him surely die. And anyone who will do any work therein, let him surely die forever so that the children of Israel might guard this day throughout their generations and not be uprooted from the land because it is a holy day and a blessed day. (2:26–28)

The author draws out of the biblical narrative several other points of law: Because Adam entered the Garden of Eden before Eve, the law for purification after childbirth extends seven days after a male and fourteen for a female (3:8–14); the fact that Abraham tithed establishes forever the rule of tithing (13:25–27); the story of Jacob, Rachel, and Leah establishes a law that the younger sister must never marry before the elder (28:6–8); the rape of Dinah sets a precedent for prohibition against taking foreign spouses (30). Overall, *Jubilees* represents a strict interpretation of biblical law.[26] Although the exact dating of *Jubilees* is uncertain, it was written during the Hellenistic period when Hellenism was perceived to be a serious threat.[27]

Although the *Biblical Antiquities* of Pseudo-Philo is not as consistently concerned with halakhic issues, the author does treat the regulations for cultic worship (13) found in Leviticus. Overall, Pseudo-Philo skips the legal material from the Pentateuch in his renarration of biblical history, but this selection process is probably due to the author's interest in creating a coherent and entertaining narrative,[28] and not to the avoidance of

---

[24] This is most evident in that the book concludes (50) with a reprisal of the laws pertaining to the Sabbath.

[25] See n. 23.

[26] Nickelsburg, "The Bible Rewritten," 100.

[27] Wintermute ("Jubilees," 44) puts the date between 161 and 140 BCE.

[28] See Frederick Murphy, *Pseudo-Philo: Rewriting the Bible* (New York: Oxford, 1993) 9–25.

halakhah. He is certainly no less interested in Jewish identity in the face of internal and external pressures than the author of *Jubilees*.

The *Biblical Antiquities* comes out of the volatile world of the First Century CE in Palestine,[29] when relations between Jews and Gentiles (especially those Gentiles who constitute the occupying power), as well as intra-Jewish sectarianism, produced intensely polemical responses similar to the time just before the Maccabean revolt. It is quite likely that the author known to us now as Pseudo-Philo sympathized with those factions who advocated resistance rather than complacence with the Romans.[30] This tendency is consistent with the essential themes that are transparent in Pseudo-Philo's retelling of the biblical story.

Among those major themes is an emphasis on covenant. The word *testamentum* occurs fifty-one times in the *Biblical Antiquities*.[31] The mention of covenant occurs at all those points in the biblical story when one would expect it—with Noah after the flood, with Abraham in Canaan, with Moses at Sinai—but the author also uses it thematically to look backward and forward in history. It is referred to several times in speeches made by various heroes in order to assure the people of Israel's continued viability in the face of adversity. Rebellion and Israel's lack of faithfulness to the covenant also comprise an important aspect of the overall covenantal theme. For instance, when God speaks to Moses at the time of his death, God forecasts Israel's future by telling Moses that the day the tablets of the covenant were smashed will be the same day in the calendar that Israel will fall victim to her enemies (the Babylonians). Of course God's fidelity to the covenant is absolutely unshakable; God must punish Israel for her sins, but God will never end the special covenantal relationship with Israel.[32]

---

[29] See discussions by Nickelsburg, ("Good and Bad Leaders in Pseudo-Philo's Liber Antiquitatum Biblicarum," *Ideal figures in Ancient Judaism: Profiles and Paradigms*, ed. John J. Collins and George W. E. Nickelsburg [Ann Arbor: Scholars, 1980] 62–63) and Saul Olyan, ("The Israelites Debate Their Options at the Sea of Reeds: *LAB* 10:3, Its Parallels, and Pseudo-Philo's Ideology and Background," *JBL* 110 [1991] 87–92). Both believe a date around 70 CE is likely.

[30] Olyan, "The Israelites Debate Their Options," 90.

[31] Murphy, *Pseudo-Philo*, 244.

[32] Both Nickelsburg ("Good and Bad Leaders," 62) and Murphy (*Pseudo-Philo*, 244–46) point out that Pseudo-Philo stresses that no matter how serious Israel's disobedience is, God will *never* abandon the covenant. Murphy also points out how striking this is, because although Pseudo-Philo is heavily dependent on the book of Judges, he does not emphasize the role of repentance so prevalent in that book. The covenant is truly unconditional.

Idolatry itself, which is seen as the ultimate violation of the covenant, is another major theme in the *Biblical Antiquities*. As Frederick Murphy says, "Pseudo-Philo enhances the element of idolatry when it appears in the biblical text and often inserts it in contexts where it is not originally present."[33] Examples abound. In recounting the story of Micah, the self-made priest whose mother manufactured an idol from silver (Judg 17), Pseudo-Philo devotes a substantial portion of his version of the story to a diatribe against idolatry which even involves a recounting of the decalogue. Murphy interprets the scene to mean thus:

> Every commandment is broken by the making of idols (44:7). Worshipping idols is equivalent to giving God's name to them and so takes God's name in vain. Idolatry defiles God's Sabbath. Dishonoring the Creator relates to dishonor of father and mother. Idolatry is the same as thievery. To seduce others (*seducere*, in this case meaning "to lead into idolatry") is the same as killing. Idolatry is adultery. Idolators accept false testimony. The connection between lust for foreign women and idolatry is implicit here but explicit throughout Pseudo-Philo. To commit idolatry is to commit every other possible sin at the same time.[34]

At the time of Moses' death, when God tells him he will not be permitted to enter the promised land, Pseudo-Philo tell us that the reason for this is to spare Moses the sight of the people who will eventually be engaged in idolatry (19:7). This example, among others, indicates that idolatry is associated with defilement of the land and with relations with Gentiles. Contact with Gentiles runs the risk of importing the worship of idols, hence Pseudo-Philo is also wary of marriage to foreigners.[35]

The interest in prevention of idolatry in the *Biblical Antiquities* is parallel to *Jubilees'* interest in insuring the celebration of the Sabbath and all the feasts. Cultic institutions and the worship of one true God are the most distinctive marks of Jewish identity. The author of *Jubilees'* emphasis on these aspects when narrating biblical history indicates a perceived threat from foreigners; it also most likely indicates that some Jews are assimilating or becoming syncretistic. Furthermore, the audience must surely be other Jews. The perspective in *Jubilees* may or may not reflect full-blown sectarianism, but at the very least it indicates internal debate. That the author of *Jubilees* and the *Biblical Antiquities* are compelled to legitimate their point of view to other

---

[33] Murphy, *Pseudo-Philo*, 252.

[34] Murphy, "Retelling the Bible: Idolatry in Pseudo-Philo," *JBL* 107 (1988) 279–80.

[35] Murphy, *Pseudo-Philo*, 264.

Jews through the use of their common history means that not all Jews of the time share the same ideas about how to handle the problem of national identity.

National identity is at the heart of the retellings of biblical history in texts like *Jubilees* and the *Biblical Antiquities*. After all, *Jubilees* was written after generations of rule by various Hellenistic powers and the *Biblical Antiquities* was written after about a century of Roman occupation. Pseudo-Philo may be unique in spending an inordinate amount of time covering the period of the Judges while grossly compressing the saga of Abraham,[36] but the interest in that period of Israelite history surely derives from the author's nationalistic impulse. The period of the Judges represents the time when Israel was in the land—having already received the inherited promises of "the covenant of the fathers"[37]—and was yet struggling for national cohesion, organization, and identity, not to mention her struggles with foreign peoples.

It is not surprising that Pseudo-Philo's version of biblical history is very much a history of heroes—"the great men" of the Bible.[38] These great men are national leaders, ordained by God, who faithfully guide the people in the covenant. Most often the leaders emerge in the midst of conflict among different groups. They make dramatic speeches either to chastise the people or motivate them to behave appropriately. Thus, the leaders are symbols of national unity. That the *Book of Biblical Antiquities* ends with the birth of the monarchy coheres with this perspective.[39]

The nation of Israel is represented by national leaders, institutions, common laws and beliefs, and the land with which it is identified. All these are seen to be at stake in these retellings of history, and so they are used as points of emphasis in the story.[40]

---

[36] According to Nickelsburg ("Bible Rewritten," 107) one-third of the *Biblical Antiquities* is drawn from Judges, while all the escapades of Abraham are compressed into one chapter.

[37] The term covenant can mean specific individual covenants or the standing relationship God has with Israel, but the phrase "covenant of the fathers" also occurs frequently; see Murphy, *Pseudo-Philo*, 245.

[38] Nickelsburg, "Good and Bad Leaders," 49–61.

[39] As it stands now, the *Biblical Antiquities* ends with the death of Saul. Some scholars have speculated that the original version may have extended into the Davidic monarchy. In any case, the plot of the story clearly points toward the establishment of the monarchy; see Murphy, *Pseudo-Philo*, 16–17.

[40] See the recent work by Betsy Halpern-Amaru (*Rewriting the Bible: Land and Covenant in Postbiblical Jewish Literature* [Valley Forge, PA: Trinity, 1994]) who discusses the concept of "peoplehood" in these texts and how notions of land and covenant have been modified by post-biblical circumstances. I regret that I was not able to take full account of

The Hellenistic Strain

We now turn to the other trajectory in Jewish historiography, which is represented best by the *Antiquities* of Josephus, and, in an earlier period, by the fragments from Jewish Hellenistic authors. The retelling of biblical history in these kinds of texts was inspired by Greek historiographical methods and is on par with similar endeavors by other "Barbarian" writers, such as Manetho's *Egyptian History*, Berossus's *Babylonian History*, and Philo of Byblos's *Phoenician History*.[41] The attempts by various nations, including the Jews, to give an account of their origins and development in Greek comprised what could be called the "culture wars" of the Hellenistic period. The motivational source of such writing was cultural pride. The goal was to outdo the other nations—the Greeks themselves as well as Barbarian peoples—in antiquity and cultural achievement. Because of this interest in competitive nationalism, the tone is always apologetic and thus directed at other nations, even though the genre is not strictly 'apology,' but rather historiography or Hellenistic romance.[42]

One of the most striking themes present in this literature is the universal perspective taken—the horizon is so much broader in writers like Eupolemus and Artapanus than in a work like *Jubilees* or Pseudo-Philo. Although both of those latter works start from the primeval period in Genesis, their ultimate goal is to establish Israel's unique relationship with God. Thus, Pseudo-Philo uses primeval history primarily for genealogical purposes, while Jubilees uses the created order to establish the eternally binding nature of Jewish law and liturgy. In sharp contrast, Eupolemus and Artapanus can take national figures and institutions and turn them into men and structures of universal significance.

For example, Moses is the cultural benefactor *par excellence*. As Eupolemus tells us, Moses invented the alphabet; "Moses was the first wise man and . . . he gave the alphabet to the Jews first; and . . . the Phoenicians received it

---

Halpern-Amaru's nuanced reading of these texts because of its very recent release.

[41] The historical writings of Hecataeus (sixth century BCE, no longer extent) were also influential. See R. A. Oden, "Philo of Biblos and Hellenistic Historiography" *PEQ* 110 (1978) 115–26; Momigliano, "The Origins of Universal History," *On Pagans, Jews, and Christians* (Middletown, CT: Wesleyan, 1987) 31–57; and Arthur Droge, *Homer or Moses? Early Christian Interpretations of the History of Culture* (Tübingen: J. C. B. Mohr [Paul Siebeck], 1989).

[42] The excerpts from Artapanus are best understood as being part of romance. For a discussion of the genre of Artapanus' work and the relationship between historiography and Hellenistic romance, see Carl R. Holladay, *Fragments from Hellenistic Jewish Authors, Volume I: Historians* (Chico, CA: Scholars, 1983) 190–91.

from the Jews, and the Greeks received it from the Phoenicians."[43] Obviously the point is not simply to re-establish the greatness of Moses as a Jewish leader, but as a world renowned figure. Artapanus attributes even more original accomplishments to Moses, including the founding of religious and political institutions in Egypt:

> This Moses became the teacher of Orpheus. When he reached manhood, he bestowed on humanity many useful contributions, for he invented ships, machines for lifting stones, Egyptian weapons, devices for drawing water and fighting, and philosophy. He also divided the state [Egypt] into thirty-six nomes, and to each of the nomes he assigned the god to be worshipped; in addition, he assigned the sacred writings to the priests.[44]

Moses accomplishes all this long before God instructs him to liberate the Jews. After these introductory comments about Moses, Artapanus reports many other non-biblical escapades which portray Moses as a world leader and adventurer. Besides his high level dealings in Egypt, he makes influential contact with Arabian and Ethiopian peoples.

Because Artapanus betrays his Alexandrian bias, one could argue that he is not really interested in reinterpreting biblical history but rather in Jewish apologetics directed at Hellenized Egypt. Obviously he is dependent on other sources for his version of biblical history besides the LXX. Still, he weaves the biblical with the non-biblical into a seamless *historia*. Whatever the source of the individual episode, the portrait of Moses is consistent: he is a superman with world-wide cultural, political, military, and religious influence. The following is the report of God's revelation to Moses to lead the people out of Egypt and Moses' response:

> While he was making his appeal to God, suddenly . . . fire appeared out of the earth, and it blazed even though there was neither wood nor any other kindling in the vicinity. Frightened at what happened, Moses fled but a divine voice spoke to him and told him to wage war against Egypt, and as soon as he had rescued the Jews, to return them to their ancient fatherland. Taking courage from this, he resolved to lead a fighting force against the Egyptians, but first he went to Aaron his brother. The king of the Egyptians, upon learning of the arrival of Moses, summoned him and inquired of him why he had come. Moses

---

43 Frag. 1 (=Clement of Alexandria, *Strom.* 1.23.153.4). All translations for the Jewish Hellenistic fragmentary historians are from Holladay, *Hellenistic Jewish Authors.*

44 Frag. 3 (=Eusebius, *PE* 9.27.4).

replied that he had come because the Lord of the universe [τὸν τῆς οἰκουμένης δεσπότην] had commanded him to liberate the Jews.[45]

Several details in this account, which is on the whole biblical, bespeak the author's universal perspective. First, it is assumed that Moses has the wherewithal to summon an army. Second, Pharaoh invites Moses to come to him. This little addition to the LXX implies that Pharaoh recognized the power and authority of Moses. Third, God is called the "Lord of the universe," a designation impressive on the one hand but generic on the other.[46]

Moses is not the only biblical hero transformed in this literature into a cultural benefactor. The writer now called Pseudo-Eupolemus characterizes Abraham not only as surpassing all men in nobility and wisdom, but as the discoverer of astrology and Chaldean science—clearly an attempt to undermine the commonly held assumption that the Babylonians were the founders of astrological science.[47] And Artapanus portrays Joseph also as a man of innumerable talents. Not only is he wise and learned but he divided the land of Egypt into fair allotments and taught them proper methods of farming.[48]

The universal perspective taken by these Jewish Hellenistic authors often means that biblical heroes have kinship ties to—or are sometimes even identified with—other nobles or heroes or admired nationalities. Among the less spectacular of these connections, Moses marries the daughter of Raguel, chief of the Arabian region whither Moses fled.[49] There are also more bombastic claims. Cleodemus Malchus claims that Abraham is the ancestor of major cultures like Assyria and Africa, even positioning him prior to the hero Heracles.[50] Furthermore, Artapanus identifies Moses with Hermes: "Moses was loved by the masses, and being deemed worthy of divine honor by the priests, he was called Hermes because of his ability to interpret the sacred writings."[51]

---

[45] Frag. 3 (=Eusebius, *PE* 9.27.21–22)

[46] Holladay (*Hellenistic Jewish Authors*, 240 n. 84) points out that δεσπότης is common as a divine appellation in Greek literature.

[47] Frag. 1 (=Eusebius, *PE* 9.17.3)

[48] Frag. 2 (=Eusebius, *PE* 9.23.2)

[49] Cf. Exod 2:10 where Zipporah is the daughter of a Midianite priest.

[50] Frag. 1 (=Josephus, *Ant.* 1.15.1 §239–241). See also Holladay's comments (*Hellenistic Jewish Authors*, 246).

[51] Frag. 3.6 (=Eusebius, *PE* 9.27.6).

The writer Eupolemus devotes a substantial discussion to the building of the Solomonic temple.[52] But the Jerusalem temple is so much more than a Jewish cultic center, it has a world-wide profile. Eupolemus, as well as Josephus, provide information about the involvement of the kings of Egypt and Tyre in the construction of the temple.[53] The kings contributed labor and resources. Both Eupolemus and Josephus include the texts of letters, one from each king as well as Solomon's requests to them for the various resources. The account, though partly dependent on the biblical text, is surely intended to emphasize the universal significance of the building of the temple.

Because the historical horizon is broad—spatially speaking that is—in these authors, the Jews always come across as one uniform people; there is no divisiveness in Israel. The deuteronomic theme of the people's recurring disobedience and the consequent punishment so common in the historical résumés and other works like Pseudo-Philo finds no place here. Furthermore, the leaders are never at odds with the people or even each other. Here is the description by Eupolemus of the succession that led to the formation of the monarchy:

> Joshua lived 110 years and pitched the holy tabernacle in Shilo. After that, Samuel became a prophet. Then, by the will of God, Saul was chosen by Samuel to be king, and he died after ruling twenty-one years. Then David his son ruled, and he subdued the Syrians who lived along the Euphrates river . . . .[54]

The painful transition from the period of the judges to the monarchy described with such narrative detail in 1 Samuel is non-existent here. The struggling saga of the people to find the right kind of leader, which was so important to Pseudo-Philo, is not pertinent to the story Eupolemus wants to tell.

Indeed, "the people" hardly play any role at all because the heroes loom so large. History is more like a string of biographies of the heroes, rather than the continuous story of a nation. This method of describing the biblical *historia* allows the writer to transcend national boundaries. "The people," collectively speaking are always identified with Israel, and Israel is one particular nation. But the heroes, while on the one hand being the symbolic

---

[52] Frag 2 (=Clement of Alexandria, *Strom.* 1.21.130.3=Eusebius, *PE* 9.30.1–34.18)

[53] The involvement of the King of Tyre is biblical (1 Kings 5:8–9), while the King of Egypt's (Vaphres) participation is not.

[54] Frag. 2 (=Eusebius, *PE* 9.30.2–3).

embodiment of the nation, are, on the other hand, individuals of noble stock who by their wits or connections have powers well beyond the nation-state.

No writer provides a better and more comprehensive example of the "great man theory of history" than Josephus in his work, the *Antiquities*.[55] Josephus not only stresses the heroic deeds of major biblical figures, but he transforms them into models of Hellenistic virtue and piety. As Louis Feldman says, Josephus' portrait of Abraham, for example, emphasizes Abraham's qualities as "a philosopher-king, scientist, rhetorician-logician, and romantic hero."[56] Carl Holladay as well as Feldman point out that all the major heroes are remarkably similar in their conformity to Hellenistic ideals of the hero, which not only demonstrates how much Josephus valued this type of portrait, but also points to its use as a unifying principle in Josephus' otherwise lengthy and disparate work.[57]

While it is true that Josephus does not have the kind of pagan flavor found in many of the earlier Hellenistic-Jewish historians—he does not for example identify Moses with Hermes—his work is no less directed at educated Gentiles. Josephus seeks to establish credibility with such an audience by several means. In addition to his Hellenized portrayal of the heroes (a trait in continuity with writers like Eupolemus and Artapanus), Josephus feels compelled to use and name numerous Greek sources, which would certainly appeal to a more critically astute audience.[58] Furthermore, Josephus imitates many stylistics and literary details of Greek authors. More than one scholar has noted that Josephus' portrayal of the bliss originally experienced by the first human beings (because they were closer to the source of creation), which is then followed by a decline in well-being, is dependent on Hesiod.[59]

---

[55] Louis H. Feldman, "Use, Authority and Exegesis of Mikra in the Writings of Josephus," *Mikra*, 480.

[56] Feldman, "Mikra in Josephus" 480–81. See also Feldman, "Abraham the Greek Philosopher in Josephus," *TAPA* 99(1968) 143–56.

[57] Holladay, *Theios Aner in Hellensitic Judaism: A Critique of the Use of the Category in New Testament Christology* (Missoula, MT: Scholars, 1977) 67–78; Feldman, "Mikra in Josephus," 481.

[58] Feldman ("Mikra in Josephus," 481) claims that Josephus names no fewer than fifty-five Greek authors.

[59] Feldman, "Hellenizations in Josephus' Portrayal of Man's Decline, " *Religions in Antiquity* (Leiden: Brill, 1968) 336–53. See also the discussion in Droge (*Homer or Moses?* 36–41) who calls Josephus' description of the intimacy between Adam and God a "Hesiodic interpretation of the biblical narrative."

The theme of providence (πρόνοια) may be the most "dominant interpretive motif"[60] in Josephus' version of biblical history, and one which is effective in adapting certain biblically specific concepts for a Gentile audience. In other words, Josephus replaces the deuteronomic themes of election and covenant[61] with a more generic form of moralizing which will appeal to a wide audience. Josephus' moralizing gives him more opportunity to discuss many of the internal conflicts in the history of Israel, and this tendency sets him apart from the earlier Hellenistic Jewish authors who neglected to mention any internal turmoil. But this is not necessarily evidence that Josephus has more of a Jewish audience in mind.[62] Josephus needs conflict in his *historia* because it allows him to narrate and assess right and wrong behavior. As he himself says in his preface to the *Antiquities*:

> [T]he main lesson to be learnt from this history by any who care to peruse it is that men who conform to the will of God, and do not venture to transgress laws that have been laid down, prosper in all things beyond belief, and for their reward are offered by God felicity; whereas, in proportion as they depart from the strict observance of these laws, things (else) practicable become impracticable, and whatever imaginary good thing they strive to do ends in irretrievable disasters. (*Ant.* 1.1.3 §14)

Thus, Josephus is not afraid to depict Jewish leaders, like Herod, in a bad light, since they provide moral examples.[63] Before Josephus tells us of Herod's execution of Antipater, he says, "I shall relate the whole story of this in order that it may be an example and warning to mankind to practice virtue in all circumstances" (17 §60).

Furthermore, Josephus' particular assessment of conflict in the history of Israel is geared toward evoking Roman sympathies for the virtuous side. In other words, Josephus argues that the Jews have gone astray or caused trouble only when they have abandoned their ancestral laws; when they and their leaders have acted in accordance with the ancient laws, they have been

---

60 Attridge, "Josephus," *Jewish Writings*, 218.

61 Attridge (*The Interpretation of Biblical History in the Antiquitates Judaicae of Flavius Josephus* [Missoula, MT, 1976] 148) discusses the lack of emphasis on covenant in the *Antiquities* and speculates that an avoidance of it is due to the Gentile audience for which the text is geared.

62 Feldman ("Mikra in Josephus," 471) argues that some episodes in the *Antiquities* seem to be directed at Jews. Not only are these episodes questionable, but Feldman himself says that the Jewish audience is ultimately only secondary to the Gentile audience Josephus has in mind.

63 Attridge, "Josephus," 218–19.

models of virtue. This apologetic strategy is in keeping with the apologetics of the *Jewish War*. Those Jews who rebel are those who are disobedient to their own tradition; eventually they receive their just desserts. In this way the *Antiquities* functions as a defense of Jewish rights.[64]

Comparison of the Palestinian and Hellenistic Strains

Although this was an all too brief overview of the two strains of antiquarian history in the relevant period, enough has been said to demonstrate the pattern. On the one hand are the Hellenistic historians, who are largely—though not exclusively[65]—writing in the diaspora for the outside world. As a result they emphasize the universal significance of Israelite history, while those characteristics that are uniquely Jewish in the history of Israel are downplayed; most notable among these is a lack of stress on the covenant. On the other hand, the texts of *Jubilees* and the *Biblical Antiquities* of Pseudo-Philo are written for an internal audience, and they take pride in distinctly Jewish institutions and the land of Israel.

As we noted earlier, God is always faithful in Pseudo-Philo, even though the Israelites do not deserve it, because of the binding nature of the covenant. Conversely, Josephus wants to demonstrate that the Israelites deserve God's attention because of their virtue, not because of an unconditional agreement.[66] Perhaps the best illustration of this is the way the two authors report the events at Mt. Sinai. For Pseudo-Philo the episode of the golden calf is a quintessential example of the Israelites' incapacity to do the right thing. When Moses pleads with God to have mercy on the people, it is not because Moses thinks the people are redeemable, but because God's nature is forever faithful. If God abandoned Israel, God would besmirch God's name (12:9–10). Although God knows that the people "will forget the covenants that [God] established with their fathers," God "will not forget them forever" (13:10). By contrast, Josephus does not so much as allude to the golden calf incident. The reason he gives for Moses twice ascending the mountain is that the people request a full law code to supplement the decalogue (3.5.6 §93). Thus, the peoples' behavior is proper and dignified throughout the whole affair. But more significantly, the picture in Josephus of the scene at Mt. Sinai is about the bringing of a law code to the people, not about the re-establishment of the covenant.

---

[64] Attridge, "Josephus," 225–26.

[65] Eupolemus is thought to be Palestinian because of his rudimentary Greek and his knowledge of Hebrew and Aramaic; see Holladay, *Hellenistic Jewish Authors*, 93–95.

[66] Attridge, *Interpretation*, 148.

Furthermore, the geographical perspective of the diaspora is evident among the Hellenistic historians. That the Jews are historically identified with a specific locale becomes almost inconsequential. Indeed, for Philo (as for the rabbis) the land becomes symbolic of an eschatological age or utopia.[67] None of the fragmentary historians mention Abraham's divine entitlement to the land, including Pseudo-Eupolemus' comparatively lengthy account of Abraham's life. Although Josephus mentions God's promise to Abraham to inherit the land of the Canaanites, it is a brief reference and is not depicted as part of the covenant (1.10.3 §185). Rather, it is due to the fact that the Canaanites deserve to be dispossessed.[68] By contrast, the theological importance of the land is an integral part of biblical history in the Genesis Apocryphon,[69] *Jubilees*, and Pseudo-Philo. Pseudo-Philo, as we have already remarked, spends one-third of his text on the period of the Judges and is consistently concerned with allotments of the land. He, like the other two authors, is not much concerned with what happens outside of Palestine. For the author of *Jubilees*, the land and the covenant are intimately connected. When God predicts the future disobedience of the Israelites to Abraham, he says,

---

67 Although Philo retains the notion of a return to the land in a messianic age, he does not make much of it. Rather, what distinguishes Jews from others is not their geography, but their laws, as this passage from the *Life of Moses* 1:278 indicates: "not because their dwelling-place is set apart and their land severed from others, but because in virtue of the distinction of their peculiar customs they do not mix with others to depart from the ways of their fathers." The rabbis' view of a symbolic/eschatological understanding of the land can be summed up in this passage from *m. Sanhedrin* 10.1: "All Israelites have a share in the world to come, for it is written, Thy people also shall be righteous, they shall inherit the land for ever . . ." (Isa 60:21). For a thorough discussion, see W. D. Davies, *The Gospel and the Land: Early Christianity and Jewish Territorial Doctrine* (Berkeley: University of California, 1974).

68 Josephus (1.6.3 §141–42) is dependent on the Bible here (Gen 9:22–28): The reason the Canaanites deserve this punishment is due to the curse upon Ham which was transferred to his son, Canaan.

69 The Genesis Apocryphon makes quite a to-do over God's giving Abraham the land: "'Go up to Ramath-Haor, which is to the north of Bethel, the place where you are dwelling; lift up your eyes and look to the east, west, south, and north, and see all this land which I am giving to you and to your descendants forever' . . . . The next day I climbed up to Ramath-Hazor and I looked at the land from this height, from the River of Egypt to Lebanon and Senir, and from the Great Sea to Hauran, and all the land of Gebal as far as Kadesh and at all the Great Desert . . . . And he said to me 'To your descendants I shall give all this land; they will inherit it forever Rise, walk about, and go (around) to see how great is its length and how great is its width. For I shall give it to you and to your descendants after you for all ages.'" (Text from Fitzmyer, Col . 21 vv. 8–14) The text continues with Abraham taking an actual tour of the land.

And great wrath from the Lord will be upon the sons of Israel because they left his covenant and have turned aside from his words. And they have provoked and blasphemed inasmuch as they have not done the ordinance of this law [circumcision] because they have made themselves like the gentiles to be removed and uprooted from the land. (15:34)

Faithfulness to the covenant means dwelling in the land, while unfaithfulness means exclusion. Furthermore, *Jubilees* winds down its narrative with a glorious vision of celebrating Passover in the land of the people's inheritance (49:18–21). This vision includes the forbidding of the Passover feast outside the land: "They shall not be able to observe the Passover in their cities or in any district except before the tabernacle of the Lord or before his house in which his name dwells." Given *Jubilees'* preoccupation with the celebration of feasts, it is no surprise that the author would advance the centrality of Jerusalem, thereby promoting the practice of pilgrimage to the holy city.

Thus, we have two very different perspectives on biblical history which circulated concurrently—one which was part of the Hellenistic dialogue, or debate, on the origins and history of civilization and was mainly directed to outsiders, and one which was part of the debate about the authentic form of Judaism and was directed to other Jews. Although works in both groups sometimes overlap in reporting similar midrashic details,[70] their agendas in recounting history could not be more different. However, there exists at least one consistent literary theme in both perspectives: the emphasis on heroes. It is not only Josephus who employs the "great man" theory of history; they *all* have a pervasive interest in heroes to a greater or lesser extent. Obviously, this interest is much greater in the Hellenistic historians and Josephus than in *Jubilees*, but even *Jubilees* gives as much space to hero-specific details like the birth and early life of Moses as to the narration of the exodus. The fact that the Genesis Apocryphon presents Abraham narrating his own story[71] is another indication of the focus on the individual lives of the heroes. The reason for this emphasis on heroes is not entirely clear, but it is surely related to the rise of individualism in the Hellenistic and post-Hellenistic age and perhaps to the entertainment value to be found in the life-stories of heroes, rather than in the chronicling of national events.

---

[70] Feldman, "Mikra in Josephus," 472.

[71] Abraham's story is told in the first person until Genesis 14, when it switches to third person.

Before moving on to the presentation of biblical history in the NT, it may be worth noting that neither one of these strains of historiography correspond exactly to the presentation of biblical heroes and history in Hebrews 11, except for the fact that the focus is on the heroes rather than the people. However, certain elements do overlap, primarily with the Hellenistic strain of historiography. The most obvious example is that the neglect of covenant and a theology of the land is a factor in both the Hellenistic texts and in Hebrews 11. At the same time this demonstrates the lack of similarity between Hebrews 11 and texts like *Jubilees* and the *Biblical Antiquities* of Pseudo-Philo. On the other hand, the heroes in Hebrews 11 in no way resemble the paragons of Greek virtue found in the Hellenistic texts. At best, the similarity between Hellenistic historiography and Hebrews 11 is only partial.

Having now completed our survey of the perception of Israelite history in ancient Jewish historiography, we can move to the equivalent in the NT. Once we cover the relevant texts in the NT, we will have a good picture of contemporary views of biblical history. This overview will in turn set the perspective of biblical history in Hebrews 11 in high relief against these contemporary perspectives. Then when we survey the Christian writings after the NT, the turning point in the early Christian understanding of biblical history that Hebrews 11 represents will be evident.

Biblical History in the New Testament

Besides Hebrews 11, the only other place in the NT where we find a comprehensive retelling of biblical history is in Stephen's speech in Acts 7. However, Paul's discussion in Romans 9–11 of the place of Israel in salvation history, though not properly a retelling,[72] does involve a biblically based construct of the history of Israel as part of his argument.[73] Although

---

[72] Paul does not start out wanting to tell the story of the Bible as we have seen in the texts so far considered. Rather, he makes an argument and enlists the Bible as evidence. Because of this orientation, Paul's agenda is up front rather than hidden in the retelling itself. What makes Romans 9–11 different than the countless other examples of speech-makers and letter-writers who cite scripture as evidence is how comprehensive Paul is in his use of the biblical text.

[73] Robin Scroggs ("Paul as Rhetorician: Two Homilies in Romans 1–11," *Jews, Greeks and Christians,* eds., Robin Scroggs and R. Hamerton-Kelly [Leiden: Brill, 1976] 271–298) argues that Rom 1–4 and 9–11 together function as one large recounting of scripture. Indeed, Scroggs (290) believes that in Rom 1–4 and 9–11 Paul has blended the "narration of the events of *Heilgeschichte* such as is found in the Song of Moses (Deut. 32) and Psalms 78 and 106" with a "more explicit midrashic tradition." Although I focus here on chaps. 9–11, Paul's orientation toward the Abraham story and its implications in chap.

quantitatively speaking Abraham receives the majority of Paul's attention in Romans as a whole,[74] in 9–11 he also mentions Isaac, Sarah, Rebecca, Jacob, Esau, Moses, Pharaoh, quotations from two prophets (Hosea and Isaiah), Elijah and David. Thus, Paul demonstrates his interest in the big picture of biblical history. The point of these much discussed chapters of Romans is,[75] on the one hand, to account for the inclusion of Gentiles into the salvation-historical trajectory established in Jewish scripture, and, on the other, to account for the fact that so many Jews have rejected the kerygma and the salvation-historical understanding that accompanies it. Does the Jews' rejection of Christian teaching represents God's rejection of them? Where would that leave God's promises to Israel, which are supposed to have eternal validity?

Paul's first response to these questions is contained in a statement particularly significant for our discussion of biblical history in 9:4–5:

> They are Israelites, and to them belong the adoption, the glory, the covenants, the giving of the law, the worship, and the promises; to them belong the patriarchs, and from them, according to the flesh, comes the Messiah, who is over all, God blessed forever.

Again, this list of Israel's possessions is not a diachronic reading of scripture. However, the list points toward many moments in scriptural history which are often found on the historical résumés, hero lists, and longer retellings like the work of Pseudo-Philo. Before discussing each of the privileges listed as belonging to Israel, we should note that Paul first makes the statement: οἵτινές εἰσιν Ἰσραηλῖται, "they are Israelites." He does not use "the common ethnic or political title *Ioudaioi*,"[76] which would have cleared up the confusion to be found in two-thousand years of commentaries over Paul's varied use of the term 'Israel.' But here Paul surely means the actual, historical, ethnic people[77]—which would have made the use of 'Ἰουδαῖοι quite appropriate. One reason that Paul chose to use 'Israel' here can be derived from the use of the term a few lines later, in v. 6, in which he makes a distinction between "those who are from Israel" and "Israel," when he says οὐ γὰρ πάντες οἱ ἐξ Ἰσραὴλ οὗτοι Ἰσραήλ, "For not all those who are

---

4 is, to be sure, a forerunner to the argument in chaps. 9–11.

[74] Paul devotes Romans 4 to Abraham.

[75] The literature on Romans 9–11 is enormous. Scholarly discussions of the finer points of the text need not detain us here; for a recent, thorough bibliography see Joseph A. Fitzmyer, *Romans* (AB; New York: Doubleday, 1993) 550–54.

[76] Fitzmyer, *Romans*, 545.

[77] Fitzmyer, *Romans*, 545.

from Israel are Israel."[78] Thus, Paul's choice to use the term 'Israelites' in v. 4 prepares the way for him to demonstrate the subtle nuances of the term 'Israelites'—that it can be both an ethnic designation and a theological one—which will in turn allow him to use it as a designation for Gentile Christians. Still, what is striking is that he uses the present tense, "they *are* Israelites." That he does not begrudge the use of the sacred term 'Israel' as a current designation for the Jews is significant. It shows that Paul perceives a seamless historical continuity between his contemporary Jews and the Israelites of the Bible.

Therefore, the privileges Paul enumerates in 9:4–5 are not merely attributes of Israel past, but describe the condition of Jews now and always. The first privilege "adoption" (υἱοθεσία) is a somewhat odd term,[79] but it clearly refers to God's unique caring relationship with Israel, analogous to that of a parent to a child. It may even be an oblique way of speaking of Israel's election, since that term (ἐκλογή) does not occur in this catalogue.[80] "Glory" (δόξα) is most likely a reference to the manifestation of Yahweh at the time of the exodus and in the wilderness, but it may also mean that the Jews are a people deserving of honor because of their special relationship with God.[81] "Covenants" (διαθῆκαι), standing third in the list of privileges and in the plural, obviously refers to the individual covenants made with various ancestors, Noah, Abraham, Moses, among others. The theme of covenant, both as a general description of the relationship between God and the people, as well the individuals convenants, may be the most typical theme to be found in the résumés, hero lists, and the longer retellings like *Jubilees* and the *Antiquities* of Pseudo-Philo. (It was, however, conspicuously absent from the Hellenistic historians.) There is no ambiguity that the fourth blessing "the giving of the law" (νομοθεσία) refers to the legislation enacted by Moses at Mt. Sinai. The fifth, "worship" (λατρεία) most likely refers to the cult.[82] The sixth, "the promises," also in the plural, must mean the multiplicity of promises connected with the covenants made with the ancestors, e.g., the promise to Abraham of inheriting the land, the promise

---

78 Translation mine. The NRSV reads "For not all Israelites truly belong to Israel . . . ."

79 The word never appears in the LXX; see BAGD, 833.

80 Paul uses the term ἐκλογή in 11:28.

81 Paul's use of the term υἱοθεσία indicates that he is not restricting himself to septuagintal referents and terminology.

82 Fitzmyer (*Romans*, 547) points out that the verb λατρεύειν is used exclusively for the cult of Yahweh in the LXX.

of a never-ending dynasty to David.[83] The seventh privilege is the claim to an ancestral lineage, (ὧν οἱ πατέρες).[84] Finally, the Jews can claim that the Messiah descended from that lineage—κατὰ σάρκα, of course.

Paul's list of privileges enjoyed by the Jews focuses on their national distinctiveness. Although Paul is sincerely interested in the universal dimension of salvation-history—and, later, in his quotations from the prophets, he will stress the universal dimension of scripture—*he does not attempt to find universal significance in the actual history of Israel*. In other words, he is not interested in portraying Abraham or Moses as a teacher of theology to other nations, like the Hellenistic historians were. The pride of Israel is not her status in the world, but her status with God, which is represented by those privileges and institutions *peculiar* to Israel.

Nevertheless, Paul wants to write Gentiles into the history of Israel. It seems strange that this goal of his did not lead him to employ the methods of his Hellenistic Jewish predecessors. Rather, Paul's two primary arguments rely on simple scripture: 1) the promise of Isaac to Abraham makes Isaac and his descendants the children of faith, which is not ethnically specific (like the law or the covenants);[85] and 2) the notion, found mainly in the prophets, but also in the promise to Abraham itself, that God is not just the God of the Jews but of all nations.[86]

---

[83] Davies (*The Gospel and the Land,* 167) points out that 'promise' in the singular would surely denote the land explicitly. The plural does not highlight the promise of the land but it definitely includes it. See Davies, 178–79.

[84] As Davies (*The Gospel and the Land,* 170) says, "In the rootless, Hellenistic world of the first century pride in pedigree was cherished."

[85] In 9:7-15, Paul picks up where he left off in Romans 4 (Scroggs, "Paul as Rhetorician," 278) to argue that God's chosen ones are not dictated by biology or human convention, but rather derive from God's own choices. Interestingly this passage contains the same quotation of God's promise to Abraham as appeared in Hebrews 11: "through Isaac shall your descendants be named." Furthermore, mention of Abraham and the children of promise is followed by a brief discussion of Jacob and Esau, and the fact that the younger son inherited, while the older was dispossessed, and this, too, was a theme we identified in Hebrews 11. That the scriptural referents in Romans 4 and 9 are so similar to those in the 'Abraham and the Patriarchs' section of Heb 11:8–22 led James Swetnam (*Jesus and Isaac: A Study of the Epistle to the Hebrews in Light of the Aqedah* [Rome: Biblical Institute, 1981] 98–109) to argue that Hebrews 11 may be as concerned about 'spiritual descendants' as Paul is. What is certain is that both texts show a profound concern for genealogical legitimation in their recounting of Israelite history.

[86] In Romans 4 Paul quotes from that part of the promise to Abraham (Gen 17:5) where God says that Abraham will be the father of many nations. Davies (*The Gospel and the Land,* 177) stresses that this part of the promise was neglected in contemporary Judaism. Abraham was essentially the father of the Jews; even proselytes were not allowed to call Abraham "our father." Davies explains, "The exigencies of Jewish history—not

Although Paul is unique in carrying these two notions as far as he did in his salvation-historical scheme, the traditional Palestinian historiography of scripture remains largely intact. The Jews are the people of the covenant and the promise. God may punish them when they are disobedient, but God never abandons them. In fact, the reason Paul is in such a conundrum about the problem of Israel's salvation is that while he promulgates an utterly novel teaching about Christ—of whom the scriptures foretold—his understanding of the biblical story is thoroughly Jewish.[87] Thus, the biblical model of God's relation to the (ethnic) people of Israel must prevail, because God is a reliable maker of promises.

Indeed, the prevailing wisdom about Romans 9–11 since Krister Stendahl's landmark work,[88] has emphasized just this point. Here Paul, himself an Israelite, writes apologetically on behalf of Jews, not polemically against them.[89] God has not rejected his people. The traditional view of the biblical story is still so much intact that the only way for Paul to picture the Gentiles as a part of it is to see them as "grafted on" at a later date (11:17–18). Although the advent of Christ is now part of salvation-history, present day Judaism remains continuous with its biblical past.[90] Belief in Christ and the continuing existence of Judaism have not yet become mutually exclusive.[91]

---

surprisingly—had pressed upon the Abrahamic promise a "national, territorial stamp which often tended to obliterate its universal range." Along similar lines, Fishbane ("The Exodus Motif/Paradigm," 130) discusses the difficulty which translators and interpreters had with the reference to the Egyptians in Isa 19:25 as "my people" ('ammi): "Unable to tolerate such a theological paradox, the Septuagint and Targum traditions renationalized the text and substituted Israel for Egypt."

[87] Scholars like Ernst Käsemann (*Perspectives on Paul* [Philadelphia: Fortress, 1971] 138–66) tend to argue for Paul's hermeneutical originality. There is no doubt that Paul's belief in Christ affected his understanding of scripture and his reading of Jewish texts. My point here is that insofar as scripture contains the narrative of events that make-up Israelite history, Paul does not see the biblical history of Israel in a way that substantially diverges from contemporary Jews. Admittedly, the story of the history of Israel ends with the post-biblical fact of the advent of Christ for Paul. But Paul's reading of the biblical history of Israel is rather conventional: he still sees scripture as the national history of the Jews.

[88] Krister Stendahl, *Paul among Jews and Gentiles and Other Essays* (Philadelphia: Fortress, 1976).

[89] Fitzmyer, *Romans*, 541.

[90] According to Alan F. Segal (*Paul the Convert* [New Haven: Yale, 1990]264) because Paul tolerated the practice of Judaism among Christian Jews, they never experienced the transforming power of their Christian belief and therefore they never could have formed a truly Christian (as distinct from a Jewish) identity.

[91] And, as John Gager (*The Origins of Anti-Semitism: Attitudes toward Judaism in Pagan and*

I turn now to Acts 7, Stephen's speech which is—at least in its literary setting—a response to charges that he has committed blasphemy.[92] Stephen's speech can be easily placed in the tradition of those speeches from Jewish scripture which rehearse the history of Israel. Indeed, the speech has been viewed as so typically Jewish that Martin Dibelius, who was otherwise disposed to believing that the speeches in Acts were Lucan compositions, asserts that this speech must be based on a source, because it is a non-polemical "*neutral* history of Israel."[93] More recently, the polemical character of the speech has been ascertained, and, therefore, the neutral history theory has been undermined.[94] (My hope is that this study will make a contribution to the eradication of the notion of neutral history in general.)

A quick glance at the text reveals why so many scholars have perceived the text as more Jewish than Christian. The list extends from Abraham to David and includes most all the major figures and events that we found on the Jewish hero lists and historical résumés we surveyed earlier.[95] The speech is comparatively comprehensive in its scope and is notably faithful to its source text, the LXX.[96]

Christian Antiquity [New York: Oxford, 1985] has shown, for many Christians of both Jewish and Gentile background, the two did not become mutually exclusive until much later than has traditionally been assumed.

[92] On the problematic relationship between the content of Stephen's speech and its literary setting in Acts, see F. F. Bruce, "Stephen's Apologia," *Scripture: Meaning and Method*, ed. B, Thompson (England: , 1987) 37–50.

[93] Martin Dibelius, "The Speeches in Acts and Ancient Historiography," *Studies in the Acts of the Apostles* ed. H. Greeven (New York: Scribner's, 1956) 138–85 (italics mine). Hans Conzelmann (*Acts of the Apostles* [Hermeneia; Philadelphia: Fortress, 1987] 53–58) and Ernst Haenchen (*The Acts of the Apostles: A Commentary* [Philadelphia: Westminster, 1971] 286–90) follow this line of thought. A redaction critical or source critical discussion of Acts 7 would unnecessarily distract us here; for a summary of thought on this matter see E. M. Boismard, "Le Martyre d'Etienne Actes 6,8–8,2," *RSR* (1981) 182; for a recent assessment and bibliography of the debate see J. J. Kilgallen "The Function of Stephen's Speech," *Bib* 70 (1989) 173–4.

[94] See Earl Richard, "The Polemical Character of the Joseph Episode in Acts 7," *JBL* 98 (1979) 255–67; and T. L. Donaldson, "Moses Typology and the Sectarian Nature of Early Christian Anti-Judaism: A Study in Acts 7," *JSNT* 12 (1981) 27–52.

[95] The figures listed in Acts 7 can be found in Appendix B.

[96] Richard ("Polemical Character," 258) commenting on the recounting of the Joseph episode, says "The amount of verbatim or nearly verbatim borrowing is truly amazing." He goes on to say that this is probably the reason why so many scholars have assumed it is a "neutral" retelling. For a more detailed study of the relation of the LXX to Acts 7, see Richard, *Acts 6:1–8:4: The Author's Method of Composition* (SBLDS 41; Missoula: Scholars, 1978). Some scholars have speculated that the Samaritan Pentateuch has influenced the telling of the biblical story; this idea began with Paul Kahle ("Untersuchungen zur

The author begins with Abraham and highlights three events in Abraham's life: his call, God's promise about the inheritance of the land which in this case includes God's forecast about the future vicissitudes of Abraham's descendants, and the covenant of circumcision.[97] The author does mention other elements but does not treat them as significant. For example, the birth of Isaac is mentioned but the story of his miraculous conception is not told. Furthermore, the offering of Isaac is not even referred to. Conversely, he offers an unusual amount of commentary about other events, namely that Abraham moved around a lot and never possessed the land his descendants inherited.

But these comments do not necessarily indicate an indictment of Abraham. On the contrary, the closest match of this portrait of Abraham is Nehemiah 9, which also includes the call, the promise of land, and the covenant. The reason for the stress on Abraham's wanderings has more to do with the overall interest of the speech, which is to demonstrate that God is not confined to Jerusalem or the land of Israel. As others have pointed out, when God reveals God's self, it is always outside the land: Abraham receives his call in Mesopotamia, God provides for Joseph in Egypt, and God appears to Moses in the wilderness.[98] This point is made clear by the last segment of Stephen's speech which is an unbridled attack upon the Jerusalem temple (which is of course the center of the promised land).[99]

In sum, the author has a bias against the temple, Jerusalem, and the land. Upon first consideration, this bias appears analogous to the Jewish Hellenistic stream of historiography.[100] But, conversely, the author mentions

---

Geschichte des Pentateuchtextes," *Theologische Studien und Kritiken* 88 [1915] 399–415) according to Robin Scroggs ("The Earliest Hellenistic Christianity " *Religions in Antiquity,* ed. Jacob Neusner [Leiden: Brill, 1968] 176–206) who follows up on this idea by arguing that Stephen's speech represents a Christian missionary document to the Samaritans. For a review and critique of the various positions of Samaritan influence upon Acts 7, see Richard, "Acts 7: An Investigation of the Samaritan Evidence," *CBQ* 39 (1977) 190–208.

[97] Marion Soards (*The Speeches in Acts: Their Content, Context, and Concerns* [Louisville: Westminster/John Knox, 1994] 62) points out how noteworthy the reference to circumcision is here. Covenant is only mentioned twice in the book of Acts (3:25 and 7:8) and circumcision only appears in one other speech in Acts (21:21).

[98] The "revelation-outside-of-Palestine" theme is commonly recognized; see A. Ehrhardt, *The Acts of the Apostles: Ten Lectures* (Manchester: Manchester University, 1969); Richard, "Polemical Character," 259–60; and D. Sylva, "The Meaning and Function of Acts 7:46–50," *JBL* 106 (1987) 261–275.

[99] Kilgallen ("Function of Stephen's Speech," 177–81) believes the attack is not on the temple per se (ἱερόν), but on the thinking that the temple is God's house (οἶκος).

[100] Some have pointed out that the comment that Moses "was instructed in all the wisdom of the Egyptians," indicates a more Hellenistic portrait of Moses. It is similar, but

the covenant of Abraham, and even mentions the sign of the covenant—circumcision! Indeed, with the exception of the bias against the land, most of what the author includes in his biblical story is typical of what we find in the Palestinian view of Jewish history. The heroes are the leaders of a defiant and conflicted nation, and there is mention of covenant and promise, the giving of the law, and entering into the land. Furthermore, the people are relentlessly disobedient—this too must be seen as a fundamentally Jewish (and biblical) theme.

What some scholars have misunderstood is that the bad light that is shed on the people of Israel in this retelling is not a peculiarly Christian attack upon Judaism *per se*, but is rather typical of the longstanding biblical indictment of Israel's bad behavior.[101] A brief look at two other segments of the speech, one dealing with Joseph, the other with Moses, will illustrate the typical nature of this polemic.

Earl Richard has persuasively argued that although the alterations to Stephen's telling of the Joseph story (7:19–26) are slight, the author's bias is evident in them.[102] First, while other biblical retellings mention that Joseph was sold into slavery (Psalm 104, Wisdom 10), they do not usually mention that it was because Joseph's brothers were jealous of him. Second, in the biblical account it is not his brothers who sell him into slavery but the Midianites (Gen 37:28, 36). However, in Acts 7 the brothers are the ones said to have sold their brother. Although Richard does not note it, this picture of the brothers is similar to the one in *Jubilees*: "And [his brothers] acted fraudulently and made a plot against him to kill him, but they repented and sold him to a band of Ishmalites" (34:11); as well the one in Pseudo Philo: "Now Jacob and his twelve sons lived in the land of Canaan. And these hated their brother Joseph, whom they delivered into Egypt to Potiphar . . ." (8:9).

The antithesis constructed between Joseph and his brothers is analogous to the contrasting images of Moses and the people in the next segment of Stephen's speech. The bulk of the author's attention here is directed toward Moses' personal biography and the people's disobedience,[103] which includes the golden calf incident. The contrast between Moses and the people is sharp:

---

in the Hellenistic historians we surveyed, Moses is the *teacher* of wisdom, not the student.

[101] Cf. Nehemiah 9 and Ezekiel 20.

[102] Richard, "Polemical Character."

[103] The actual exodus receives a scant one line, "He led them out, having performed wonders and signs in Egypt, the Red Sea and the wilderness . . ." (v. 36).

[Moses] is the one who was in the congregation in the wilderness with the angel who spoke to him at Mount Sinai, and with our ancestors; and he received living oracles to give to us. Our ancestors were unwilling to obey him; instead they pushed him aside, and in their hearts they turned back to Egypt, saying to Aaron, "Make gods for us who will lead the way for us; as for this Moses who led us out from the land of Egypt, we do not know what has happened to him." (vv. 38–40)

Again, the description for this incident is similar to the one given by Pseudo-Philo:

And while [Moses] was on the mountain, the heart of the people was corrupted, and they gathered to Aaron, saying, 'Make gods for us whom we may serve, as the other nations have, because that Moses through whom wonders were done before our eyes has been taken away from us." (12:2).

The people here are not as antagonistic toward Moses as they are in Acts 7, but the image of them asking Aaron to help them to become idolaters is equally negative in both texts. The details of Moses being pushed aside by the people in Acts 7 derive from a Jesus-Moses typology[104] that Pseudo-Philo obviously did not have. But as strong as the invective against the people is in Acts 7, it is not any worse than the claims by the Qumran community that the whole nation of Israel has fallen into irredeemable apostasy.[105]

Thus, Acts 7 is not a particularly Christian reading of biblical history. Claims by scholars that the vituperative attack upon Israel is "completely aberrant"[106] from anything that came before, or that the speech is a "vital manifesto of the breakaway of the Church from its Jewish moorings"[107] is to

---

104 On this see Donaldson ("Moses Typology," 39–45) and Conzelmann (*Acts*, 53–53).

105 Although the writer of the retelling in the Covenant of Damascus (see my discussion of this text in chapter two) does not literally describe the golden calf incident, surely he has it in mind when considering the people's recurring disobedience: "Through [the evil inclination] the first members of the Covenant sinned and were delivered up to the sword, because they forsook the Covenant of God and chose their own will and walked in the stubbornness of their hearts, each of them doing his own will" (3.); and a few lines later: "Yet they wallowed in the sin of man and in ways of uncleanness, and they said 'This is our way.'" This is in no way the nastiest example of the Qumranic attack on Israel; see CD 8 for worse. For discussions of the ubiquity of intra-Jewish polemic, see Luke T. Johnson, "The New Testament's Anti-Jewish Slander and the Conventions of Ancient Jewish Polemic," *JBL* 108 (1989) 419–41; and Craig Evans, "Faith and Polemic: The New Testament and First Century Judaism, " *Anti-Semitism and Early Christianity: Issues of Faith and Polemic,* eds. Craig Evans and Donald Hagner (Minneapolis: Fortress, 1993) 1–17.

106 Marcel Simon, *St Stephen and the Hellenists in the Primitive Church* (London: 1958) 98.

107 William Neil, *The Acts of the Apostles* (New Century Bible; London: 1973) 116, quoted

ignore a long tradition—which, to be sure, became more exaggerated with the advent of Jewish sectarianism—of inner Jewish polemic. In addition to the emphases we have already pointed out, the repeated phrase "our ancestors" and terms like "our race" (7:19) indicate how much a part of Jewish history the author feels himself to be. Scholars are right to identify the polemical nature of Acts 7, but it is however, an intra-Jewish polemic, insofar as the early Christian movement is a Jewish sect. "Finally," as T. L. Donaldson has said, "nowhere does the polemic of Acts 7 show evidence of a *Gentile* Christian standpoint. Gentiles are nowhere in view in the passage."[108] Perhaps no one put it better than A. F. J. Klijn:

> In Stephen's speech we are dealing with problems still arising within a Jewish community where a minority holds opinions different from the rest. The speech is an introduction to a (Jewish) Christianity outside Jerusalem and its temple.[109]

Hebrews 11 as a Christian Reading of Biblical History

As we concluded in chapter three, the most striking characterization of the heroes in Hebrews 11 is that they are outsiders, rather then national leaders, as they typically had been. To be sure, in other retellings the heroes of the Bible are at odds with the people, but the heroes are still portrayed as leaders. For Pseudo-Philo, the successful leaders of the Bible are those who can curtail the people's disobedience or act as a mediator on their behalf before God. Thus, disobedience and leadership form a symbiotic relationship in Pseudo-Philo's retelling. But in Hebrews the nation is not even in view. The author of Hebrews concentrates on the personal odyssey of the heroes. They are individuals. While they are connected to each other by their lineage, their connection to the people or the nation is virtually nonexistent. Thus, the reading of biblical history in Hebrews 11 constitutes a denationalized understanding of that history.

We also saw how the heroes in Hebrews 11 have lost all their glamour and glory. They are diminished personages in comparison with the portraits found on other lists and in other retellings. This reduction in the stature of the heroes is due to a specific hermeneutical attitude on the part of the author, who viewed the biblical figures as part of an old world order that

---

in Bruce ("Stephen's Apologia," 40) who seems to concur.

[108] Donaldson, "Moses Typology," 29.

[109] A. F. J. Klijn, "Stephen's Speech—Acts vii 2–53," *NTS* 4 (1957–8) 26, also quoted in Donaldson, 29.

pre-dated Christ. The heroes' primary accomplishment is their ability to see beyond that old world order toward a better future. What happens as a result is the transvaluation of the biblical hero. The author of Hebrews did not formulate his list of heroes merely for the sake of demeaning them. Rather, he now values them for different reasons—their independence is to be prized over their leadership skills, and their hope in the future is more meaningful than their accomplishments on behalf of the people in their own time.

As far as I can tell, no one before the author of Hebrews viewed Jewish scripture this way. We saw how the Palestinian strain of historiography was preoccupied with defining national identity. National themes like the law, worship, covenant, and the land were in the forefront of the telling of history. The Hellenistic strain by contrast was concerned with none of these things, but was nevertheless also nationalistically motivated. The lives of the heroes represented the greatness of the Jewish nation.

Paul and the writer of Stephen's speech in Acts, both Christians, fit— albeit not perfectly—into the tradition of Palestinian historiography. The heroes and the nation are the people of the promise, even if the people reject the covenant and the promises that are attached to it. The Christian orientation of Paul and the writer of Stephen's speech is evident in that they understand Christ as a salvific element which gets attached to biblical history, but they do not so revise their vision of biblical history itself that it deviates significantly from contemporary exegetes of the Palestinian strain. We can at least say that their conception of Jewish history has more in common with other Jewish sectarian retellings of history than it has originality.[110]

This is not so of Hebrews 11, and I hope that by now the vision of Hebrews 11 is evident. The heroes of Hebrews have none of the pious Jewish qualities of the Palestinian type and none of the Greek virtues of the Hellenistic type. The heroes of Hebrews are alienated individuals with no national affiliation but who nevertheless form a historic lineage of the community. The reason I wish to call the vision of biblical history found in

---

110 Paul's post-biblical-christological ending to the story of the history of Israel may not be a conventional understanding of the teleology of Jewish history, but the idea that only a remnant participate in eschatological salvation (Rom 11:5–7) is parallel to the Qumran sect. As for Stephen's Speech, its only 'unJewish' element was its negative assessment of the land. Again, a negative attitude toward the land is found at Qumran: Since the land had been defiled by the temple establishment, withdrawal from the land became desirable (CD 4).

Hebrews 11 'Christian' is because it represents an important stage in a paradigm shift which occurred in biblical interpretation in the early church. To be sure, Paul and others helped initiate such a shift, but Hebrews 11 reflects a perception of biblical history that has gone further. While Paul and the author of Stephen's speech simply attached the advent of Christ onto the story of Israel, the author of Hebrews no longer sees scripture as the history of Israel; it is now the pre-Christ history of Christians. Abraham and Moses are not Israelites or Jews, they are *Christians.*

Scholars often assume that what is Christian about the early Christians' reading of the Bible was their interpretation of the text through the lens of the death and resurrection of Jesus. No doubt the christological interpretation of specific passages of scripture played an important role in early Christianity. But claiming that the history of one particular ethnic group, i.e., the Jews, is really Part I of the theological history of Christians is a different hermeneutical endeavor. Indeed, christological readings are evident right from the dawn of Christianity, and may be associated with the earliest stage of Jewish-Christian sectarianism.

Based on the previous analysis of Romans 9–11 and Acts 7, the larger hermeneutic that read the OT as Christian history most likely derives from a later stage of development, when Christianity moves from being a sect to an independent religion. From the second century onwards, Christianity was primarily a Gentile affair. Hebrews, written at the end of the first century, opened the way for Gentile Christians to read Israelite history as if it were their own history. Furthermore, non-Jewish Christians (with the exception of some gnostics) retained Jewish scripture as myth—in Lincoln's sense of the word—which enabled the ultimate retention of the OT as scripture. While it is true that most of the legal material was probably not observed by Gentile Christians, the Jewish Bible in Greek was considered the source of divine authority both before and after the canonization of the NT. More than one Gentile Christian in antiquity was converted by reading Jewish scripture.[111] To be sure, Jewish scripture was radically reinterpreted—and only through such interpretation did it become the Christian OT. Nevertheless, the majority of Christians never seriously doubted its status as scripture.[112] That Christians retained the mythic quality of scripture—even as they reinterpreted it—can be demonstrated by patristic writers' extensive use of it

---

[111] William Horbury, ("Old Testament Interpretation in the Writings of the Church Fathers," *Mikra,* 728) cites Theophilus, *Ad Autol.* 1.14; Justin Martyr, *Dial. Tr.* 8; and Tatian *Ad Gr.* 29 as proof of authority of Jewish scripture.

[112] Ellis, "The Old Testament Canon in the New Testament Church," 655–56.

and defense of it when threatened by marcionites.[113] Indeed, the very fact that Christians reinterpreted Jewish biblical writings proves that these writings were authoritative for Christians. If they had not been authoritative, no one would have cared to reinterpret them.[114]

Although the document we know as the Epistle to the Hebrews was not quoted or interpreted with frequency in the earliest period of Christian history and suffered from a lack of acceptance in the West,[115] the historiographical vision expressed in Hebrews reflects the earliest version of what became the standard Christian reading of the OT. Such Christian reading came to view the OT not as the national history of the Jewish people, but as a trans-ethnic history of Christians which accounted for the time before the coming of Christ. The result was not just the simple inclusion of non-Jewish Christians at the latter end of the biblical story (à la Paul), but a reorientation of that story which made the heroes pre-Christ Christians, and, most unfortunately, excluded post-biblical Jews as the heirs.

Although we do not possess a Christian author who gives us a comprehensive retelling of OT history until that first serious historian of the church, Eusebius, there are many not-so-subtle statements by various early Christian writers that indicate that they understand themselves as heirs to the biblical tradition, while the Jews are dispossessed of their national historical heritage. The *Epistle of Barnabas*[116] argues, for example, that circumcision cannot possibly be a sign of God's covenant with the Jewish people, since many other peoples, such as Arabs, Syrians, and Egyptians, practice circumcision (9.6–8). Barnabas goes beyond Hebrews' notion that the Jews

---

113 Ellis ("Old Testament Canon," 655) also notes that when it came to defining the extent and number of biblical books, Christians (such as Melito, Origen, and Jerome) looked to Jewish authoritative teaching.

114 In chapter two we discussed the author's devaluation of certain elements in the biblical narrative. To be sure, most Christian interpreters from the second century onwards engaged in a similar hermeneutic. Nevertheless, the use of allegorical interpretation and other methods to reinterpret the legal and historical sections of scripture, means that these exegetes still valued the text as authoritative. Devaluing certain of the *contents* of the biblical text is not the same as devaluing the text itself.

115 As Harry Y. Gamble (*The New Testament Canon: Its Making and Meaning* [Philadelphia: Fortress, 1985] 47) briefly discusses, although some Western writers know of Hebrews (like 1 Clement and Tertullian), it does not command much interest. In the East it seems to have enjoyed much better acceptance; it is included in P46 and Clement of Alexandria quotes it as scripture. For a more detailed discussion, see W.H.P. Hatch, "The Position of Hebrews in the Canon of the New Testament," *HTR* 29 (1936) 133–51.

116 Interestingly, Tertullian (*De Pudicitia* 20) believes Barnabas is the author of Hebrews.

possess the old covenant (which is becoming obsolete) to believing that the Jews were *never* the heir to the covenant (13). The promises to Abraham refer to Christ and the hope of resurrection (6). When Barnabas at one point refers to Gen 17:5—that Abraham will be the father of all nations—his use of the text moves far beyond Paul's inclusive understanding to an exclusionary one. He writes:

> What then does [God] say to Abraham, when he alone was faithful, and it was counted him for righteousness? "Behold I have made thee, Abraham, the father of the Gentiles who believe in God in uncircumcision." (13.7)

No longer is Abraham father of "*all* the nations," but simply "the nations" (or Gentiles), i.e., in place of the Jews.[117]

Perhaps the fullest expression of Christians as the heirs to the biblical heritage while at the same time excluding Jews can be found in Justin Martyr. In Justin's *Dialogue with Trypho* Abraham is not only the father of the nations, he is the father of the Christians. Thus, the promises to Abraham are promises to Christians:

> But we Christians are not only a people, but a holy people, as we have already shown: "And they shall call it a holy people, redeemed by the Lord." [Isa 62:12] Wherefore, we are not a contemptible people, nor a tribe of Barbarians, nor just any nation as the Carians or the Phrygians, but the chosen people of God who appeared to those who did not seek Him. "Behold," He said "I am God to a nation which has not called upon My name." [Isa 65:1] For, this is really the nation promised to Abraham by God, when He told him that he would make him a father of many nations, not saying in particular that he would be father of the Arabs or the Egyptians or the Idumeans, since Ishmael became the father of a mighty nation and so did Esau; and there is now a great throng of Ammonites. Noah was the father of Abraham, and indeed, of all men. And other nations had other ancestors. What greater favor, then did Christ bestow on Abraham? This: that He likewise called with His voice, and commanded him to leave the land wherein he dwelt. And with that same voice He has also called of us, and we have abandoned our former way of life in which we used to practice evils common to the rest of the world. And we shall inherit the Holy Land together with Abraham, receiving our inheritance for all eternity, because by our similar faith we have become children of Abraham. For, just as he believed the voice of God (which was spoken again to us

---

[117] The LXX text of Gen 17:5 reads: ὅτι πατέρα πολλῶν ἐθνῶν τέθεικά σε. *Barn* 13:7 reads: τέθεικά σε, Ἀβραάμ, πατέρα ἐθνῶν τῶν πιστευόντων δι' ἀκροβυστίας τῷ θεῷ.

by the Prophets and the Apostles of Christ), and have renounced even
to death all worldly things. Thus, God promised Abraham a religious
and righteous nation of like faith, and a delight to the Father; but it is
not you, "in whom there is no faith." [Deut 32:20] (119.3–6)

The nation of the Jews is completely out of the picture.[118]

Of course, both the *Epistle of Barnabas* and Justin's *Dialogue with Trypho* are
polemical works, in which Christian identity vis-à-vis Judaism is still a critical
issue—probably because Christians at this time held various positions about
Jews and the role of Jewish history in salvation history.[119] The position of
Marcion was that Abraham was so quintessentially the father of the Jews, he
could in no way be the ancestor of Christians.[120] If we were to summarize
Marcion's historiographic reading of Jewish scripture, it would be that he
inverted the traditional understanding of Jewish history: All the biblical
heroes are indeed Yahweh's chosen people and the ancestors of the Jewish
nation, but, as a result, this heritage bespeaks *damnation history*, instead of
salvation history (Abraham ends up in hell according to Marcion), because
Yahweh is not the one true God but a creator god who is imperfect.[121]
Perhaps part of the reason that the church fathers vociferously exiled the
Jews from their own history and claimed Abraham as a Christian was to
counteract such claims.

Although it is a jump into the future, we can look to Eusebius to see
where Christian historiography of the Jewish Bible ended up. Eusebius is
particularly instructive because he does not write polemically against Jews,
and the birth pangs of forming a Christian identity are not as prominent as
they are in earlier authors. In his *Preparation for the Gospel* Eusebius—after
spending several chapters surveying the history and doctrines of other
cultures—explains why Christianity is founded upon the oracles of the
Hebrews. First on his agenda is the distinction between "Hebrews " and
"Jews."

---

118 For a full discussion of this text in particular and the role of Abraham in early
Christian-Jewish debate, see Jeffrey S. Siker, *Disinheriting the Jews: Abraham in Early
Christian Controversy* (Louisville: Westminster/John Knox, 1991).

119 See the conclusions of Gager, *Origins of Anti-Semitism.*

120 For other gnostic views of Abraham, see Siker, *Disinheriting the Jews,* 153–56.

121 Irenaeus, *Against Heresies,* 1.27.3. For Marcion, the god of the OT is a 'just' god,
while the god of the gospel is the 'good' god. Marcion's dualistic theology understands
'justice' and 'mercy' as two mutually exclusive concepts. The just god of the OT is petty
and exhibits no mercy. See Hans Jonas, *The Gnostic Religion* (Boston: Beacon, 1963) 141–
42.

And you may know the difference between Hebrews and Jews thus: the latter assumed their name from Judah, from whose tribe the kingdom of Judah was long ages afterward established, but the former from Eber, who was the forefather of Abraham. And that the Hebrews were earlier than the Jews, we are taught by the sacred writings. (7.6c)

He then goes on to explain the Jews' "manner of religion," which is dependent upon the laws of Moses. We later learn that the Mosaic legislation and the establishment of the Jewish nation was caused by the people's "moral weakness" at that time, making them unable "to emulate the virtue of their fathers, inasmuch as they were enslaved by passions and sick in soul . . ." (7.9d). The law represents a symbolic and enigmatic statement of the nature of the divine (7.9d), as opposed to the direct revelation of earlier times. Before the giving of the law, the Hebrews

> having never heard of all the Mosaic legislation, enjoyed a free and unfettered mode of religion, being regulated by the manner of life which is in accordance with nature, so that they had no need of laws to rule them, because of the extreme freedom of their soul from passions, but had received true knowledge of the doctrines concerning God. (7.6d)

After his discussion of the difference between Hebrews and Jews, Eusebius gives us a brief historical overview of the Hebrews beginning with creation (7.8). He includes many of the usual heroes, and a few not-so-usual ones,[122] but he stops his review promptly with the Mosaic legislation. Throughout his survey he pauses numerous times to remind his readers that the heroes are Hebrews and not Jews. After this point he tells us that he will now turn to an analysis of the doctrines contained in the oracles of the Hebrews, including the prophets. He also points out that although the prophets come after the Mosaic legislation, they are properly called Hebrews, and not Jews (7.11b), because they lived in accordance with their earliest forefathers.

Eusebius does not take as extreme a position as authors like Barnabas and Justin; neither does he have their vituperative tone. Furthermore, unlike earlier Christian authors, Eusebius' understanding of Jewish scripture has been influenced by Jewish Hellenistic writers and non-Jewish ethnographers.[123] Nevertheless, his compulsive distinction between Hebrews and Jews

---

[122] Such as Enoch and Job.

[123] See Droge, *Homer or Moses?*, 168–93. We could characterize the reading of Jewish history in Eusebius as a combination of the trajectory which we are discussing here, which begins with Hebrews, and that of Jewish Hellenistic historiography. Since in Eusebius'

remains a means of dispossessing the Jews of their ancestry. The Hebrew heroes are not connected to the Jewish nation. Moses only acts as lawgiver and leader out of necessity. Eusebius ignores the covenant(s) and the promises, even though he speaks of the new covenant. He takes for granted that the lives of the patriarchs are not part of the trajectory of history that led to the establishment of the Jewish nation. In general, Eusebius sees the heroes of the Bible as great theologians. At the same time they form an ancestral heritage for Christians.[124]

Conclusion

My hope is that this all too brief survey of Christian views of ancient Jewish history will aid in illustrating the role played by the reading of the same history in Hebrews 11. No one before the author of Hebrews had ever claimed that the patriarchs "did not receive what was promised." Paul had explicitly said of the Jews "to them belong the promises." The only mid-way point between the relatively traditional position of Paul and the extreme positions of Barnabas and Justin is Hebrews 11. By concentrating on what the heroes accomplished apart from the national destiny of Israel, the author of Hebrews so modified the teleology of biblical history that an opening was created for Gentile Christians to fully identify with scriptural history. No longer did biblical history center on the establishment and well-being of a nation. Rather, it culminated with the theological realization of Christian teaching. Thus have we moved from a national history to a supra-national one.

Obviously, Gentile Christians came to see biblical history as their own mythic history in stages. Hebrews 11 was part of a gradual evolution. In one sense, this evolution began even before the writing of Hebrews with the increasing emphasis in Jewish historiography on individual heroes of the Bible at the expense of the story of the people. The retelling of biblical history was a discourse constantly in flux, adapting to the needs of the tellers and hearers. Nevertheless, the denationalization of Hebrews' portrait of biblical heroes and history must be seen as a significant stage in the development of Christian thought—a stage which surely aided in the formation of Christianity as a separate religion from Judaism.

---

time Christianity was beginning to merge with the State, it no surprise that Eusebius would want to once again portray the biblical heroes as world leaders.

124 The central concern for Eusebius is proving the antiquity of Christianity. See Arthur Droge, "The Apologetic Dimensions of the Ecclesiastical History," *Eusebius, Christianity, and Judaism*, ed. Harold Attridge and Gohei Hata (Detroit: Wayne State, 1992) 492–509.

The author of Hebrews sparked the innovation he did through the subtle modification of discourse. The foundation of that discourse was the retelling of biblical history. Because it was such a familiar discourse at the time, retelling biblical history was non-threatening and allowed the speaker an open channel of communication with his audience. The alterations or modifications the author made in his retelling were performed by the manipulations of sentiments. Many of these sentiments derive from the biblical text itself, but were lying dormant in the traditional discourse on biblical history of the time. For example, Abraham never does come to live in the promised land as an heir, and Moses may have been the greatest leader of the Jewish people, but the Bible does relate many tragic events in his life that indeed portray him as a man without a nation.

Other sentiments derive from the audience's cultural setting which, when brought to bear on the biblical story, modify their reading of it. For example, the de-emphasis on the land in Hebrews 11 dovetails with the sentiments (or lack thereof) of Jews in the diaspora. Similarly, the neglect of the covenant and the emphasis on the individual in Hebrews 11 fit nicely with those in the audience who were influenced by Greek ideals and ethics— which probably included everyone.

What is important to recognize is that the author's retelling of biblical history highlighted the non-national or trans-national elements of that history. My sense is that the implementation of these sentiments in the biblical story must reflect an ethnically mixed community and not an exclusively Jewish one. But, as I said earlier, by describing the biblical figures and their deeds the way he did, the author did not merely mirror any marginalization that may have been felt by his community, he turned it into a bonding agent. Ironically, by marshaling the sentiment of marginalization to strengthen the ties between Christian individuals, the author probably helped to diminish the feeling of marginalization. Obviously those who identified themselves as Christians possessed the common affinity of belief in Christ. But the Christian reading of scripture gave what was most likely an ill defined group of people an ancestral heritage and the undeniable identity that comes with that. Thus, these non-national sentiments were constitutive of the formation of this early Christian community and aided in the development of a Gentile Christianity which came to see the OT as its own heritage. The emphasis on the independent individual is a sentiment which could appeal to almost anyone in the post-Hellenistic age; a retelling that stressed the fate of the people of Israel could never have had a broad appeal. Hebrews 11 joined in the common Jewish discourse of recounting the mythic past and in so doing took one significant step toward redefining that past as a Christian, rather than a Jewish, one.

Appendix A

OUTLINE OF HEBREWS 11

⨏⨎

The following outline corresponds to the exegesis in chapter three.

A. Introduction (vv. 1–3)
　Definition of Faith (v. 1)
　Introduction to the Testimony of the Ancestors' Lives (v. 2)
　Reference to Understanding of Creation by *Present* Community (v. 3)

B. Primeval Figures (vv. 4–7)
　Abel (v. 4)
　Enoch (vv. 5–6)
　Noah (v. 7)

C. Pilgrim's Promise: Abraham, Sarah, and the Patriarchs (vv. 8–22)
　1. Abraham (vv. 8–19)
　　i) Part 1 (vv. 8–12)
　　　A Wanderer (vv.8–10)
　　　Sarah (v. 11)
　　　A Father (v. 12)
　　ii) Heavenly Homeland, a Commentary (vv. 13–16)
　　iii) Part 2: The Offering of Isaac (vv. 17–19)
　2. The Patriarchs (vv. 20–22)
　　Isaac (v. 20)
　　Jacob (v. 21)
　　Joseph (v: 22)

D. Exodus and Entropy: Moses, the Israelites, and Rahab (vv. 23–31)
　1. Moses (vv. 23–28)
　　i) Part 1 (vv. 23–25)
　　　An Orphan (v. 23)
　　　A Defector (vv. 24–25)
　　ii) Disgrace of Christ, a Commentary (v. 26)
　　iii) Part 2 (vv. 27–28)
　　　Departs Egypt (v. 27)
　　　Performs the Passover (v. 28)

2. The Israelites (vv. 29–31)
   Red Sea Pedestrians (v. 29)
   Jericho Victors (v. 30)
   Rahab (v. 31)

E. Summary Allusions to Remaining History (vv. 32–37)
   1. Names named (v. 32)
      Gideon
      Barak
      Samson
      Jepthah
      David
      Samuel
      The Prophets
   2. Deeds Done (vv. 33–38)
      Positive (vv. 33–35a)
      Negative (vv. 35a–38)

F. Conclusion (vv. 39–40)
   Conclusion of Testimony (v. 39)
   Reference to Perfection in *Past and Present* Community (v. 40)

HERO LISTS IN PARALLEL COLUMNS

Sir 44–50	1 Macc 2:51–60	Wis 10	4 Macc 16:16–23	4 Macc 18:11–19
		Adam		Abel
		Cain		(Cain)
[Enoch]				
Noah		Noah		
Abraham	Abraham	Abraham	Abraham	
Isaac		Isaac	Isaac	Isaac
		Lot		
Jacob		Jacob		
	Joseph	Joseph		Joseph
Moses		Moses		
Aaron				
Phinehas	Phinehas			Phinehas
Joshua	Joshua			
Caleb	Caleb			
the judges				
Samuel				
(Saul)				
Nathan				
David	David			
Solomon				
(Rehoboam)				
(Jeroboam)				
Elijah	Elijah			
Elisha				
Hezekiah				
Isaiah				
Josiah				
kings				
Jeremiah				
Ezekiel				
Job				
Prophets	Hananiah		Daniel	Hanainiah
Zerubbabel	Azariah		Hananiah	Azariah
Jeshua	Mishael		Azariah	Mishael
Nehemiah	Daniel		Mishael	Daniel
				Isaiah
				David
				Solomon
				Ezekiel
				Moses

HERO LISTS IN PARALLEL COLUMNS

CD 2–3	4 Ezra 7:105–111	Acts 7	Hebrews 11
mighty heroes			Abel
Watchers			Enoch
sons of Watchers			Noah
sons of Noah			Abraham
Abraham	Abraham	Abraham	Sarah
Isaac		Isaac	Isaac
Jacob		Jacob	Jacob
		12 patriarchs	(Esau)
sons of Jacob		Joseph	Joseph
sons in Egypt	Moses	Moses	Moses
		(Aaron)	the people
			Rahab
	Joshua	Joshua	
			Gideon
	Samuel		Barak
			Samson
			Jephthah
kings	David	David	David
	Solomon	Solomon	Samuel
	Elijah		
	Hezekiah		
		prophets	prophets
			women
			others
mighty heroes	many others		

BIBLIOGRAPHY

Albertz, Rainer. *A History of Israelite Religion in the Old Testament*. OTL. Louisville: Westminster/John Knox, 1994.

Amir, Yehoshua. "Authority and Interpretation of Scripture in the Writings of Philo." In *Mikra*. See Mulder.

Anderson, A. A. *The Book of Psalms*. New Century Bible. London: Oliphants, 1972.

Attridge, Harold. *The Epistle to the Hebrews*. Hermeneia. Philadelphia: Fortress, 1989.

—————. *The Interpretation of Biblical History in the Antiquitates Judaicae of Flavius Josephus*. Missoula, MT: Scholars, 1976.

Aune, David. *The New Testament in Its Literary Environment*. Library of Early Christianity. Philadelphia: Westminster, 1987.

—————. *Prophecy in Early Christianity and the Ancient Mediteranean World*. Grand Rapids: Eerdmans, 1983.

Austin, J. L. *How to do Things with Words*. Cambridge: Harvard, 1975.

Baltzer, Klaus. *The Covenant Formulary*. Philadelphia: Fortress, 1971.

Barilli, Renato. *Rhetoric*. Theory and History of Literature 63. Minneapolis: University of Minnesota, 1989.

Barth, Markus. "The Old Testament in Hebrews: An Essay in Biblical Hermeneutics." In *Current Issues in New Testament Interpretation*, ed. W. Klassen and G. F. Snyder. New York: Harper, 1962.

Betz, H. D. *Greek Magical Papyri*. Chicago: University of Chicago, 1986.

Blenkinsopp, Joseph. *Ezekiel*. Louisville: John Knox, 1990.

—————. *Ezra-Nehemiah, A Commentary*. OTL. Philadelphia: Westminster, 1988.

Boismard, E. M. "Le martyre d' Etienne Actes 6,8–8,2." *RevScRel* (1981).

Booth, Wayne. *The Rhetoric of Fiction*. 2nd ed. Chicago: University of Chicago, 1983.

Bovon, Francois. "Le Christ, la foi et la sagasse dans L'Epître aux Hébreux." *RTP* 18 (1968).

Boyarin, Daniel. *Intertextuality and the Reading of Midrash*. Indianapolis: Indiana University, 1990.

Braun, Herbert. *An die Hebräer*. HNT 14. Tübingen: Mohr [Paul Siebeck], 1984.

Brawley, Robert. "Discoursive Structure and the Unseen in Hebrews 2:8 and 11:1: A Neglected Aspect of the Context." *CBQ* 55 (1993) 81–98.

Brice, B. J. "Paradeigma and Exemplum in Ancient Rhetorical Theory." Ph.D. Diss., University of California, Berkeley, 1975.

Brooke, George J. *Exegesis at Qumran. 4Q Florilegium in its Jewish Context.* JSOTSup 29. Sheffield, England: JSOT, 1985.

Bruce, F. F. *The Epistle to the Hebrews.* New International Commentary of the NT. Grand Rapids: Eerdmans, 1990.

————. "Stephen's Apologia." In *Scripture: Meaning and Method,* ed. B. Thompson. Hull: Hull University, 1987.

Buchanan, George Wesley. *To the Hebrews: Translation, Comment and Conclusions.* AB 29. Garden City, NY: Doubleday, 1972.

Burch, Varcher. *The Epistle to the Hebrews, Its Sources and Message.* London: Williams & Norgate, 1936.

Burgess, Theodore. "Epideictic Literature." In *University of Chicago Studies in Classical Philology III,* 89–261. Chicago: University of Chicago, 1902.

Caird, George B. "The Exegetical Method of the Epistle to the Hebrews." *CJT* 5 (1959) 44–51.

Charlesworth, James H., ed. *The Old Testament Pseudepigrapha.* Garden City, NY: Doubleday & Company, Inc., 1985.

Clark, D. L. *Rhetoric in Greco-Roman Education.* Westport, CT: Greenwood, 1957.

Cohen, Shaye. *Josephus in Galilee and Rome: His Vita and Development as a Historian.* Leiden: Brill, 1979.

————. "History and Historiography in the Against Apion of Josephus." In *Essays in Jewish Historiography.* See Rapoport-Albert.

Combrink, H.J. "Some Thoughts on the Old Testament Citations in the Epistle to the Hebrews." *Neot* 5 (1971) 22–36.

Conte, Giam. *Latin Literature: A History.* Baltimore and London: Johns Hopkins University, 1994.

Conzelmann, Hans. *Acts of the Apostles.* Hermeneia. Philadelphia: Fortress, 1987.

Cosby, Michael. *The Rhetorical Composition and Function of Hebrews 11: In Light of Example Lists in Antiquity.* Macon, GA: Mercer, 1988.

Cross, Frank Moore. *Canaanite Myth and Hebrew Epic.* Cambridge, MA: Harvard University, 1973.

————. *The Ancient Library of Qumran.* London: Duckworth, 1958.

Culler, Jonathan. *The Pursuit of Signs.* Ithaca, New York: Cornell University, 1981.

Culpepper, Alan R. "A Superior Faith: Hebrews 10:19–12:2." *Rev Exp* 82 (1985) 375–390.

D'Angelo, Mary Rose. *Moses in the Letter to the Hebrews.* SBLDS 42. Missoula: Scholars, 1979.

Damrosch, David. *The Narrative Covenant: Transformations of Genre in the Growth of Biblical Literature.* San Francisco: Harper & Row, 1987.

Dautzenberg, Gerhard. "Der Glaube im Hebräerbrief." *BZ* 17 (1973) 161–77.

Davies, John H. *A Letter to Hebrews.* CBC. Cambridge: Cambridge University, 1967.

Davies, W. D. *The Gospel and the Land: Early Christianity and Jewish Territorial Doctrine.* Berkeley: University of California, 1974.

Dibelius, Martin. "The Speeches in Acts and Ancient Historiography." In *Studies in the Acts of the Apostles,* ed. H. Greeven. New York: Scribner's, 1956.

Dilella, A. A. and P. Skehan. *The Wisdom of Ben Sira.* AB. New York: Doubleday, 1987.

Dimant, Devorah. "Use and Interpretation of Mikra in the Apocrypha and Pseudepigrapha." In *Mikra.* See Mulder.

Donaldson, T. L. "Moses Typology and the Sectarian Nature of Early Christian Anti-Judaism: A Study in Acts 7." *JSNT* 12 (1981) 27–52.

Dodd, C. H. *According to the Scriptures: The Substructure of New Testament Theology.* New York: Charles Scribner's Sons, 1952.

Droge, Arthur. "The Apologetic Dimensions of the Ecclesiastical History." In *Eusebius, Christianity, and Judaism,* eds. Harold Attridge and Gohei Hata. 492–509. Detroit: Wayne State, 1992.

—————. *Homer or Moses? Early Christian Interpretations of the History of Culture.* Tübingen: J. C. B. Mohr [Paul Siebeck], 1989.

Duban, Jeffery. *Ancient and Modern Images of Sappho.* Lanham, MD: University Presses of America, 1983.

Dunn, James D. G. *The Parting of the Ways: Between Christianity and Judaism and Their Significance for the Character of Christianity.* London; Philadelphia: SCM; Trinity, 1991.

Ehrhardt, A. *The Acts of the Apostles: Ten Lectures.* Manchester: Manchester University, 1969.

Ellingworth, Paul. *Commentary on Hebrews.* New International Greek Testament Commentary, Grand Rapids: Eerdmans, 1993.

—————. "Hebrews and 1 Clement: Literary Dependence or Common Tradition." *BZ* 23 (1979) 262–9.

Ellis, E. E. "Biblical Interpretation in the New Testament Church." In *Mikra.* See Mulder.

—————. *Prophecy and Hermeneutic.* WUNT 18, Tübingen: J. C. B. Mohr [Paul Siebeck], 1978.

Emerton, J. A. "The Riddle of Genesis xiv." *VT* 21 (1971) 403–39.

—————. "Some False Clues in the Study of Genesis xiv." *VT* 21 (1971) 24–27.

Eskenazi, Tamara. *In an Age of Prose: A Literary Approach to Ezra-Nehemiah.* SBLMS 36. Atlanta: Scholars, 1988.

Evans, Craig. "Faith and Polemic: The New Testament and First Century Judaism." In *Anti-Semitism and Early Christianity: Issues of Faith and Polemic*, eds. Craig Evans and Donald Hagner. 1–17. Minneapolis: Fortress, 1993.

Feldman, Louis. "Use, Authority and Exegesis of Mikra in the Writings of Josephus." In *Mikra*. See Mulder.

—————. "Abraham the Greek Philosopher in Josephus." *TAPA* 99 (1968) 143–56.

—————. "Hellenizations in Josephus' Portrayal of Man's Decline." In *Religions in Antiquity*, ed. Jacob Neusner. Leiden: Brill, 1968.

Fishbane, Michael. *Biblical Interpretation in Ancient Israel.* Oxford: Clarendon, 1985.

—————. "The Exodus Motif/Paradigm in Historical Renewal." In *Text and Texture: Close Readings of Selected Biblical Texts.* New York: Schocken, 1979.

Fitzmyer, Joseph. *Romans.* AB. New York: Doubleday, 1993.

—————. *The Genesis Apocryphon of Qumran Cave I.* Rome: Biblical Institute, 1971.

—————. "Now This Melchizedek … (Heb 7:1)." In *Essays on the Semitic Background of the New Testament.* London: Scholars, 1971.

—————. "The Use of Explicit Old Testament Quotations in Qumran Literature and in the New Testament." In *Essays on the Semitic Background of the New Testament.*

Frankfurter, David. "The Origin of the Miracle List Tradition and Its Medium of Circulation." *SBL Seminar Papers* (1990) 344–71.

Gager, John. *Moses in Greco-Roman Paganism.* SBLMS 16. Nashville and New York: Abingdon, 1972.

—————. *The Origins of Anti-Semitism: Attitudes toward Judaism in Pagan and Christian Antiquity.* New York: Oxford, 1985.

Gamble, Harry. *The New Testament Canon: Its Making and Meaning.* Philadelphia: Fortress, 1985.

Geertz, Clifford. *The Interpretation of Cultures.* New York: Basic Books, 1973.

Genette, Gérard. *La littérature au second degré.* Paris: Editions du Seuil, 1982.

Gilbert, M. "La place de la loi dans la priére de Néhémie 9." In *De la Torah au Messie: Mélanges Henri Cazelles*, ed. P. Grelot J. Doré and M. Carrez. 307–16. Paris: Desclée, 1981.

Ginzberg, Louis. *Legends of the Jews.* Philadelphia: Jewish Publication Society, 1937.

Goldstein, J. A. *1 Maccabees*. AB 41. Garden City: Doubleday, 1976.

Gordis, Robert. "Quotations in Wisdom Literature." *JQR* 30 (1943)

—————. "Quotations as Literary Usage in Biblical, Oriental, and Rabbinic Literature." *HUCA* 22 (1949) 157–219.

Graham, William. *Beyond the Written Word: Oral Aspects of Scripture in the History of Religion*. Cambridge: Cambridge University, 1987.

Grant, Michael. *History of Rome*. New York: Charles Scribner's Sons, 1978.

Grasser, Erich. *Der Glaube im Hebräerbrief*. Marburg: Elwert, 1965.

Greenberg, Moshe. *Ezekiel 1–20*. AB 20. Garden City: Doubleday, 1983.

Gunkel, Hermann. *The Psalms: A Form-Critical Introduction* Philadelphia: Fortress, 1967.

Haenchen, Ernst. *The Acts of the Apostles: A Commentary*. Philadelphia: Westminster, 1971.

Hagner, Donald A. *The Use of the Old and New Testaments in Clement of Rome*. NovTSup 34. Leiden: Brill, 1973.

Hall, Robert G. *Revealed Histories: Techniques for Ancient Jewish and Christian Historiography*. JSOTSup 6. Sheffield: JSOT, 1991.

Halpern-Amaru, Betsy. *Rewriting the Bible: Land and Covenant in Postbiblical Jewish Literature*. Valley Forge, PA: Trinity, 1994.

Hamm, Dennis. "Faith in the Epistle to the Hebrews: The Jesus Factor." *CBQ* 52 (1990) 270–91.

Hanson, Paul D. *The Dawn of Apocalyptic*. Philadelphia: Fortress, 1979.

Harnack, Adolf von. "Probabilia über die Addresse und den Verfasser des Hebräerbriefes." *ZNW* 1 (1900) 16–41.

Harris, William V. *Ancient Literacy*. Cambridge, MA; London: Harvard University, 1989.

Hatch, W. H. P. "The Position of Hebrews in the Canon of the New Testament." *HTR* 29 (1936) 133–51.

Hay, David. *Glory at the Right Hand of God: Psalm 110 in Early Christianity*. SBLMS 18. Nashville and New York: Abingdon, 1972.

Hays, Richard. *Echoes of Scripture in the Letters of Paul*. New Haven & London: Yale University, 1989.

Hering, Jean. *The Epistle to the Hebrews*. London: Epworth, 1970.

Hewitt, Thomas. *The Epistle to the Hebrews*. Vol. 15. Tyndale NT Commentaries, Grand Rapids: Eerdmans, 1960.

Hofius, Otfried. *Die Vorstellung von endseitlichen Ruheort im Hebräerbrief*. WUNT 2. Tübingen: Mohr, 1970.

Holladay, Carl. *Fragments from Hellenistic Jewish Authors, Volume I: Historians*. Chico, CA: Scholars, 1983.

—————. *Theios Aner in Hellenistic Judaism: A Critique of the Use of the Category in New Testament Christology.* SBLDS 40. Missoula, MT: Scholars, 1977.

Hoppin, Ruth. *Priscilla: Author of the Epistle to the Hebrews and other Essays.* New York: Exposition, 1969.

Horbury, William. "Old Testament Interpretation in the Writings of the Church Fathers." In *Mikra.* See Mulder.

Horgan, Maurya. *Pesharim: Qumran Interpretation of Biblical Books.* Washington: Catholic Biblical Association, 1979.

Horton, Fred. *The Melchizedek Tradition: A Critical Examination of the Sources to the Fifth Century and in the Epistle to the Hebrews.* Cambridge: Cambridge University, 1976.

Howard, George. "Hebrews and the Old Testament Quotations." *NovT* 10 (1968) 208–16.

Hughes, Graham. *Hebrews and Hermeneutics: The Epistle to the Hebrews as a NT Example of Biblical Interpretation.* SNTSMS 36. Cambridge: Cambridge University, 1979.

Hurst, I. D. *The Epistle to the Hebrews: Its Background of Thought.* Cambridge: Cambridge University, 1990.

Jaeger, Werner. *Paideia: The Ideals of Greek Culture.* New York: Oxford, 1981.

Janssen, Enno. *Das Gottesvolk und seine Geschichte: Geschichtsbild und Selbstverstandnis im palästinensischen Schrifttum von Jesus Sirach bis Jehuda ha-Nasi.* Neukirchen-Vluyn: Neukirchener, 1971.

Jewett, Robert. *Letter to Pilgrims: A Commentary on the Epistle to the Hebrews.* New York: Pilgrim, 1981.

Jobes, K. H. "Rhetorical Achievement in the Hebrews 10 'Misquote' of Psalm 40." *Bib* 72 (1991) 387–96.

Johnson, Luke T. "The New Testament's Anti-Jewish Slander and the Conventions of Ancient Jewish Polemic." *JBL* (1989) 419–41.

Johnson, Marshall. *The Purpose of Biblical Genealogies.* SNTSMS. Cambridge: Cambridge University, 1988.

Johnsson, William G. "The Pilgrimage Motif in the Book of Hebrews." *JBL* 97 (1978) 239–51.

Jonas, Hans. *The Gnostic Religion.* Boston: Beacon, 1963.

Juel, Donald. *Messianic Exegesis: Christological Interpretation of the Old Testament in Early Christianity.* Philadelphia: Fortress, 1988.

Käsemann, Ernst. *Perspectives on Paul.* Philadelphia: Fortress, 1971.

—————. *The Wandering People of God: An Investigation of the Letter to the Hebrews.* Minneapolis: Augsburg, 1984.

Katz, Peter. "The Quotations from Deuteronomy in Hebrews." *ZNW* 49 (1958) 213–23.

Kennedy, George. *New Testament Interpretation Through Rhetorical Criticism.* Chapel Hill and London: University of North Carolina, 1984.

—————. *The Art of Persuasion in Greece.* Princeton: Princeton University, 1963.

Kilgallen, J. J. "The Function of Stephen's Speech." *Bib* 70 (1989).

Kistemaker, Simon E. *The Psalms Citations in the Epistle to the Hebrews.* Amsterdam: Soest, 1961.

Klijn, A. F. J. "Stephen's Speech—Acts vii 2–53." *NTS* 4 (1957–8).

Kobelski, Paul J. *Melchizedek and Melchiresa.* CBQMS 10. Washington D. C.: C. B. A., 1981.

Koester, Helmut. *Introduction to the New Testament.* Berlin and New York: Walter De Gruyter, 1982.

—————. "'Outside the Camp,' Hebrews 13:9–14." *HTR* 55 (1962) 299–315.

Kristeva, Julia. *Semiotiké.* Paris: Seuil, 1969.

Kugel, James. *In Potiphar's House: The Interpretive Life of Biblical Texts.* San Francisco: Harper, 1990.

—————. "Two Introductions to Midrash." In *Midrash and Literature,* ed. Geoffrey Hartman. New Haven and London: Yale, 1986.

————— and Rowan Greer. *Early Biblical Interpretation.* Library of Early Christianity. Philadelphia: Westminster, 1986.

Kümmel, Werner Georg. *Introduction to the New Testament.* Nashville: Abingdon, 1975.

Lamparter, Helmut. *Die Apocryphen I: Das Buch Jesus Sirach.* Die Botschaft des Alten Testament 25.1. Stuttgart: Calwer, 1972.

Lane, William. *Hebrews 9–13.* WBC. Dallas, TX: Word, 1991.

—————. *Call to Commitment: Responding to the Message of Hebrews.* Nashville: Nelson, 1985.

Lee, Thomas R. *Studies in the Form of Sirach 44–50.* SBLDS 75. Atlanta: Scholars, 1986.

Lehne, Susanne. *The Covenant in Hebrews.* JSNTSup 44. Sheffield: JSOT, 1990.

Levenson, Jon. "The Davidic Covenant and Its Modern Interpreters." *CBQ* 41 (1979) 205–19.

Lincoln, Bruce. *Discourse and the Construction of Society.* Oxford: Oxford University, 1989.

Lindars, Barnabas. "The Rhetorical Structure of Hebrews." *NTS* 35 (1990) 382–406.

—————. *The Theology of the Letter to the Hebrews.* Cambridge, U. K.- New York: Cambridge, 1991.

Lührmann, Dieter. "Henoch und die Metanoia." *ZNW* 66 (1975) 103–16.

MacDonald, Dennis. *Christianizing Homer: The Odyssey, Plato, and the Acts of Andrew.* New York and Oxford: Oxford University, 1994.

Mack, Burton. *Rhetoric and the New Testament.* Minneapolis: Fortress, 1990.

——————. *Wisdom and the Hebrew Epic: Ben Sira's Hymn in Praise of the Fathers.* Chicago: University of Chicago, 1985.

MacRae, George. "Heavenly Temple and Eschatology in the Letter to the Hebrews." *Semeia* 12 (1978) 179–99.

Maertens, Thierry. *L'Eloge des pères (Ecclèsiastique XLIV-L).* Bruges: Editions de L'Abbaye de Sainte-André, 1956.

Manson, Thomas W. "The Argument from Prophecy." *JTS* 46 (1945) 125–37.

Manson, William. *The Epistle to the Hebrews: An Historical and Theological Reconstruction.* London: Hodder and Stoughton, 1953.

Marrou, H. I. *A History of Education in Antiquity.* Madison, WI and London: University of Wisconsin, 1956.

McCarthy, Dennis. "Covenant and Law in Chronicles-Nehemiah." *CBQ* 44 (1984) 25–44.

——————. "Covenant in Narratives from Late OT Times." In *The Quest for the Kingdom of God,* eds. Spina Huffman Green. 77–94. Winona Lake, IN: Eisenbrauns, 1983.

Metzger, Bruce. "The Fourth Book of Ezra." In *OTP.* 1.540–41. See Charlesworth.

——————. "The Formulas Introducing Quotations of Scripture in the NT and the Mishnah." *JBL* 70 (1951) 297–307.

Michel, Otto. *Der Brief an die Hebräer.* Göttingen: Vanderhoeck and Ruprecht, 1949.

Michie, Donald and David Rhoads. *Mark as Story.* Philadelphia: Fortress, 1982.

Milikowsky, Chaim Joseph. "Seder Olam: A Rabbinic Chronography." Ph.D. Diss., Yale, 1981.

Miller, Merland Ray. "What is the Literary Form of Hebrews 11?" *JETS* 29 (4 1986) 411–17.

Moffat, James. *A Critical and Exegetical Commentary on the Epistle to the Hebrews.* ICC. New York: Scribner's, 1924.

Momigliano, Arnaldo. "The Origins of Universal History." In *On Pagans, Jews and Christians,* 31–57. Middletown, CT: Wesleyan, 1987.

——————. *The Classical Foundations of Modern Historiography.* Berkeley, Los Angeles, Oxford: University of California, 1990.

Montifiore, Hugh. *A Commentary on the Epistle to the Hebrews.* New York: Harper, 1964.

Mulder, Martin Jay, ed. *Mikra. Text, Translation, Reading and Interpretation of the Hebrew Bible in Ancient Judaism and Early Christianity.* CRINT 2.1. Assen; Maastricht; Minneapolis: Van Gorcum; Fortress, 1990.

Müller, Karlheinz. "Geschichte, Heilsgeschichte und Gesetz." In *Literatur und Religion des Fruhjudentums*, eds. Johann Maier und Josef Schreiner. Wurzburg: Echter, 1973.

Murphy, Frederick. *Pseudo-Philo: Rewriting the Bible.* New York: Oxford, 1993.

——. "Retelling the Bible: Idolatry in Pseudo-Philo." *JBL* 107 (1988) 279.

Neil, William. *The Acts of the Apostles.* New Century Bible. London: 1973.

Nickelsburg, George. "The Bible Rewritten and Expanded." In *Jewish Writings of the Second Temple Period.* See Stone.

—— and John J. Collins. *Ideal Figures in Ancient Judaism: Profiles and Paradigms.* SBLSCS 12. Ann Arbor: Edwards Brothers, 1980.

Noack, Bent. *Spätjudentum und Heilgeschichte.* Stuttgart: W. Kohlhammer, 1971.

Oden, R. A. "Philo of Biblos and Hellenistic Historiography." *PEQ* 110 (1978) 115–26.

Oesterley, W. O. E and G. H. Box. "The Book of Sirach." In *Apocrypha and Pseudepigrapha of the Old Testament in English*, ed. R. H. Charles. London: Oxford University, 1971.

Olbrechts-Tyteca, L. and Ch. Perelman. *The New Rhetoric: A Treatise on Argumentation.* Notre Dame: University of Notre Dame, 1969.

Olyan, Saul. "The Israelites Debate Their Options at the Sea of Reeds: LAB 10:3, Its Parallels and Pseudo-Philo's Ideology and Background." *JBL* 107 (1991) 87–92.

Ong, Walter. *Orality and Literacy.* New York and London: Methuen, 1982.

Padva, P. *Les citations de l'Ancien Testament dans l'Epître aux Hébreux.* Paris: N. L. Danzig, 1945.

Patte, Daniel. *Early Jewish Hermeneutic in Palestine.* SBLDS 22. Missoula: Scholars, 1975.

Perlman, S. "The Historical Example, Its Use and Importance as Political Propaganda in the Attic Orators." In *Scripta Hierosolymitana VII*, eds. A. Fuks and I. Halpern. Jerusalem: Magnes, 1961.

Peters, F. E. *Children of Abraham.* Princeton: Princeton University, 1982.

Peterson, David. *Hebrews and Perfection.* Cambridge: Cambridge University, 1982.

Ploeg, J. van der. "L'exégèse de l'Ancien Testament dans L'Épitre aux Hébreux." *RB* 54 (1947) 187–228.

Podlecki, Anthony J. *The Early Greek Poets and Their Times.* Vancouver: University of British Columbia, 1984.

Rad, Gerhard von. *Old Testament Theology.* New York: Harper & Row, 1965.

Rapoport-Albert, Ada, ed. *Essays in Jewish Historiography.* Wesleyan University, 1988.

Reese, J. M. *Hellenistic Influence on the Book of Wisdom and Its Consequences.* AnBib 41. Rome: Pontifical Biblical Institute, 1970.

Rendall, Robert. "The Method of the Writer to the Hebrews in Using Old Testament Quotations." *EvQ* 27 (1955) 214–220.

Richard, Earl. "The Polemical Character of the Joseph Episode in Acts 7." *JBL* 98 (1979) 255–67.

—————. *Acts 6:1–8:4: The Author's Method of Composition.* SBLDS 41. Missoula: Scholars, 1978.

—————. "Acts 7: An Investigation of the Samaritan Evidence." *CBQ* 34 (1977) 190–208.

Riggenbach, Eduard. *Der Brief an die Hebräer.* Kommentar zum Neuen Testament 14. Leipzig: Deichert, 1922.

Robinson, J. A. T. *Redating the New Testament.* Philadelphia: Westminster, 1976.

Sanders, James. *Torah and Canon.* Philadelphia: Fortress, 1972.

Savran, George W. *Telling and Retelling. Quotation in Biblical Narrative.* Bloomington: Indiana University, 1988.

Schille, Gottfried. "Katechese und Taufliturgie." *ZNW* 51 (1960) 112–31.

Schmitt, Von Armin. "Struktur, Herkunft und Bedeutung der Beispielreihe in Weish 10." *BZ* 21 (1977) 1–22.

Schröger, Friedrich. "Das Hermeneutische Instrumentarium des Hebräerbriefverfassers." *TGl* 60 (1970) 344–59.

—————. *Der Verfasser der Hebräerbriefes als Schriftausleger.* Biblische Untersuchungen 4. Regensburg: Pustet, 1968.

Scroggs, Robin. "Paul as Rhetorician: Two Homilies in Romans 1–11." In *Jews, Greeks and Christians,* eds. Robin Scroggs and R. Hamerton-Kelly. 271–298. Leiden: Brill, 1976.

—————. "The Earliest Hellenistic Christianity." In *Religions in Anitiquity,* ed. Jacob Neusner. 176–206. Leiden: Brill, 1968.

Segal, Alan F. *Paul the Convert.* New Haven: Yale, 1990.

Seters, John Van. *In Search of History: Historiography in the Ancient World and the Origins of Biblical History.* New Haven and London: Yale, 1983.

Siebeneck, Robert T. "The Midrash of Wisdom 10–19." *CBQ* 22 (1960) 176–82.

—————. "May Their Bones Return to Life!—Sirach's Praise of the Fathers." *CBQ* 21 (1959).

Siker, Jeffery S. *Disinheriting the Jews: Abraham in Early Christian Controversy.* Louisville: Westminster/John Knox, 1991.

Simon, Marcel. *St. Stephen and the Hellenists in the Primitive Church.* London: 1958.

Soards, Marion. *The Speeches in Acts: Their Context, Content and Concerns.* Louisville: Westminster/John Knox, 1994.

Sowers, Sidney. *The Hermeneutics of Philo and Hebrews.* Basel Studies of Theology 1. Zurich: EVZ, 1965.

_____. "On the Reinterpretation of Biblical History in Hellenistic Judaism." In *Oikonomia*, eds. Felix Christ. Hamburg-Bergstedt: Herbert Reich Evang., 1967.

Spicq, Ceslas. "L'Epître aux Hébreux et Philon. Un cas d'insertion de la littérature sacrée dans la culture profane du 1er siècle (Hebr V, I-VI, 20 et le 'De sacrificiis Abelis et Caini' de Philon)." In *ANRW* 2/25 (1987) 4.3602–18.

_____. "L'Epître aux Hébreux, Apollos, Jean-Baptiste, les Hellénistes et Qumrân." *RevQ* 1 (1959) 365–90.

_____. *L'Epître aux Hébreux.* SB. Paris: Gabalda, 1952–3.

_____. "Alexandrismes dans l'Epître aux Hébreux." *RB* 58 (1951) 481–502.

Stendahl, Krister. *Paul Among Jews and Gentiles and Other Essays.* Philadelphia: Fortress, 1976.

Stern, Menahem. *Greek and Latin Authors on Jews and Judaism.* Jerusalem: The Israel Academy of Sciences and Humanities, 1976.

Stone, Michael E., ed. *Jewish Writings of the Second Temple Period. Apocrypha, Pseudepigrapha, Qumran Sectarian Writings, Philo, Josephus.* CRINT 2.2. Assen; Philadelphia: Van Gorcum; Fortress, 1984.

Suggs, M. J. *Wisdom, Christology, and Law in Matthew's Gospel.* Cambridge: Cambridge University, 1970.

Swetnam, James. *Jesus and Isaac: A Study of the Epistle to the Hebrews in the Light of the Aqedah.* Rome: Pontifical Biblical Institute, 1981.

_____. "On the Literary Genre of the 'Epistle' to the Hebrews." *NovT* 11 (1969) 261–269.

Sylva, Dennis. "The Meaning and Function of Acts 7:46–50." *JBL* 106 (1987) 261–75.

Synge, F. C. *Hebrews and the Scriptures.* London: SPCK, 1959.

Thackeray, H. St. J. et. al. *Josephus. Greek Text and English Translation.* LCL. Cambridge; London: Harvard; William Heinemann Ltd., 1926–65.

Thiselton, Anthony. *New Horizons in Hermeneutics: The Theory and Practice of Transforming Biblical Study.* Grand Rapids, MI: Zondervan, 1992.

_____. *The Two Horizons: New Testament Hermeneutics and Philosophical Description.* Grand Rapids, MI: Eerdmans, 1980.

Thomas, Kenneth J. "The Old Testament Citations in Hebrews." *NTS* 11 (1964–5) 303–25.

Thompson, James W. *The Beginnings of Christian Philosophy: The Epistle to the Hebrews.* Washington D. C.: Catholic Biblical Association of America, 1982.

Thyen, Hartwig. *Der Stil der Jüdisch-Hellenistischen Homilie.* Göttingen: Vandenhoeck and Ruprecht, 1955.

Towner, Wayne Sibley. *The Rabbinic Enumeration of Scriptural Examples: A Study of a Rabbinic Pattern of Discourse with Special Reference to the Mekilta D'R. Ishmael.* SPB. Leiden: E. J. Brill, 1973.

Vanhoye, Albert. "'Fidelis ei qui fecit eum,' Heb 3,2." *VD* 45 (1967) 291–305.

——————. *La structure litteraire de L'Epitre aux Hebreux.* StudNeot 1. Paris: Desclee de Brouwer, 1963.

Vermes, Geza. *Post-Biblical Jewish Studies.* SJLA. Leiden: E. J. Brill, 1975.

——————. *Scripture and Tradition in Judaism.* SPB. Leiden: E. J. Brill, 1961.

Vernard, L. "L'utilisation des Paumes dans l'Epître aux Hébreux." In *Mélanges E. Podechard.* 253–69. Lyon: Facultés Catholiques, 1945.

Weiser, Artur. *The Psalms.* OTL. Philadelphia: Westminster, 1962.

Westcott, Brooke F. *The Epistle to the Hebrews.* London: Macmillan, 1909.

Whitaker, G. H., R. Marcus and F. M. Colson. *Philo. Greek Text and English Translation.* LCL, Cambridge; London: Harvard; William Heinemann Ltd., 1929–53.

Williams, Michael, Collet Cox, and Martin S. Jaffe, ed. *Innovation in Religous Traditions: Essays in the Interpretation of Religious Change.* Berlin: Mouton de Gruyter, 1992.

Williamson, H. G. M. *Ezra, Nehemiah.* WBC 16. Waco, TX: Word Books, 1985.

Williamson, Ronald. *Philo and the Epistle to the Hebrews.* Leiden: Brill, 1970.

Wills, Lawrence. "The Form of the Sermon in Hellenistic Judaism and Early Christianity." *HTR* 77 (1984) 277–99.

Wilson, Robert R. *Genealogy and History in the Biblical World.* New Haven and London: Yale, 1977.

Windisch, Hans. *Der Hebräerbrief.* HNT 14. Tubingen: Mohr [Paul Siebeck], 1931.

Winston, David. *The Wisdom of Solomon.* AB. Garden City: Doubleday, 1979.

Wright, R. Boling and G. E. *Joshua: A New Translation with Introduction and Commentary.* AB 6. Garden City: Doubleday, 1982.

Wuellner, Wilhelm. "Where is Rhetorical Criticism Taking Us?" *CBQ* 49 (1987).

Yadin, Yigdal. "The Dead Sea Scrolls and the Epistle to the Hebrews." In *Aspects of the Dead Sea Scrolls.* Scripta hierosolymitana 4. Jerusalem: Magnes, 1958.

INDEX

ᴄᴏ ᴏᴅ

I. Hebrew Scripture

245

II. New Testament

III. Ancient Jewish Literature

IV. Greco-Roman Literature

V. Ancient Christian Literature